TRUE MYTHS

TRUE MYTHS

The Life and Times of
ARNOLD
SCHWARZENEGGER

Nigel Andrews

A Birch Lane Press Book
Published by Carol Publishing Group

A Birch Lane Press Book
Published by Carol Publishing Group
Birch Lane Press is a registered trademark of Carol
Communications, Inc.

Editorial, sales and distribution, rights and permissions inquiries
should be addressed to Carol Publishing Group, 120 Enterprise Avenue,
Secaucus, NJ 07094

In Canada: Canadian Manda Group, One Atlantic Avenue, Suite 105,
Toronto, Ontario, M6K 3E7

Carol Publishing Group books may be purchased in bulk at special
discounts for sales promotion, fund-raising, or educational purposes.
Special editions can be created to specifications. For details, contact
Special Sales Department, 120 Enterprise Avenue, Secaucus, N.J. 07094.

Printed with permission from Bloomsbury Publishing Plc

Manufactured in the United States of America
10 9 8 7 6 5 4 3 2 1

Library of Congress Cataloging-in-Publication Data

Andrews, Nigel.
True myths : the life and times of Arnold Schwarzenegger / Nigel
Andrews.
p.   cm.
"A Birch Lane press book."
Includes bibliographical references and index.
ISBN 1-55972-364-5 (hc)
1. Schwarzenegger, Arnold.   2. Motion picture actors and
actresses—United States—Biography.   I. Title.
PN2287.S3368A53   1996
791.43'028'092—dc20

[B]

96-27124
CIP

For Holly

CONTENTS

TRUE MYTHS

INTRODUCTION

'Why are you writing this book?' a friend asked. Picturing a
fellow film critic seduced by the whorish charms of Hollywood,
he was concerned that I was not writing one of the books he
wanted me to write; or that he wanted to write himself and was
projecting onto me: like 'The Influence of German Expressionism
on Postwar American Angst', or 'Montage after Godard', or 'Jim
Jarmusch, Man or Myth?'

I rounded on him with four reasons. One, I am a Schwarzenegger
fan. Two, Schwarzenegger is the most intriguing and improbable
movie phenomenon of the millennium's climactic years. Three, I
suspect – we all suspect – that rather than being a human being he
is some bizarre construct of the PR industry, or of late-century
Teutonic transcendence, or of a team of biomechanical scientists
working out of Silicon Valley. Fourth and finally, I could claim,
like the nine-stone weakling who was the 'before' symbol in the
old Charles Atlas ads, to have once had sand kicked in my face
by Mr Schwarzenegger.

This happened on a beach in Cannes during Arnold's first
ever film festival epiphany. (Let us save eight letters a time
for the length of this book by staying on first-name terms.)
I was preparing for an al fresco interview with a medium-
famous director, when I sensed something huge, slow and
heavy-breathing displacing the air to my right. The sand made
chuffing noises beneath the yet-unseen feet; a group of strolling
seagulls were frightened into take-off; and there moved into my
eyeline something resembling a large, animated redwood tree.

1

Two hundred and fifty pounds of muscle, oil and ear-to-ear Austrian grin, it stood surveying the beach. Then it kicked away a few carefully laid towels – that was when the sand hit me – and prepared a circle for himself, his media following (then smallish) and the statutory 'bevy' of girls.

Then Arnold held forth as only Arnold can. With one ear – the other was attending to the words of the now-arrived medium-famous director – I listened to this stream of Austrian charm and polished, impudent narcissism, delivered in the thickest Teutonic accent since Sig Ruman, that much-loved character actor with squashed-bagel face who played comic Germans in the 1930s and 40s.

Arnold's Cannes talk-in was around the time of *Pumping Iron* (1977), his bodybuilding docu-feature that also began building his name among filmgoers. Twenty movies later that name is still one of the wonders of Hollywood.

'Schwarzenegger.' Four syllables of lexical torment for the average movie fan. Fourteen letters of constructional hell for the average movie marquee. And a name that would smash known records on a Scrabble board. Try thinking of any other top-billed Hollywood name, ever, that could compete.

What else does the most famous nomenclature in modern cinema tell us? That the 48-year-old Austrian-born bodybuilder turned screen action hero is a paragon of obstinacy. No other actor would have kept that doorstopping surname in the age of Tom Cruise, Brad Pitt, Bruce Willis and other make-it-snappy monikers. That Arnold is not afraid of being hissably Teutonic in white-bread, well-elocuted America. Above all, that Arnold has the sense to know that a name you can't forget always begins as one you can't remember.

'Schwarzenegger' in Austrian means 'black ploughman'. That's one role the actor hasn't yet played in a career spanning cops, robots, hitmen, special agents, macho kindergarten teachers and oversize twin brothers. *Conan The Barbarian, The Terminator, Commando, Red Heat, Total Recall, True Lies.* Arnold has become the biggest hero in the world by playing the biggest heroes in the world. One hundred years after the birth of cinema, some mad evolutionary process has produced this barbie-doll he-person; this guttural, bulging, preening savage in love (at least on screen) with his own machismo.

Physical perfection, ferocity, primitive charm, programmed quips, interspersed with long stretches of smouldering taciturnity. This last item is no surprise. No one expects custom-made machismo dolls to speak, except when you turn them upside down and they growl out their speciality one-liners. 'Hasta la vista, baby,' 'Beeg mistake' . . . What does surprise is the speed with which Arnold's taciturnity has yielded recently to something like – let's not get overexcited and call it articulacy, but at least an ironic, well-groomed, on-screen wit.

Like many oversized men of talent – from Orson Welles to Pavarotti – Arnold can move lightly on his feet, physically, gesturally, emotionally. Hollywood myopia began by casting him as a musclebound Nemesis. In movies from *The Terminator* to *Red Heat*, via *Commando* and *Predator*, he stood there like a Colossus wired for sound while opponents broke their knuckles and wits on his impassivity. But with *Twins* and *Kindergarten Cop* he came to play comedy. And with the reality-juggling *Last Action Hero* he came to play – what? Surrealism? Postmodernism? Actually he played two different roles (three if you count a spoof Hamlet) and lost large sections of the ticket-buying public by looking as if he had sold out to the avant-garde.

But Arnold has always been avant-garde. What makes him a freak achiever is not just his origin – the only sportsman ever to become a Hollywood superstar, let alone the only Austrian – but his ability to be several pairs of complete opposites. Outlaw and establishment warrior; patrician and peasant; untried android and grizzled human veteran; hero and villain; Cybernetics Age demigod and New Stone Age buffoon.

He has also been the mascot of an era in which America has been going through a dozen varieties of agony – tragic and comic – about its role as a global policeman. We saw Hollywood wear its gloom-and-doom mask about the country's failures in the *Rambo* series, starring the man who has long been Arnold's closest rival Sylvester Stallone. Those films tried to restore US pride with a hero who first cleaned up the Missing-in-Action problems of the Vietnam war (*Rambo*) and then kicked the Russians out of Afghanistan (*Rambo III*). Unfortunately the Russians had already kicked themselves out by the time that film was released. And in the same way the music-backed, flag-wrapped lectures about US–USSR entente in *Rocky IV* seemed otiose in the dawn of an age when all that was happening anyway.

Stallone's heroes made the mistake of taking themselves too seriously and then the bigger mistake of being politically unpunctual. Audiences tired of seeing Rocky Rambo beat his patriotic-pugilistic chest while history raced by. So enter Schwarzenegger: not so much an American hero, more a living robot created by the New World Order.

This man came from over there; now he is over here. He appears at rallies for the Republicans; now he has married into the Democrats. (We need a new series of *Dynasty* to do justice to the soap-opera farfetchedness by which a bodybuilding prole from Austria gets spliced to JFK's niece.) He is a frowning machine for destruction; he is a graceful light comedian. Wrap it all up, take it away, look at it at home, and what do you have? Something like a symbol for the West itself.

A star tells us all about the country and culture in which he or she rises. Arnold has been the age's most effective incarnator of an ultimate wish: for the power of absolute strength – America as the world's licensed and invincible knight errant. And he has been the age's most effective incarnator of an absolute fear: that given the right opposition, even absolute strength is powerless. Put America in Vietnam or confront America with the insoluble problem of Bosnia, and the machine for justice cannot function. Put Arnold in front of a classroom of kids (*Kindergarten Cop*) or hand-in-hand with a pintsize, hellraising twin brother (*Twins*) – yes, this enfeebled-America idea is so frightening that it has to be turned into comedy – and the he-man is undone by the homunculi.

Not that audiences are going to let him get tripped up too often. They like him winning. My first experience of seeing a Schwarzenegger film in America is one I shan't forget. Place: the Egyptian Theatre, Hollywood Boulevard. Audience: assorted bikers and psychos. In a once proud movie theatre that had been ruthlessly duplexed, we all sat crammed in an auditorium about the size of a boxing ring. The film was *Commando*, in which a couple of hundred people get put away by Action Arnie with weapons ranging from fists to bazookas. The front-of-screen mood became progressively hysterical: 'Yeah, get 'im, Arnie!'; 'Blast 'im'; 'Kill the motherfucker!' And each time the hero delivered one of his own one-liners – the favourite was 'Now let off steam', when he impales the baddies' henchman with a heating pipe – the place erupted in exultant guffaws.

The spectators were not responding to the film's direction, script or production design. They were turned on by the star's marmoreal machismo. This was the American hero they had long wanted – a biomechanical stud in whom you couldn't tell the muscle-bulging limbs from the bristling armoury of portable weapons; they all seemed equally organic, exoskeletal. And if Hollywood had had to go to Austria to get him, complete with accent, so what? America *is* the world's proverbial melting pot.

So what created this mythopoeic bruiser, this Knight Template from the other side of the western world? A biography starts with a pile of questions and then tries to throw definitive answers at them. Did Arnold grow up with dreams of power or pop-cultural influence? When did he lift his first weight? *Why* did he lift his first weight? Was his father a Nazi? As a child, did he know or care about movies? Once in Hollywood, how did he make the moguls love his accent? Why was he so rude so often about Sylvester Stallone – before years later founding a chain of hamburger restaurants with, among others, Stallone? After weight-lifting, acting and the restaurant business, is there any logical career step left short of politics? Taking into account his past tendency to pop up beside R. Reagan or G. Bush on celebrity platforms, are we looking at a future contender for high office?

It is, of course, a wonderful joke that a non-American has become the filmgoer's Mr America. But after Mr Europe and Mr Universe and Mr Olympia, that is almost a climbdown for the boy who rose without trace from a small village in rural Austria; a village where his policeman father could have had no idea that sonny would follow, more or less, in Dad's footsteps, except that Arnold would do his policing for another country in another language in another medium (than real life) and in front of the entire watching and listening world.

1

In Search of Schwarzenegger

Hollywood is a strange town. It is, of course, no town at all, but the most famous jumped-up suburb in the world. It still suffers from the inflated ego that comes with over-promotion. Eighty-three years ago it was a one-horse sprawl on the edge of Los Angeles, full of dust and orange groves and clapboard shacks, and farmers who gazed at a camera – even a still camera – as if it was a machine from outer space. But in 1913 Cecil B DeMille chose to make a Western there, *The Squaw Man*, and the place never recovered. Fools and angels rushed in in equal numbers. Real life and nature became backdrops for make-believe. And the world's biggest magic factory has spent decades trying to make up its mind how many of its *secrets*, if any, it should reveal to prying guests.

Today Hollywood's welcome to journalists or chroniclers goes as follows. 'We talk and always will talk to the world through our movies. But you are going to have a hell of a time getting us to speak directly to you.'

Tinseltown the talkative has become Lotusland the laconic. Stars and directors used to be wheeled out by the studios for you to interview *ad lib*. Now they sit in their private Spanish-style mansions – in Beverly Hills, Malibu or Pacific Palisades (Arnold's dwelling place) – like Charles Foster Kane, nursing their whims and paranaias, and protected by those walking 'Keep Out' notices called agents and publicists. To get to the VIPs, let alone their friends and fellow eminences, you must perform an elaborate courting dance by telephone with their functionaries.

'Hello, my name is Nigel Andrews, I'm in Los Angeles for two weeks researching a book on Arnold Schwarzenegger. I believe you represent the film director, Mr X, Y or Z. I would be very keen to meet and talk with him for this book.'

'I see. Is this an authorised work, Michael? Has Arnold given his okay?'

'Mr Schwarzenegger and his people are fully aware of the book, and his publicist Charlotte Parker and I have been in regular contact.'

'I see. And how much time would you need with Mr X Y Z?'

'Oh, an hour would be fine. In person, or we could do it over the phone if that would be more convenient.'

'And where are you staying?'

'The Hyatt on Sunset. Room 911.'

'Oh-ho! Very appropriate!! (laughter) Well, we'll see what we can do, Andrew, and get back in touch.'

It took me days, back in that balmy Los Angeles April in 1994, first to get everyone to get my name right – 'Nigel' is an unheard-of locution anywhere west of Bermuda – and then to find out why my room number created such mirth. Finally an American friend reminded me that 911 is the emergency services number in the USA.

In nine cases out of ten the agent or publicist never did get back in touch. Or if they did, it was to say that the client in question was a 'close friend' of Arnold and would not want to do anything without the great man's approval or participation.

And the great man? I was told by Charlotte Parker, Arnold's publicist and the sole official conduit to him, that it was unlikely he would co-operate. As she put it in her crisp, rapid telephone voice: This was not a book Arnold was commissioning or requesting, nor did he truly have control over the result, and this wasn't necessarily the place where he wanted to make a stand about his life.

But if I wrote her a fax Charlotte would present the project to Arnold. And if *he* did not participate she would try to smooth my way to the Arnold circle of top directors and stars.

Tinseltown rule: 'a fax' means three to four faxes. The first ones get lost, ignored or used to light the client's cigars. So an array of tortured scribblings outlining my deep and absorbing fascination with Arnold passed from me to Charlotte, with little initial effect. Half way through my thirteen-day stay in Dreamtown I still did not have my planned hand of interviewees, let alone the man himself.

A few months later, off my own bat, I would have collected enough witnesses to start exerting leverage on the Arnie A-team. But back in that first spring Charlotte's telephone routine went roughly like this. 'Nigel, I'm still trying to convince Arnold. Would you take me off the speakerphone, Nigel, those things give me a headache. I mean, this is from a "No" position. Arnold already wrote me back a memo after my request saying no. But I'm trying for you. Intuitively, Nigel, I've a feeling this is going to be a very pleasant experience. Arnold's not saying "Let's go get him" or "I hate him"! It's nothing like that.'

At least she got my name right. But as days went by, more and more witnesses seemed to fall silent after 'checking with Charlotte'.

Finally, the lady who had cancelled one previous lunch engagement, agreed to tryst with me on a Friday evening at the Hyatt bar: a room, once elegant, that over the years has come to resemble some nightmare video arcade. Against one wall sat a Terminator game machine, with Arnold's own blackglassed face gazing impassively at the summit to come.

Or not. Fifteen minutes after official meeting time, no Charlotte. Phone rings in bar. Charlotte is still at her office finalising, she says, a new memo to Arnold. But she's coming. I and my support system (one friend, one researcher) order another round of whisky sours. Half an hour and three Budweiser chasers later, the phone rings again. Charlotte is prolix with her apologies: she has gone to the 'wrong hotel'. She has confused the Hyatt with the Holiday Inn. She has been wandering around the place, she says, vainly paging Nigel Andrews. Now it is not worth her coming over to the Hyatt – she is sure I will understand – because the Holiday Inn is on her way home.

So I still had not met Charlotte. Arnold would have to be approached by a different route. I got out my map of Los Angeles and spread it, crackly and omniscient, across the floor of my room. I felt like Kirk Douglas in *Spartacus* planning his approach to Rome. Where and how to strike?

Arnold, we know, owns a restaurant in Venice, California. Was he not sometimes rumoured to breakfast there, before or after working out at his favourite nearby gym?

Tomorrow morning was Saturday. He would have a day off from filming *Junior*, which had started shooting that week. Assuming that Arnold was still Arnold, and would not be lying in bed having a tray brought him by wife Maria, he might well go to Schatzi (his restaurant) and make with the muesli before visiting the gym.

Like Spartacus, I slept. Like Spartacus, I rose at dawn. Unlike Spartacus, I climbed into a hired red Toyota Corolla. A little later I was outside the patio entrance to Schatzi, peering in. At one table a group of four men sat in earnest conversation, among whom I recognized the film-maker Paul Verhoeven. He had directed Arnold in *Total Recall* and according to the trade press was soon to direct him again in *Crusade*. I went in, ordered breakfast and pondered the tactics of buttonholing Mr Verhoeven. As I did so, I looked again at the table for four. Seated next to Verhoeven was someone who had been obscured from my view before. He was a large-built man with light carrot hair, a big jawline and a lighted cigar. He seemed to be speaking with an Austrian accent.

2

Child Arnold

'There was no refrigerator, no flushing toilet, no doctor – only a radio.'

(i) Heimat

He should have been flung to earth in a fork of lightning, naked and glistening, and devoid of any provenance save some god-given mandate to stomp the earth righting wrongs or re-programming other people's destinies. Instead Arnold Alois Schwarzenegger was born in the Austrian village of Thal (pronounced 'Tahl') in the early hours of July 30th 1947 to Gustav and Aurelia Schwarzenegger. He inherited from his parents, he notes in the slim volume of autobiography he wrote thirty years later, 'an excellent bone structure and an almost perfect metabolism'. He also found himself, this future Hercules, stuck in a tiny village five miles west of Graz: a village bursting with bucolic beauty – you expect Julie Andrews to come prancing over the high green hills dotted with cows and chestnut trees – but also notable for its lack of every luxury that would be awaiting him thirty years later in Hollywood.

'Nobody had a phone except the village restaurant, the priest and the police station, where my father worked,' recalled Arnold. 'There was one TV set, in the village restaurant.'

Schwarzenegger senior was the local police chief and a former member of the Nazi party. He joined in July 1938, four months after it became legal for Austrians to do so when

11

Germany annexed the country on March 12th. Though Gustav Schwarzenegger seems to have signed up willingly, he was far from being one of his first countrymen to do so – the impression left by one previous Arnold biography. Between 1934 and 1938 it was technically *verboten* to join the party, but no fewer than 38,000 Austrians still became Nazis and were known as 'the Illegals'. The date of registration on Gustav's membership document – I am looking at it now with its stamp-obscured membership number 8439?80 – is July 4th 1938. In the light of his son's own later destination and filial 'declaration of independence', the day and month seem awesomely symbolic.

According to Arnold's later descriptions and the memories of his schoolfriends, Gustav was everything that a father, mentor, policeman and National Socialist might be expected to be. Descended from locksmiths and steelworkers, he put the disciplinary manacles on Arnold and his older brother Meinhard (b. July 17th 1946) whenever possible. He required them to polish the buckle of his police uniform belt. He made them keep their own clothes clean and tidy. He seems to have had a particular obsession with shoes. As Arnold grew up, Gustav developed the habit of opening the boy's cupboard and inspecting his footwear: 'These look a little dirty to me. Maybe we don't go out tonight, Arnold?'

And Gustav always had an answer whenever his young son was at a loss. 'Sit in front of this book for two hours and read.' The boy said he would love to have a bicycle. 'Get it yourself. Work.'

Then there were the essays. The family would enjoy a weekend of, say, museums and galleries and trips into the country. Then on Monday, says Arnold: 'We would have to write an essay about what we had learned. I mean, a lot of fun, right? I hated music because he [Gustav] was a musician and played six instruments. I hated art and antiques because of the essays.'

Nor did Gustav just skim-read the ten-page compositions he ordered and slap on a casual 'B minus, could do better'. 'He would correct [them] with a red pencil, putting marks all over the place. "This sentence makes no sense. This sentence is not true; we did not go there. We did not see this exhibit. You made a mistake in the spelling: write this word fifty times."' If the essay was approved, the most that Gustav would say was 'That's not too bad'.

In this well-disciplined Roman Catholic family, which attended Mass every Sunday and had religious study sessions every week, obedience to one's parents was a rule of life, and from Gustav there would be no emotional pampering. 'He had no patience for listening to understand your problems,' Arnold says. 'There was a real wall; he established that wall.'

Arnold's childhood friends remember that whenever they all went out together – to go to the cinema, swim in the Thalersee, or play mediaeval knights in the castle ruins lying opposite the Schwarzenegger home – he was the only boy who had to be back home sharp by a particular hour.

'He had to do what his father said,' recalls classmate Josef Heinzel. 'He was never allowed to answer back. And he had to be very polite and correct with neighbours or friends. On a bus he wasn't allowed to sit if a grown-up was standing.'

Gustav fancied himself an athlete and was an amateur ice-curling champion. So from tender years Arnold and Meinhard were drummed into sporting activities. Both were out on the soccer field; both put on boxing gloves and bashed at each other or at schoolmates; and Arnold had no sooner reached puberty than he was throwing javelins, putting shots and following Dad onto the curling rink. (He later became a junior champion.)

Arnold's schooling was at the Hans Gross School in Thal and later the Frobel School in Graz. He was 'in the middle' academically, but he stood out as being loud and goodhumoured in class. 'Lustig' – cheerful, exuberant – is his contemporaries' favourite word to describe him.

Just how exuberant Arnold was seemed to depend on the proximity of his brother. About Meinhard there is an awesome unanimity among those who knew him. 'A sadist, a thief, a bully,' one former schoolmate says with a visible shudder. Meinhard took delight in hurting other boys during 'mock' fights and would sometimes bring out pugnacious qualities in Arnold when the two were together.

Meinhard was later expelled from school and sent to a reformatory.

Gustav had his work cut out dealing with filial misconduct.

Arnold remembers that even minor misbehaviours at school would result in Dad greeting him at home with 'You really screwed up!' and vigorous slaps 'across the cheek or arse'. For especially heinous crimes, the paternal belt was removed and deployed.

Meanwhile the police chief, when over-pressured by a life of crime and punishment both at home and at work, had his own soothing worlds to escape into. One was alcohol: on the right day he could drink steadily from noon and then be carried home drunk in the evening from the local bar. Fellow villagers confirm – often with that time-honoured miming motion of hand and wrist – that he was a steady tippler. At the same time there was little visible deterioration in his manner or temper before collapse-point was reached.

Gustav's other escape was music. The only time he was publicly sighted doing anything serene or euphoric was when he plied his brass-playing skills.

A skilled flugelhorn player, he led the Graz Gendarmerie Band, of which he was a founding member and whose twice-weekly get-togethers he attended for thirty-four years (1938–72). His passion was for military music. Pictures show a gaunt, balding man leading his little infantry of musicians across the town square. Sashed, capped and uniformed, he towers head if not shoulders above everyone else.

Gustav seems to have been an obsessional figure for his son. In an interview for the promotional film *Champions* (1990) Arnold can scarcely stay off the subject. There is the actor, waving his stogie about in a blood-spattered shirt on the set of *Total Recall*, as the interviewer is deluged with memories of Stalag Thal. 'Dizzipline' – the word given an extra frisson by the Arnold accent – is the key concept. 'We always had a bit of a military environment at home,' says Arnold. But his perspective on Gustav seems to depend on what he feels the interviewer wants to hear. For the *Champions* film Dad's 'dizziplinary' ways were a fact of life: 'That's the way you were brought up in those days.' For young readers of one of his fitness books, 'My father played soccer with me, he was out sledding with me. I had a fantastic upbringing.' For an interviewer who tells him one of her children is having nightmares, he says: 'I remember having nightmares, and no one coddled me. They just let me cry.' And for *Playboy* interviewer Joan Goodman in 1988, Arnold leavens his account of the essay regime with all's-well-that-ends-well philosophising: 'I thought everything my father said was wrong, but then you get to be twenty-five or thirty and you think back and say, "Goddam it, can you believe it? All the things that I like now my father was saying I should learn!"'

So where was his mother in all this? She was doing what most mothers do: providing love while father provides the lectures. Aurelia Schwarzenegger, nee Jadrny, met Gustav after the end of the war and married him on October 20th 1945. Family pictures show a kindly, worried-looking, somewhat bucktoothed lady, wearing Arnold's cheekbones and wide-smiling mouth. He called her one of the best mothers a boy could have: you could eat off the floors, he recalled; the towels would all be neatly folded with sharp corners.

She was also the parent who listened to him and his problems. She was less likely to go through the roof when Arnold misbehaved; and later, when he began bodybuilding, she would defend the weird fad against Gustav's fulminations.

Aurelia could lay down her own laws, though. She designed a 'daily routine' for Arnold and his brother, so that they knew when to play and when to work. And she had a gung-ho attitude to the boy's health and well-being. Brought up in the austerity years after World War 2, Arnold recalls the hardships. Despite her part-time work at the local *gasthaus*, she 'had to go around with us to various farms until she got enough food and sugar and stuff. I had only shelter and love from parents; but after that, nothing. We had no television set in my house when I grew up. There was no phone, no bathroom in the sense that we know it.' And no refrigerator – until it arrived one day in the late 1950s, to rapt and silent astonishment from the Schwarzenegger family. 'I remember, we were all standing around the kitchen looking at it. Then my mother opened it up, and we all stuck our hands in there, and it was cold, and we were freaking out like this was the strangest thing you could imagine.'

Doctors too were a luxury. 'If I got sick in the middle of the night my mother or father would take me on his or her shoulders and walk over a big mountain for two hours to the main town of Graz.'

With parental examples like this, are we surprised that Arnold grew up devoid of wimpishness? The advantage of muscular parenting is that when Mum or Dad finally deal out the praise and appreciation they are all the more gratifying. Years later, when the boy brought home his first weight-lifting trophy, Aurelia was the first to go berserk with reflected glory. She took it and ran from house to house in Thal, he remembers, showing the neighbours what he had done.

On another occasion, Arnold seems to recall that it was Gustav. Either way, someone of parental status ran around the village waving a shiny object and crying 'My son the champion bodybuilder!'

(ii) Thal Tales

Does the inconsistency matter? Maybe not. Or maybe it offers the first evidence for the 'true myths' syndrome of our title.

The birth and upbringing of a famous person are read for major significance, or have that significance read into them, by every fan, student and biographer of the later life. That 'reading' becomes a kind of retrospective life-designing. 'He was dropped on his head as a child, so he became Galileo'; 'She had her doll taken away at age three, so she became Louisa May Alcott.' The search to clinch these cause-and-effect conclusions asks – or begs – one major question. Who is providing the evidence for the supposed formative experiences? In many cases, where the subject recalls moments that took place in solitude, or where the biographer's trawling net cannot reach other sources, it is the famous person himself. There is no surer way to build a legend about yourself than to create or to control – or even to re-inflect out of an *innocently* hazy memory – the stories about your own past.

Arnold Schwarzenegger is one of the great media magicians of this century. The world loves his tales even when they sound like what Huck Finn would call 'stretchers'. It's a minor solecism to tell the trophy-carrying story twice and to be inconsistent about which parent was involved. But it lodges a question-mark in the biographer's mind. So does the tale of parental piggy-backs to the doctor. A former schoolfriend of Arnold's says that the practice, if there was an illness at night, was to call out the nearest doctor who lived just west of Graz. The caller would use the telephone in the local guesthouse. So did Arnold's parents really keep slogging over that mountain – or is Arnold re-wishing mundane reality into a more resonant form? Consider again his father's objections to the boy's essays. They are not routine red-pencillings about grammer or spelling but – 'This sentence is not true; we did not go there. We did not see this exhibit . . .'

One of Arnold's favourite stories about his childhood is fascinating just because of its mythopoeic quality. The young Schwarzenegger apparently developed an *amour fou* with Dad's police uniform.

> I remember as a boy dressing up in his uniform. I was a little kid standing on a chair, and the jacket was hanging down, like a raincoat, all the way to my toes. I had this hat on which covered me all the way to my nose. I always played dress-up with his uniform. I loved his uniform. But I didn't want to be a cop.

On another occasion, though, Arnold says he did want 'to be in the military or to be a police officer or with the Gendarmerie, which is the country police . . . That was my first dream.' With or without that imprimatur of boyhood ambition, his story – recounted in two major interviews and referred to in others – provides fuel for the Arnold detractors: those who gaze solemnly at *The Terminator* or *Commando* or *Raw Deal* and believe that Schwarzenegger the movie hero is right-wing totalitarianism's last laugh at a West that thought it had got that nightmare out of its system fifty years ago.

Not subscribing to that view, I suspect that a minor event – a boy's dressing-up caper – has been magicked into a formative fable by Arnold himself. It is a playful designer concession to those love-hate commentators who iconise or demonise him as Mr Ubermensch. The vagueness over vocational underpinning (did he or didn't he want to be a cop?) is part of the general swell of reminiscence turning to mythmaking. For Arnold is also vague about the physical logistics of donning Dad's uniform. On the one hand it was so large that he could wear it only by standing on a chair. On the other, 'I always ran around with [it] on.' Either this is self-contradictory or it suggests a seriously chronic dressing-up habit: one that stayed with Arnold over several, growing years.

Biographer Wendy Leigh leaps at the child-psychologising possibilities. Arnold 'tried to defuse his fear of his father by dressing up . . . and pretending he *was* his father. As he grew older his unrequited love for Gustav drove him not only to don his father's uniform but also to imitate his actions. Gustav had taught him to hate and humiliate rather than to love. Gustav had terrorized him; now Arnold, incited by his brother, began to terrorize other people.'

If Arnold's story is biographer bait, it has caught one hefty mackerel. For Leigh the shuffling on of the police drag goes with the boyhood delinquencies and anticipates the later Arnold she will draw, of the violent screen image and ruthless ambition. For me there is an element of playacting about the whole dressing-up story, real or false. In either case Arnold the future actor is 'trying on' an image. And what could be more histrionic – more of an endearing charade of strength and power, rather than a practical or threatening application of those things – than the first vocation he goes on to choose? Bodybuilding.

3

Arnold Starts Building

'I felt like Leonardo Da Vinci. I was a sculptor sculpting the body.'

(i) Building the Body

There are several different versions of how Arnold came to body building: not least from the man himself. The most scenic occurs in his book *Arnold's Fitness for Kids, Ages Birth to Five.* At age fourteen, he recalls, he used to play with friends at the village lake. They would chase each other along the shore, or have swimming races, or dive to the lake floor to collect mud for mud-fights. More and more, Arnold noticed the older, bigger boys who worked out with weights and did exercises. He remembers staring at them and thinking 'how wonderful it must be to have a body like theirs.' Soon he asked them to teach him; he wanted to be able to do more 'chin-ups' than any of them.

The better-known story, also from Arnold's own mouth, was that he started working out with weights as part of football training: His coach decided that lifting weights for an hour once a week would be a good way to condition the boys for playing soccer.

In another version he was in the school gym and saw a magazine featuring Mr Universe pictures. 'It fascinated me. I decided that was the way to be different.'

It could be none or one or all of these stories, swirling around in the mythmixer of Arnold's head. But however the

19

boy actually opened the door to his first vocation, there was no doubting the Damascene light shining inside. During his first visit to the bodybuilding gym he remembered the weight-lifters shining with sweat and their powerful Herculean looks. There it was before him – 'my life, the answer I'd been seeking.'

Soon the self-obsessed mystique of bodybuilding was spreading through Arnold like a virus. For him it was a way to escape team sports – 'I disliked it when we won a game and I didn't get personal recognition' – and develop a romance with his body and his power to shape it. 'The worst thing I can be is the same as everybody else. I hate that. That's why I went into bodybuilding in the first place. It was the idea of taking the risk by yourself rather than with a whole team.'

In due course Arnold was waving aside the horrified reaction of his parents to sculpt the body beautiful.

Aurelia: 'Why, Arnold, why do you want to do it to yourself?'

Gustav: 'What will you do with all these muscles once you've got them?'

Arnold: 'I want to be the best-built man in the world. Then I want to go to America and be in movies.'

Gustav: 'I think we better go to the doctor with this one, he's sick in the head.'

But with Arnold's body swelling by the minute, piggy-back rides over the mountain to Graz were a whole new proposition. And if the boy was sick in his head, he seemed to be possessed of a startling clarity of thought and purpose. Where fellow iron-pumpers trained two or three times a week, Arnold trained daily. Where others packed it in around dinnertime. Arnold would be there in the Graz gym until ten in the evening. After his first workout he started riding home and fell off his bike. 'I was so weak I couldn't make my hands hold on,' he writes in his autobiography. 'I had no feeling in my legs: they were noodles. I was numb, my whole body buzzing.'

Arnold's boyhood trainer was Kurt Marnul. The reigning Mr Austria and future Mr Europe 1965 had founded the Atletic Union Graz in the late 1950s: the town's only weight-lifting gym, located under a concrete stand in the town's football stadium. Marnul had built his own weight-machines there, based on pictures he had seen in American bodybuilding magazines.

Marnul met Arnold in 1961, introduced by a mutual friend, a schoolteacher, at the Thalersee. At first the new mentor saw more promise in the boy's older brother. 'Arnold was tall but thin,' he remembers. 'Meinhard looked much more like a potential bodybuilder.' Meinhard, though, had no powers of discipline or application, while his brother seemed to have both.

'The first day Arnold trained,' Marnul recalls, 'he said, "I will be Mr Universe." He trained six, sometimes seven days a week, about three hours a day. Within three to four years he had put on twenty kilos of pure muscle.' The Graz gym was closed on Sundays, says Marnul, but Arnold would break in by forcing open a window. Usually he missed the last bus home, so he would walk back or his trainer would give him a lift on his motorbike.

Back at home his mother was more tolerant than his father of the boy's new fad. 'She said she'd rather he trained three hours a day than be in bars and restaurants or smoking or taking drugs or being with women,' recalls Marnul. A regime of conspiratorial acceptance set in.

'After he had finished his preparation for school and thought his father was asleep,' remembers Aurelia, 'Arnold would hitchhike down the mountains to the soccer stadium.' After a few hours' heaving and humping he would come home, 'arriving in the early light to be picked up by a tank that took him to school. It was an American tank, because they were still occupying Austria and Arnold was very friendly with the soldiers.' (This must have been a rogue American tank; locals today insist that the area was under British occupation at that time).

In those early iron-pumping years Marnul was astonished at his pupil's zeal and progress. There were also early signs of Arnold's expertise at gamesmanship. The one weakness Marnul remembers in the boy's early development was his stomach. 'You're supposed to have three muscles showing there, but Arnold only had two. However much he trained, he couldn't get that third muscle, so he used to stand like this when he posed.' Marnul mimes holding an arm in a shielding position across his stomach.

To help boost the swelling body, Marnul introduced Arnold to steroids which were then legal. Back in the early 1960s, the trainer claims, 'There was no weightlifter in the world who did not take them. You could get prescriptions for them from the doctor. Arnold never took them, though, without my supervision.'

Marnul says he learned about steroids from famed bodybuilder Steve Reeves. That name brings us to another energizing influence on Arnold: the imagery which inspired him; the pictures in the magazines and movie-house.

(ii) Building The Myth

Arnold had seen Steve Reeves on the movie screen and what body fetishist is the same after that? Reeves, an ex-Mr Universe, was a bronzed demigod who strutted through a dozen Italian-made muscle epics in the 1950s and early '60s. These rejoiced in semi-interchangeable titles (*Hercules Unchained, Goliath and the Barbarians, The Last Days of Pompeii*) and in half-baked plots borrowed from history or mythology. Heroes, gods and other mythic beings, plus skimpy-clad damsels in states of permanent distress. The films circuited the world soon after they had penetrated the American market thanks to an inspired publicity ploy by independent producer-distributor Joseph E. Levine. Levine crammed all the best moments from the first Reeves film he bought into a bulging, blazing 'trailer'. Everyone then went to the movie itself, expecting an action masterpiece. By the time they realised it was the seen-before stuff plus longueurs, the money was in the till and Reeves's name in lights.

Arnold had also seen the British-born muscle champion Reg Park. Park, like Reeves, was a former Mr Universe; he had won the title in 1951 and 1958 and would win again in 1965. Like Reeves too, he pumped his pectorals and ballooned his biceps in a series of discount epics made in Italy, in Park's case after 1960. Sample titles included *Hercules Conquers Atlantis* and *Hercules and the Vampires*.

'Reg Park looked so magnificent in the role of Hercules I was transfixed,' wrote Arnold in his *Education of a Bodybuilder*. Sitting there in the theatre, he writes, he knew he was looking at his own future. His friends idolised Reeves, but Arnold preferred

Park's rough, animal look. He knew in his mind that he was not geared for elegance. He wanted to be massive. It was the 'difference between cologne and sweat.'

Movies, with their hi-fi inflated vision, fed Arnold's imagination throughout his childhood. 'When I was ten and twelve and fifteen, I only went to R-rated movies. I would refuse to go to PG movies. Who wants to see people talk and have a good time? I wanted to see violence and hanky-panky.'

Since these movies were forbidden to children, he and his friends snuck in illicitly. 'I'd have to walk in backwards when the exit doors opened,' says Arnold. Josef Heinzel, who used to go to the movies with Arnold, doesn't remember this elaborate manoeuvre but says that 'The man in charge of the cinema turned a blind eye'.

Even when Arnold was old enough to see the films legally, Gustav could be relied on to provide the missing forbidden-fruit factor. 'I remember when my father would say, "Don't go to see this movie," I would run twice as fast. That's how I could tell how much I would like a movie: by how much my father disapproved of it.' All this contraband blood and thunder 'released a kind of desire of violence in me and I could let it go through fantasy by seeing it on the screen'.

But it was more than a love of violence. The movies Arnold liked – despite their mixed cultural pedigree, including Italian epics about Ancient Greece starring (in Park's case) a South African-based Englishman – seemed to suggest one word to him, 'Hollywood'. And Hollywood in turn was the mythic centre of a larger enchanted kingdom: America. 'Everything I wanted as a kid was American. I hated everything about Austria – the classical music and the museums. I hated this old shit.'

Everything was not only new in America, it was big. The culture of size to which Arnold was subscribing with his own body existed spiritually and scenically over there. He saw filmed documentaries about New York and Chicago and California: towering cities, infinite landscapes.

'I loved the huge cars, '57 Cadillacs with their wide wings, the freeways, the whole idea of America,' he says. 'While my friends were dreaming about working for the government so they would get a pension and that shit, I was talking about big things.'

But how much was he talking? Though two schoolfriends. Brigitte Verschink and Josef Heinzel, claim to recall Arnold airing his American dreams from around age fourteen, Arnold himself says that he *didn't* talk a lot about goals and ambitions. Least of all about film stardom. 'They would say I was totally insane. "What's he doing talking about Hollywood and the movies? He's going off the deep end." And so I kept it all inside.'

Arnold's friends were already poking fun at him for his bodybuilding obsession and 'showing him the bird': the Austrian equivalent of the finger-to-temple gesture indicating 'You're crazy.' But Arnold, they claim, was careless of the ridicule. He would jokingly pump a bicep back at his pals or pose for muscle-flexing photos that would end up in their albums.

Movie stardom, however, was a more serious credibility-strainer. No sportsman – let alone a boy muscle-wonder from Middle Europe – had ever turned into a major film star; though Arnold claims he once saw in the flesh the man who had come closest. Before he ever lifted a weight, let alone saw a Reg Park or Steve Reeves film, he recalls being taken to Graz to watch Johnny Weissmuller. The Olympic swimming champion turned Hollywood Tarzan was opening a new pool.

We can almost see the boy there and envisage the cartoon thought-bubble that future Arnographers, rejoicing in hindsight, would conjure from his head. 'If *that* lump of prime-condition, German-extracted muscle can conquer the movie world, by swinging from one custom-made adventure script to another, so can I.'

The halls of Hollywood were the ultimate pantheon. Over there one kind of super-hero, the muscled movie star, spent his life playing an even bigger kind: the mythic or ancient-historical figure. So building a great body could become a beautiful metaphor – or dress rehearsal – for building a great life or myth. He had always been impressed by stories of greatness and power. 'Caesar, Charlemagne, Napoleon were names I knew and remembered.' He wanted to do something special, to be recognized as the best.

To create the legend of Arnold – the super-body leading to to the super-career – it was vital to make the story of *getting* that body the best story of its kind. So the tale of Arnold's training, polished by him as the years and decades go by, becomes a mediaeval trial by the elements, something out of *Idylls of the King* by way of *The Magic Flute*.

Ice! He remembers the chin-ups late at night in the unheated Graz gym, as his fingers stuck to the frozen bars, ripping off the skin. *Air*! The wind whistling through the cracks in the walls and roof! *Fire*! The searing burn in his straining muscles. *Earth*! The pounding of the ground under his feet during the daily two-hour walk home through the snow to Thal.

Soon the boy's participation in the mysteries of body-sculpting has become so all-demanding, of time and passion, that he brings his work home. Gustav, playing the myth-hallowed role of the father depriver, has forbidden Arnold to visit Graz more than three times a week. Arnold gets round the curfew by lugging his own gym equipment into the home. The house was built like a castle, he records. The floors were solid and the walls were about five feet thick.

Casual passers-by, gazing at number 145 Thal-Linak, might be surprised to learn that its interior was built like Neuschwanstein. But here Arnold pumped, pulled, pushed, perspired. He was *in*spired by the photos of his heroes stuck on his wall. Glistening male torsos straining against nature and gravity: pin-up *ubermenschen* torn from imported physical-culture rags like *Muscle Builder* and *Mr America*.

These photos caused some comment. Mr and Mrs Schwarzenegger looked at them; then looked at Arnold's empty dating diary; then thought about Arnold spending all that time checking himself in the mirror. 'All the other boys have got *Playboy* photos up on the wall, naked girls.' they complained, 'and you hang up pictures of naked guys!'

According to Arnold, he *was* interested in girls: only not sure if they were interested in him – more specifically, in his incredible expanding body. 'There were a certain number who were knocked out by it and a certain number who found it repulsive.' In his *Education of a Bodybuilder* Arnold claims that one of the second group, Herta, was on his romantic hit list. He finally summoned up the nerve to ask for a date. 'I wouldn't go with you in a million years,' said the girl. 'You're in love with yourself, you're in love with your own body.

You look at yourself all the time. You pose in front of the mirror.'

Another girl, though, a schoolfriend now grown up and married as Brigitte Verschink, remembers Arnold squiring her with considerate old-world chivalry on and off buses, in and out of shops.

Arnold's male ex-schoolfriends don't remember him giving time to girls at all. 'Sport was more important to him,' they say. He himself explained: 'I didn't allow myself to get (romantically) involved – period . . . I couldn't afford to have my feelings hurt during heavy training or just before a competition.' He also went out less and less socially and seldom touched a drop of alcohol; though that may have owed as much to the admonitory example of Gustav as to the demands of the gym.

All this to triumph in a sport that had no perceived kudos or prestige, at least before Schwarzenegger himself put them there years later: only a faintly sleazy odour of body oil, auto-erotism and cod-Hellenic posing routines.

To psych himself into the monastic masochism required, Arnold had two transcending assets. One was the ability methodically to set a 'vision' before himself. The other was that he fell in love with the training process.

The 'vision' was nothing mystical, more a sort of DIY orientation technique. 'I set a goal, visualise it very clearly, and create the drive, the hunger, for turning it into reality. There's a kind of joy in that kind of ambition, in having a vision in front of you. With that kind of joy, discipline isn't difficult, or negative, or grim.' 'A lot of people do it in a conditional way,' Arnold explained some years later to a Hollywood friend. 'Wouldn't it be nice *if* that happened. That's not enough. You have to put a big emotional commitment into it, that you want it very much, that you love the process and will take all the steps to achieve your goal.'

On the way, of course, you risk becoming the kind of vocational fanatic that people flee from at parties: the guest who has found God or macromy. Even Arnold once volunteered, 'I'm not that different from those religious people who don't worry about dying because they're sure they'll go to Heaven.'

Arnold's whole life at this time seemed poised between a brute, ambitious egotism and a transcendent muscle-mysticism. Was he, after all, a 'team player'? – the difference being that his team consisted of those Hall of Fame immortals who had triumphed by rising *above* the throng. The team of nonteamsters: the leaders and achievers.

Another, connecting, paradox is that despite Arnold's reaction against Gustav and his martinet ways, and the boy's own stated distaste for *esprit de corps*, he wanted to go into the army. According to one friend, Franz Hermann, he had wanted to begin his year's compulsory National Service at seventeen, a year before qualifying age. When he did join in 1965, Gustav used his influence to secure Arnold a coveted post as tank driver, although the official minimum age for that was twenty-one. Arnold seems to have relished the conformist aspects of army life. He liked the regimentation, the firm, rigid structure. He even pays retrospective tribute to Gustav. 'I'd grown up in a disciplined atmosphere. My father always acted like a general.'

What Arnold surely responded to was a milieu that provided a dream combination of two extremes. It was a controlled environment where *he* could do much of the controlling. And it was an ego-subordinating institution where, in one notable respect, he could refuse to have his ego subordinated. For even in army camp nothing was going to dislodge the bodybuilding passion. Arnold and a friend used to get up at five, open the tool compartment of the tank where they kept their barbells, and exercise for an hour before anyone else woke up. After finishing manoeuvres for the day, they would train for another hour.

Like any good hero in any good legend, Arnold had to overcome one last powerful obstacle to fulfil his dream of winning his first title. Serving in the army, he was not free to compete in the 1965 junior Mr Europe contest. But he competed anyway. He went AWOL, as he recalls, climbing over a barracks wall in his army clothes and buying a third-class ticket for a train which tottered out of Austria towards Stuttgart, Germany, stopping at every station.

Arnold won the title. The Wulle Rooms in Stuttgart, where the contest was held, contained a prophetic assortment of the men who would soon play major roles in the boy's early bodybuilding career. Germany's Rolf Putziger owned the Munich gym where Arnold would soon get a job as trainer. Britain's Wag Bennett would be his friend and trainer in London. And Italian bodybuilder Franco Columbu would accompany Arnold on his later leap into fame and America, becoming everything from his business partner to his best friend and – at his wedding twenty years on best man.

A triumphant Arnold returned to camp. Back there, though, rules were still rules. He was caught climbing back over the wall and marched off to be punished. He sat in jail for seven days with only a blanket on a cold stone bench and almost no food. But he had his trophy and he didn't care, he says, if they locked him up for a whole year.

This meant that as soon as he was out of the army, he could get out of that other detention centre, Austria. In doing so, he could smuggle the one priceless weapon – his body – with which he would ally himself, as an iconic guerrilla fighter, with the land of freedom and reckless fantasy against the fraying, fogeyish culture of Old Europe. No more essays, no more concerts. No more sitting on the cold stone bench.

Arnold left Thal in 1966, heading first towards more body-building titles in Germany and a job at a Munich health club. 'I was like a black trying to get out of Harlem,' he remembered. 'I knew when I left home that I'd never go back except as a visitor. On the train, leaving, I looked back and knew, it wasn't home anymore.'

4

Mr Everything

*'I knew I was a winner. I knew I was destined for great things.
People will say that kind of thinking is totally immodest. I agree.
Modesty is not a word that applies to me in any way.'*

Between 1966 and 1975 Arnold won five Mr Universe and six
Mr Olympia titles. He was two hundred and fifty pounds of
writhing muscle and shining sinew and almost every time he
took his clothes off he won a trophy.

British bodybuilder Gordon Allen, later Chairman of NABBA
(National Amateur Body Building Association), the organisation
that had founded the Mr Universe contests, remembers his
first glimpse. It was at an East London gym run by the
husband-and-wife team soon to become Arnold's friends and
trainers, Wag and Dianne Bennett. 'Wag had told me there was
someone incredible. And I went along and Reg Park was also
there and Wag said, "Come and meet Arnold." He'd just arrived
and he was in a back room. He was wearing a sweater and Wag
told him to take it off, and I was absolutely flabbergasted. So
was Reg. I don't think he was used to seeing someone bigger
than himself: someone who was only 19 years old.'

The stupefaction was mutual. This was *that* Reg Park. The
idol, encountered in the flesh. Arnold kept staring at him and
smiling, he recalls, like a girl who has a crush on a boy and
she doesn't know what to say. He ran around looking at Park's
muscles, trying to talk to him – which was difficult, since 'at
the time I didn't know English well.'

Wag Bennett promptly laid on an exhibition show in which the youngster and the veteran could flex for each other and for the multitudes. According to Park, Arnold paid the older muscleman-movie star his debt of verbal gratitude – 'He said that he was inspired with the movies that I'd done and the photographs of me in the magazines' – and soon after that the two would be dashing off to the equator to seal their newfound friendship.

But for the moment Arnold was this strange, large piece of Austrian flotsam trying to find a home outside Austria. His stay in Munich, where from August 1966 he worked as a trainer and helper in Rolf Putziger's gym, sleeping on the floor before moving into a modest one-room apartment, leaves a bizarre picture of Arnold the supplicant limbering up to become Arnold the superman and psych-out artist.

The supplicant was seen in his determined street vigil one night outside the front door of German bodybuilding champion and ex-Mr Universe Reinhard Swolana, whose friendship and blessing he sought. Swolana finally let him in, warmed to the Arnold *braggadoccio*, and ended up organising a collection for the boy's trip to the Mr Universe contest in England.

Meanwhile the superman was getting bigger by the minute in the Munich gym, aided by the competitive friendship of Franco Columbu who arrived in Germany in 1976. And the psych-out artist's development consisted of demonic practical jokes visited on those around him: including the American iron-pumpers to whom Arnold taught helpful German phrases of greeting such as the one that meant (unknown to the Americans), 'Hello, you old pig. Do you still masturbate so much?'

In London, though, it was Arnold's turn to be a disoriented misfit. 'He wore a German-style corduroy suit when he first came here,' remembers Wag Bennett. 'But his trousers were flying at half mast, they were half way up his calves. So Dianne took him off to buy some boots to close the gap.'

Other gaps had to be closed: such as the one in Arnold's bank account. 'I used to get him shows around the country that would earn him some pocket money,' says Bennett. 'And we gave him bed and board, so he had no expenses when he was staying with us.'

Arnold kipped in the Bennetts' front room on a bed-settee he sometimes had to share with other career hunks who were passing through. When Cuban-born iron-pumper Sergio Oliva came to stay, Wag Bennett – like Arnold a practical joker – slipped a full-size picture of a nude girl between them while they slept, propping it on a pillow. Then he waited to pounce with his camera, snapping the general confusion when Dianne opened the door with the morning tea.

Arnold's own hoaxing instincts, Munich-honed, were keener. When Franco Columbu, whose English was worse than Arnold's, came to stay with the Bennetts, Arnold would help him out by naming the food Franco pointed to on the table. One day Franco pointed to some cake. 'Go to Dianne,' said Arnold helpfully, 'and tell her that you want some "fuck".' Franco went off to the kitchen. Seconds later, the sound of a slap was heard. Then Dianne came into the living room and slapped Arnold.

The rumours that Arnold himself was amorously involved with Dianne around this time cannot be confirmed or denied. Bennett gives a sheepish '*I* don't know' when asked if it is true, and Dianne is unavailable for comment. Gordon Allen, who knew them both, says the affair, though brief, was common knowledge among their friends.

If true, it accords with Arnold's now practised enthusiasm for repudiating father figures even while still, after a fashion, obeying them. Wag Bennett was no Gustav Schwarzenegger, but he was *in loco patris* as Arnold's semi-official trainer, manager and landlord. Another tale of Wag-baiting, told by Bennett himself, is a shaggy dog story with an intriguing slap in its tail. Coming in from London airport after a contest, Arnold arranged to be picked up at a tube station by Wag's orange Volkswagen. Not realising Wag had been delayed, Arnold twice stopped what he thought was the right car by doing a mock 'pose-off' in the middle of the street. The first car contained a puzzled woman: 'Are you all right?' she got out to ask. The second car contained a policeman: 'What exactly are you doing sir?' Finally, an infuriated Arnold stomped off towards Wag's home on foot, refusing a lift even when the older man's car did catch up.

The story is striking for its Scheherazade-style improbability. Since only Arnold could vouch for its veracity – the story requires that Wag could not have seen the rival cars – we are left pondering the likelihood of three orange VWs convoying in so short a time. Has Arnold been busy creating another mini-myth? Within one deftly layered fable he presents himself as the man who plays matador with moving cars; the star who brings self-display to the humblest streets; finally the man who leaves his mentor trailing in a smoky cloud of dudgeon.

The mentor after all had let Arnold down at the first hurdle. Though the Austrian won three bodybuilding titles in Europe in 1966 – Best Built Man of Europe, Mr Europe, and International Powerlifting Champion – he lost his first crack at the all-important Mr Universe contest in London in the same year. He came second to America's Chester Yorton. 'His legs were his faulty part when he came to England,' says John Citrone, who was the reigning Mr Britain at this time. 'His whole development there was weak,' concurred Irish bodybuilder Ivan Dunbar, writing in the late 1960s as *Health and Strength* magazine's man in the front row. 'Had his legs – particularly his calves – been equal to his upper body size he may well have won.'

Arnold took the leg criticism seriously, says Wag Bennett.

After he came second, he cut his trousers off at the knees so that everyone in the gym would ridicule him. He would be a figure of fun to those with better legs, and that would make him hammer those calves. He did, and they responded. If they hadn't, the whole Schwarzenegger story might be different. He would never have won Mr Universe; he wouldn't have got to America on the strength of it; he wouldn't have gone on to be a movie star.

Despite his physical shortcomings. Arnold was already a favourite with the spectators. 'Not since Reg Park appeared some years ago,' wrote Ivan Dunbar, 'have we been treated to a display of such massive muscle. And how the crowd at the judging loved him. One felt that if it had been left to the audience Arnold would have been declared winner then and there.'

He returned in 1967 to try again. This time the problem was not legs but leglessness, or the closest the normally sober Arnold

came. Wag Bennett had worked with the challenger to perfect
both his physique and his presentation, even to the point of
setting the Austrian's final pose-off to the stirring strains of the
music from *Exodus*, Otto Preminger's epic about the founding
of Israel. On the big night, however, Bennett was aghast at
what came up from the training room.

> One of the other bodybuilders had been down in the
> pumping-room with a bottle of whisky, which makes the
> veins expand, and Arnold had been having a mouthful. And
> when he goes on to be judged, he keeps almost falling asleep.
> He's standing there like this big packet of shit, all sagging, his
> belly hanging out, and I'm telling him to stand up straight and
> he stands up straight; then in a few minutes he sags again and
> I shout again. He could've lost the title as easy as that.

For other witnesses, Arnold outshone every rival, especially
in stage presence. 'He had the biggest dose of charisma I've ever
seen in a bodybuilder,' says Ivan Dunbar. And for Jimmy 'Jim'll
Fix It' Savile, a former NABBA president and one of the contest
judges, 'he just steamed in and it was like Boadicea's chariot.
He'd lop everybody's legs off and they were, like, four inches
shorter when Arnold was about. He wouldn't walk on like a
bodybuilder. He'd stroll on like an ordinary fellow, waving and
smiling to the crowd. Then suddenly – zonk! – he'd get on with
the business and that was that.'

Even before the contest, Savile recalls, Arnold was busy
honing his gamesmanship. 'He'd say to me in front of all
the other bodybuilders, "Jimmy, come and meet some of my
skinny friends."'

Aged twenty, Arnold won the contest and became the youngest
Mr Universe in history. Look at him in film records of that period,
or even in the footage recorded later for the feature *Pumping Iron*,
and you see why an entire judging panel could melt like butter
before this man's radiant arrogance. Arnold comes on stage.
Arnold looks like a demigod. Arnold stands there smiling, half
intoxicated with the applause and half derisive of it.

'Posing is pure theatre,' Arnold wrote in *Education of
a Bodybuilder*. 'I understand that and I love it. There are

bodybuilders who put almost no time into posing. And, of course, they don't win.'

Arnold on the platform started doing things never done in bodybuilding before, or never done so well. According to Gordon Allen, he would go through his set positions with a confidence no one else matched. 'He'd get four or five poses off, very flowing, while another guy is standing like a zombie in one position. He was like a ballet dancer.' He was learning too to vary his style for different audiences. 'In Paris you get more response from the classical poses,' said Arnold, 'in New York from the brutal poses, the most muscular poses.'

Below the neck, the body and its gestures seem tutored as much by Nijinsky as by Charles Atlas. Above the neck he looked like a schoolboy, even a choirboy: close-cropped hair, baby complexion, bright aspiring eyes. Hence the surprise experienced by two men one night in Ireland, when they first saw the Face and then felt the Body. Ivan Dunbar, who had invited Arnold to Belfast for an exhibition contest, remembers that he, Arnold and a couple of friends were driving through the city after a late-night meal.

> We didn't get finished until half past two in the morning. And on the way home there was an army patrol that stopped us, and everybody had to get out. And Arnold put his hands on the top of the car and they frisked him. And I remember one of the soldiers saying, 'Jesus, sarge, will you feel this here?' And it turned out one of the soldiers was a bodybuilder and I can still hear Arnold laughing! . . .

Arnold himself was 'a great mickey-taker,' recalls Dunbar. He always saw the absurd side of the sport. He'd joke about the idiocy of grown men stripping down to posture for prizes. 'There is one very important thing I can do,' says Arnold, 'and that is step back out of myself and laugh at myself when I am doing something, because it is all so ridiculous anyway.'

He would also pour scorn on the sport's traditional regimes of self-denial: 'In the old days, bodybuilders talked about eating two pounds of meat and thirty eggs a day and about how they couldn't have sex, and so on. And I said to myself, "Who the fuck wants to be part of that sport?"'

Friends in Britain testify that Arnold had a healthy interest in the opposite sex. Gordon Allen remembers trips to discos and nightclubs in Portsmouth where, speaking barely a word of English, Arnold would home in with alarming speed on the girl of his choice. He also, they claim, besmirched his copybook with another Portsmouth friend, gym-owner Bob Woolgar (father of Arnold's London patroness Dianne Bennett), by being discovered *in flagrante*, or close to it, with a girl late at night in Woolgar's gym. She was Arnold's then girl-friend Jackie.

John Citrone, who invited Arnold to stay in Newcastle, confirms his startling directness as a chat-up artist. 'He'd literally insinuate anything to a girl. He'd ask them straight out, "Do you want to come to bed with me?" He was very forward, any time we were in hotels or bars.'

Arnold was forward wherever he went, whether flirting with girls or socialising with fellow Goliaths. Remembers British bodybuilder John Bubb, 'I once went with him to Bristol and Wales for a long weekend of bodybuilding shows and demos, and he was like the scout leader. Every time there was a group of people talking, he was always the chairman, he just naturally took over.'

Reg Park witnessed the dominating personality when Arnold stayed with him in his adoptive South Africa over Christmas and New Year 1967/8, during which the two men did a barnstorming tour of bodybuilding shows across the country. 'He was very ambitious. He had a list of things he wanted to do and he ticked them off as he did them. He could be completely single-minded, as if he had blinkers on.'

At the same time, says Park, there was a carelessness, even derisiveness about him. 'Chutzpah,' says Park. 'Not quite arrogance, but leaning towards it. It's tongue-in-cheek too. It's like being serious but not taking yourself seriously. It's a very fine dividing line, and it's knowing you're good. You can only do it if you know you're good because otherwise you finish up with egg on your face.'

By 1968 it was time for Arnold to take his overweening

confidence to the country where it naturally belonged: America. He went to Florida to compete in the prestigious Mr Olympia contest, annual climax to an iron-pumper's dreams. This is the show where the winners of all the year's other bodybuilding battles gather: a vast acreage of human flesh, pumped and primed, marinaded in oils, strafed by the photographers' flashlights glancing off their polished bulges.

Arnold could have been the Cinderella at this gathering. He had no money, he recalled: only one gym bag since he had no plan to move to America at that point. 'I was kind of like a helpless kid in a way.'

Mentally, though, he wasn't helpless at all. After London and Mr Universe, he recalls, the 'heat of victory' was in his blood. The Americans, he says, were amazed by his size. There were gasps as he came on stage. The spectators moved to the edges of their seats. He rose up and expanded every muscle fibre in his body. The crowd sensed it and cheered. He heard Americans shouting 'Arnold!' He felt fantastic.

Until the verdict came in. Arnold had come second.

5

Go To Olympus,
Do Not Pass Olympia

'I feel that I must have lived here once before in a previous life because I feel so at home in America.'

The day after landing in Miami at the end of September 1968, Arnold ceded that Mr Olympia contest to Frank Zane. The top-weight Austrian prodigy came second to the medium-weight American prodigy whose body, in Arnold's own words, 'seemed to have been tooled down with the chisels and gouges a sculptor would use on mahogany'. Arnold cried all night. He felt he had disappointed his friends and supporters. He vowed to make good the defeat.

That was Miami. It is the stuff of myth that a hero is sometimes dealt a large blow across the ego, so that later triumphs are the more resonant. It is important that the hero seem a greenhorn, even a booby, like the young Arthur or the young Parsifal. The setback would be brief, for now that Arnold was in America, he was 'home'.

This was the land where he would settle and which he had long dreamt of: Anti-Austria. No museums or concerts or that 'old shit': just a vast nation berserk with entrepreneurialism. 'America is still the only country where you can do things . . . I love the mentality and openmindedness. The spirit of America is so free. I love the way this country welcomes new ideas; it's so different from Europe.'

So different. But good lord, who is this geezer swaggering over the horizon, auditioning for Gurnemanz to Arnold's Parsifal? It looks like a squashed, fairground-mirror version of Arnold's Dad Gustav. Stocky, medium-height and with a Groucho Marx moustache, it is Joseph E. Weider: owner of America's muscle empire, founded of the IFBB (International Federation of Bodybuilders) and the man who has brought Arnold over on a one-year contract.

'I asked my agent when he was in London to persuade Arnold to compete in the Mr Olympia contest,' recalls Weider today. 'He wasn't really of the calibre of the bodybuilders in America and I explained to him he had to have more definition, proportion, shape. In Europe the bodybuilders were bulky and very massive, but not aesthetically defined or "cut". That's why Arnold lost in Miami.'

Weider had zeroed in on Arnold after seeing pictures of him in *Iron Man* magazine. Impressed by the Herculean frame, he purchased a black-and-white side chest shot from British photographer George Greenwood. He then had it hand-coloured and used as a cover photo for his *Muscle Power* (later *Muscle & Fitness*) magazine. The response was huge. Realising he had found a star, Weider dangled the appropriate financial bait to try to persuade Arnold to come to America and train in California. Arnold asked Reg Park for his advice. 'Sounds great,' said Park. 'But work with a legal contract and ask for a car.'

The wage was a modest $200 a week, in return for which Weider had Arnold write articles for his magazines. 'We helped him edit them,' says Weider – according to some sources they all but wrote them for him – 'and later we encouraged him to sell his own correspondence courses.'

Weider says a car was included in the Arnold package but cannot remember what car. Canadian muscle magazine editor Robert Kennedy, a longtime Arnold fan and chronicler, says it was a yellow Volkswagen. A third source disputes there was a car at all. Bodybuilder Paul Graham, who met Arnold at Vince's Gym in North Hollywood and shared rooms with him nearby, says Arnold could not yet drive. Graham himself conducted him around Los Angeles.

We'd train at Vince's in the morning, then in the afternoon after we'd had a sleep we'd motor over to Santa Monica to

Gold's Gym. This was because Vince had no squat machine for leg exercises.

Vince – Vince Gironda, a veteran trainer who owned the oldest and most famous iron-pumping centre in California – was a law unto himself. Not least in his attitude to the Austrian muscle marvel.

Joe Weider paid me to get Arnold into shape and I got him an apartment a few blocks away [he says]. He lived around here for nine months. The guy was a cissy. I'd demonstrate exercises to him he couldn't do. He didn't have the balls.

The first day he came to see me, he walked up to my desk. He'd put on a pair of trunks and he came up from the back room. He told me who he was and he wanted me to assess his body. I looked him over and I said, 'You look like a fat fuck to me.'

He took off mad. He came on wanting me to adore him and I told him he was a big fat German sausage. He was a plodder, a typical German plodder. Nothing spectacular. Not a good student at all. His tenacity is all that's got him where he is today.

'I was supposed to get publicity in Weider's magazine, and anything else that would help my business,' Gironda goes on, airing a related grievance. 'But Joe Weider wouldn't run a picture of me, or my name, if hell froze over. He used to come into the gym after waiting to make sure I was gone, to see if there were any movie personalities on the floor he could interview.'

Relations between Arnold and Vince went from cool to freezing. Arnold finally thought about moving south to sunny, laidback Santa Monica. Better leg-squat facilities; and a growing population of bodybuilders. 'There was a potpourri of every kind of humanity in the world down there,' Gironda says, with undisguised distaste. 'Plus steroids.'

Ah. Steroids. Was Arnold taking them then?

Is a frog's ass waterproof? He was said to be using steroids like nobody had ever heard before.

Rick Wayne, though, a fellow bodybuilder and former Mr Universe who had known Arnold from London days, says he took Dianabol in much the same quantities as other top weight-pumpers. Wayne also disputes Gironda's claim that Arnold was lazy: 'He was a fanatical trainer. Vince has his own criteria about these things.'

Down in Santa Monica – where he and Arnold moved at the same time – Paul Graham witnessed the fanaticism.

Arnold was learning to drive in one of my cars at the time, and he had an accident. I was in the apartment, heard the crash and walked up to the corner. The car was smashed and the gear lever on the steering wheel had somehow gone through Arnold's leg. It must have missed an artery, though, because no blood was coming out at all. Looking back, it was like one of Arnold's films; it was as if he was from another planet. We got the wound sewn up in the morning and he still went to train that evening on his legs. Most people would have taken the week off.

The annunciation of superhuman status came at the right time. 1969 was a tough year. Arnold was making little money and taking few prizes in America. Despite notching a third successive Mr Universe victory in London, he failed again at the Mr Olympia title, losing to the rippling Cuban Sergio Oliva. Arnold confessed to Rick Wayne that he had been out-psyched and out-prepared.

In compensation he starred in, or stumbled into, his first movie. *Hercules Goes to New York* is the best and worst film an actor could begin with. Arnold got to play a demi-god, but he also battled with all-too-mortal dialogue, skimpy sets and the most sophomoric plot of the decade. The film is a collector's piece today, but back then it was more like a calling card from hell. It is barely mentioned in Arnold's early interviews and publicity, and according to actor James Karen he made attempts to buy up the negative. Karen, who co-starred, says that whenever he meets the star, 'I do not mention the movie. He does not like to know about the movie. He *hates* the movie.'

But it was surely decreed by destiny that a longtime toga-movie fan like Schwarzenegger should receive his acting baptism in a piece of total-immersion costume kitsch, made on a wing and a prayer.

Arnold secured the role through Joe Weider, who wanted to get some serious *danegeld* out of his new protégé. When two producers called Aubrey Wisberg and Lawrence F. Fabian contacted the entrepreneur to ask for a muscleman who could star in a movie, Weider recommended Arnold. 'They asked me if he could act. I said, Of course he can, in England he was a Shakespearean actor. And they fell for it.'

'Weider was such a hype artist,' recalls Arnold. 'I didn't speak English well. I didn't understand most of what I was saying. I slipped off the boat and starred in a motion picture. It was crazy.'

The film was a knockabout adventure aimed at a quick killing in theatres and on television. It was not, insists its director Arthur A. Seidelman today, made for Italian TV (as several modern reference books as well as Wendy Leigh's biography claim). In the script written by writer-producer Wisberg, Arnold as Hercules comes down to Planet Earth after pleading with Zeus for a terrestrial vacation. Planet Earth is represented by New York and Mount Olympus by Central Park, complete with audible noise of traffic and passing aeroplanes. The film cost $300,000 and Arnold got $1,000 a week for twelve weeks' work.

The movie has become a joke in ensuing years, but Seidelman claims it was largely meant as one; as a comic riff on the muscleman-in-toga movie tradition that Arnold grew up with. The director says he was at variance with the writer-producer over the film's tone, and also over whether or not they should keep Arnold's thick Austrian accent. 'I frankly was against dubbing him with an American actor's voice, because I thought he'd worked very diligently on his English. He most certainly had an accent, but it was a rather charming one.' Seidelman approached the movie as a 'lighthearted spoof', but he recalls Wisberg grabbing his arm after an early screening of one day's footage and saying 'if I hear one more laugh at dailies, you're off this film'. For Arnold's voice – as a precaution against more unwanted hilarity – Wisberg went for the dubbing option. The actor-athlete is now ventriloquised in the film with a flat-ironed

American voice that could be narrating a documentary on petrochemicals.

They could hide the Schwarzenegger voice, but they couldn't hide the bulk and wouldn't want to. 'He was enormous,' says Seidelman. 'I spent the first three days talking to his right arm.' James Karen says; 'I'd never seen anyone like him before. He was at the absolute peak of his physical development. When I first saw him, my mouth literally fell open. Later I introduced him to my son during the filming and Arnold was naked from the waist up; I said, "Arnold, give him a treat" and Arnold did the pec jiggle.'

Arnold does the pec jiggle in the film too. Indeed he is asked to do little else for the whole ninety minutes. He lays out the muscleman goods while the plot skitters dementedly around him. He fights a gang of thugs on a dockside in a scene that constitutes Seidelman's bid to be Sergei 'Battleship Potemkin' Eisenstein (eighteen different acute-angled shots in forty seconds). He struts about with a bare torso sometimes adorned with hellenic blue sash. He singlehandedly – or two-armedly – upends a yellow cab. And he flexes his face in tireless response to the lame one-liners delivered by his comical fellow protagonist Arnold Stang.

Stang, a New York comedian who resembles an anorexic Phil Silvers, plays Pretzie the pretzel-seller, who befriends our hero. Since Schwarzenegger was asked to shelve his own unwieldy surname and appear on posters as 'Arnold Strong', there is some name confusion for the uninitiated. Seidelman claims that Arnold (Schwarzenegger) was reluctant to trade in his four-syllable handle. But he settled for the substitute when it was agreed to put 'Mr Universe' in small letters under his new name in the advertising.

The one stirring passage in the entire production is Arnold (Mr Universe)'s chariot race. Escaping from assorted baddies, he hops on a passing horse-drawn Graeco-Roman vehicle and rides it through Times Square, turns around to pass Radio City Music Hall and ends up lashing the patient nags through Central Park – or such parts of it as have not been set aside for Mount Olympus.

Did he do the driving himself? Seidelman says yes. 'He had a couple of practice sessions driving round the park, two days before, with a trainer, and got to the point where he could handle it.' It was shot in the early morning and though James Karen is not sure whether they had a permit from the city to drive chariots through it, Seidelman maintains they could not have done the scenes without the authorities' co-operation. 'Even at six o'clock we had to have police holding back the traffic.'

Today *Hercules in New York* (later titled *Hercules Goes Bananas* after Wisberg and Co had given up all struggle to leave some seriousness in it) seems a piquant play-off between one man's kismet – Arnold's first step on the road to stardom – and the ludicrous obstacles placed in his path. Connoisseurs of Z-movie dialogue will treasure the script. 'Yo, Hercules' is how New York sailors apparently address passing demi-gods. And 'Mind yer own business, Venus' is a sample of how the fat is chewed on Olympus.

Arnold himself seems charmingly at sea, though any promise of star impact is sabotaged by the voice. The dubbing actor's all-American delivery of 'I'm Hercules' is no substitute for the sound we want and expect to come out of Arnold's mouth, namely 'Uh'm Hoorc-yuliss'. But there is still a half-shy, half-crazed confidence about the young actor. The face with its baby pout and upswing of jaw has a cartoon innocence mixed with caricature strongman contour; Desperate Dan meets Peter Pan. And when Arnold gets to lift weights in a show-contest with bodybuilder Tony Carroll (a scene casually bunged in for the Schwarzenegger body groupies), his face takes on the rainbow of expressions – smiling, mocking, pained, taunting, tortured, triumphant – that eight years later will clinch his starmaking turn in *Pumping Iron*.

But at this stage did he want to do other films at all? James Karen recalls him as a pleasant-mannered, shy fellow who took direction obediently, played basketball with the cast and crew and ate enormous meals. No movie future was discussed. Arthur Seidelman, though, does remember the glimmering of a career plan. 'He said to me very early on that he had come to the United States to make a lot of money. He was very serious, very determined to be successful. And he was looking towards films as a major source of that success.'

★   ★   ★

Hercules in New York, however, hurtled into oblivion, leaving its star high and dry on the muscle beaches of California. To extend his adoptive family, Arnold persuaded Joe Weider to bring Franco Columbu to America on a similar training and competing contract to his own. The Sardinian bodybuilder, who at five foot five looked like a shorter, wider version of Franco Nero, had enjoyed pre-careers as a jockey and as lightweight boxing champion of Italy. He would soon be the world's number one bodybuilder in his height class, winning Mr Olympia in 1976 and 1981.

In Germany he and Arnold had become fast, womanising friends. In America Franco moved in with Arnold, sharing a Santa Monica bachelor pad, plus the terrors of learning English, plus a fondness for the candle-burning social life.

There was already the beginning of a circle forming around Arnold. Paul Graham, muscle photographer Art Zeller, Joes Weider and Gold (of Gold's Gym) . . . and now Franco. The gang would eventually become known as the 'Arnia': in tribute to their undisputed leader and to the group's faintly threatening, Mafia-style solidarity.

It all helped to make Arnold feel at home in the new country. When he was enjoying himself, there were not enough hours in the day. 'Arnold hates to go to sleep because he feels it's a waste of time,' Franco Columbu recalls. 'When he has a party and people start to go home, he likes a small clique to stay behind. Then we light up cigars, have a little drink and sit down and talk about all our crazy friends and crack up.'

However, among Angelenos who knew nothing of either bodybuilding or the Arnia, the newcomer with the thick Teutonic accent and thicker build may have been known merely as a large, convivial fellow who did PR for muscle magazines. An article in the Santa Monica College magazine – Arnold joined the school to study English soon after settling in California – gives a stranger's-eye glimpse. 'You may have seen walking about our halls, a fellow who appears to be slightly larger than most of the student bodies . . .' Arnold, the piece goes on, is 'under contract to Weider International, a health food company, which sends him all over the world to demonstrate its products.'

Weider says Arnold's publicity efforts on the company's behalf were voluntary, not contractual. 'When we came out with a food-supplements line, Arnold said to me, "You're a pal, I'll try the products and if I like them I'll be happy for you to use my name".'

A picture of Arnold survives from his student phase. Wearing a skin-tight white sports shirt with plunging lace-up neckline, and a pair of thigh-hugging, psychedelically striped trousers, he sits in pouting enormity while a classful of girls peer with nervous admiration. In his right hand Arnold holds an exercise book, as if idly fantasising that it is one of those telephone books that strong men tear in two to impress beautiful women.

His education gathered pace and mass. 'Being at the beginning on a visitor's visa, I was only allowed to take two courses in one college. So I had to take two classes at Santa Monica City College, then I took two classes simultaneously at the West Los Angeles College.' He also started taking evening classes in business at UCLA (University of California in Los Angeles). Then he added American Indian history and American history 'and went on and on and on'.

Meanwhile he had won a few titles and was about to win a few more. His sweetest conquest must have been his 1970 Mr Universe title in London, when he vanquished his one-time idol Reg Park, who had emerged from retirement for a hoped-for comeback. The victory was swathed in more than its fair share of 'true myths'. According to a favoured version of events, Arnold's UK mentor Wag Bennett lured Park over to the contest by pretending that Arnold was out of condition. Bennett (goes the tale) sent the South Africa-based veteran a photo of the young champion's supposedly current, off-peak physique. But it was an old Arnold snap and Park fell for the scam: he came, competed and trailed second to a younger man now bigger and better defined than ever.

Wendy Leigh prints this tale as unassailable fact. Reg Park, though, denies it ever happened. 'I've read that story and there's no truth in it whatsoever.' Bennett too denies it. 'It's absolute nonsense. Someone made it up'.

Park, however, admits that he wasn't in great shape for the showdown. And Gordon Allen remembers Arnold playing a

game of hide-and-seek with his older rival during the build-up
to the contest. Arnold's aim, speculates Allen, was that Park
should not glimpse the New Improved Body before it was
ready for unveiling. On contest night Allen himself, sitting
twelve yards away in the front row, was startled when he saw
the works. 'Arnold had gone from being smooth to looking
cut to ribbons. It was something we'd never seen before: the
definition, the muscles, the veins. It was amazing.'

In America, under Weider, Arnold had developed the 'cut'
look: the look he had envied on Chet Yorton and Frank
Zane, the first two men to defeat him in major contests. 'In
bodybuilding you don't only try to train the pectoral muscles,'
Arnold explains. 'You then try to separate the upper pectoral
from the lower pectoral muscles. Then within those muscles
are muscle fibres. You're trying to get the skin so thin, burn
off all the fat underneath, so that all those little fibres, all those
little striations and muscles that touch the bone – everything is
shown.'

In the process many bodybuilders take diuretics to reduce
water and bring the body's fat content down to less than
eight percent. The said body ends up looking – to the uninitiated – like a painting of St Bartholomew after his flaying.
The Arnold who had wanted 'veins' now had them with a
vengeance. They snaked over his body like a road-map of
hell, preparing us for the SciFi-arterial look of Arnold in
The Terminator, with that fine line between cybernetic fantasy
and emetic anatomical realism. (Gasp at the gouging of an
eye. Gag at the slicing open of an arm for surgical-robotic
fine-tuning.)

The other weapon Arnold deployed in these victory years
was his 'psyching' talent. 'He didn't just have physical potential,
he had mental skills,' says Wag Bennett. Rick Wayne recalls
two psych-outs that became famous – or infamous – in the
Mr Olympia annals. Both involved Sergio Oliva, and the
first one clinched Arnold's breakthrough victory in 1970. His
first Mr Olympia title would be the beginning of a run of
victories in the top contest which no bodybuilder had matched
before.

The two men were on stage together in the final pose-off when

Arnold whispered something in Oliva's ear: apparently to the effect that he (Arnold) had had enough of this whole circus, so why didn't they both walk off. Oliva walked. Arnold remained on stage, struck his most dazzling pose and took the prize. 'The judges thought Sergio had thrown his hat in,' says Wag Bennett, who was there. 'Sergio was very upset with Arnold afterwards.'

Two years later, again trying to shrug off Oliva at the finishing tape, Arnold exercised once more his gamesmanship skills. He arranged to have the wall of a contest room repainted a darker colour so that his body would stand out better than his dark-skinned rival's. The judges gave him the contest. 'To this day I believe that was how I got the edge,' Arnold told Wayne. 'Sergio suffered for his blindness.'

Standing behind Arnold, through all these years and victories, was Joe Weider. He helped to promote the Arnold psyching talent plus the Arnold physique, plus most of the other conquering things Arnold got up to in the late 60s early 70s – PR stunts; exhibitions; magazines; mail-order enterprises. Might Arnold have begun to resent this? Here, after all, was another 'father' ordering his life for him: almost a replacement for Gustav, who had by now retired into the role of affably nagging Dad. ('This is great,' Schwarzenegger Snr would say of the body-building feats. 'But you can't do this forever. When are you going to get a job, make some money, have some security?')

Weider had a number of characteristics in common with Schwarzenegger Snr. He was domineering and single-minded; a work-pusher and Stakhanovite. And he had a weakness for culture, showing off his art and antiques collection to Arnold or dragging the lad off to museums or auctions. Weider rejoiced in having this ready-made innocent as a pupil.

At one point we went into a shop selling English furniture. I asked Arnold, 'What do you think of this table? How much you reckon it costs?' 'A hundred dollars?' said Arnold. I called the sales guy over and asked him. 'Sixteen thousand dollars.'

As with Gustav, the mentor-protégé relationship developed a love-hate dimension. During his business administration course at UCLA, Arnold was asked to write two essays: one on the person he most admired, the other on the person he most hated or despised. He wrote both essays on Weider.

The older man claims Arnold never resisted instruction or resented patronage. Why would he? Apart from anything else, Arnold was a stranger in a strange land, still struggling with a new language. 'If he didn't understand something – a word – he was never embarrassed to ask' says Weider.

Yet Weider's power over Arnold began to irk. Even the impresario's own proudest monument, the Mr Olympia contest, became a source of friction. The show was already regarded by some bodybuilders as an overgrown gimmick: says John Bubb, 'It was initially a circus put on by Weider as a kind of publicity stunt. It started out of a "sulk" when America lost a Mr Universe contest in London.' Now the contest was wielded anew as a fretful bargaining counter between patron and sportsman. After 1970 Weider forbade Arnold to compete in the British contest again. Says Wag Bennett: 'Weider had the IFBB and he wanted the number one contest. Obviously he didn't want his top man boosting NABBA.'

In the printed programme for the 1971 Mr Universe show at London's Victoria Palace theatre, NABBA President Oscar Heidelstam bemoans the absent giant. 'Arnold, after assuring me for many months that he would be there come what may, had to send me a last-minute letter stating that he had received two letters from the Weider organisation forbidding him to enter. Arnold, being on contract, had no alternative but to obey instructions, but he sent me the letters as proof of the pressure put on him.'

To get away from these accursed father figures, what more can Arnold do? In Austria he had dealt with his father by defying him. In Britain he had dealt with his substitute father Wag Bennett by, whispered the rumours, sleeping with the man's wife.

Would Weider be next? Arnold's serial mission in these early years is to put a halt to this imprinting by alien authority figures. What attracted him to America was the spirit of self-moulding enterprise. He is tired of people training him to be the toy of *their* dreams. He will train himself to be his own creation and creative superforce: Mr Autonomy, not Mr Automaton. As if placing history's own punctuation point at this moment of Arnold's will to filial emancipation, Gustav Schwarzenegger dies.

6

Father Figures

'When you have parents who mould you in a certain way, it's a great effort for them. You have a chance of paying them back, making them feel that all that effort meant something. Then that's all cut off.'

(i) Two Funerals and an Inquest

In May 1971 Arnold's brother Meinhard died in a car crash in Kitzbuhel, Austria. A year later, Gustav died of a stroke in Graz hospital, two months after seeing his son triumph in the 1972 Mr Olympia contest held in Essen, Germany. Arnold's failure to attend either man's funeral has since been filed simplistically under U for 'Unfeeling'. But it also confirms that, then and later in a life of high achievement and tunnel-vision determination, he saw and felt strictly what he allowed himself to see and feel.

The grown-up Arnold had spent years distancing himself from both men, while maintaining a vestigial protocol of family loyalty. In interviews and his own writings, he has little to say about Meinhard except to record that the older boy was the parents' favourite. Astonishingly, Meinhard is not mentioned at all in the childhood remembrances of *Arnold: Education of a Bodybuilder*. And from other Arnold utterances we receive a hazy view of an artistic type who did 'wonderful paintings' as a child, was more 'the thinking type' than his younger brother and was 'a typical Cancer – very creative'.

This is almost frighteningly at variance with the Meinhard

50

remembered and vilified by his schoolmates. Did Arnold lacquer the truth out of fraternal loyalty? As children the two brothers must have been close, if only as sons born a mere year apart and growing up in the same small, marooned village. Even when not mentioning Meinhard by name, Arnold uses 'we' almost as much as 'I' in discussing his childhood. But when Arnold became famous and moved abroad and Meinhard stayed in Austria, failing to hold down a steady job or to make up his mind whether to marry the girl (Erika Lohrer) who was carrying his child, we seem to have the perfect set-up for a legend of sibling jealousy, with the stock unhappy ending. Meinhard died in a car crash one night after a heavy drinking session.

Wendy Leigh's treatment of this chapter in the Schwarzenegger family story illustrates the two-way flow of the true myth syndrome. Leigh sees Meinhard's death in fatalistic terms: the tale of a failed brother burning out. Her title for this section could be 'Arnold the Brute Success Story': in which the protagonist's victims are not just his competitors and opponents in bodybuilding. They are also his nearest and dearest from home, sacrificed on the altar of Arnold's vision and ambition.

Meinhard may, if his life did fall apart before ending in this drink-driving harakiri, have had other, unknowable reasons than his brother's triumphs for depression and career failure. (One former schoolfriend claims he was being chased by the police on the night of his death.) In addition, the Arnold of 1971 was not the public super-achiever of today; he may have conquered the recherché bodybuilding world, but his film career was still grounded after one toga'd turkey. Leigh's interpretation, though, is remorselessly Arnie-centric. The penalty for being a supporting character in a sibling's story – as she sees Meinhard – is that you must fit into the symbolic pattern.

In the same way Gustav, who died on December 11th 1972, must pass away of 'a broken heart, still shattered by Meinhard's death' (Wendy Leigh). There is no evidence at all that Gustav's death was hastened by unassuageable grief for his son: a son on whom he never appeared to shower much love as a child, any more than on Arnold. But it suits Leigh's myth. The son who is to blame for Meinhard's death by despair must be to blame, by a domino destructiveness, for the death by grief of the bereaved father.

Meanwhile Arnold's own version of Gustav's death, and the events following it, turn this period into a spaghetti junction of myths and counter-myths. Undisputed fact: Arnold did not go to Gustav's funeral, held on December 18th at Weiz Cemetery, just outside Graz. Unresolved question: Why not? Arnold himself started this second, belated inquest by a casual anecdote delivered to camera a few years later in *Pumping Iron*. Lolling on a sofa in a snappy red-and-white-striped sports shirt, Arnold delivers thus.

> If you want to be a champion you can't have any kind of outside negative force coming in to affect you. So I trained myself for that. To be totally cold and not have things going through my mind. And it was a sad story when my father died. Because my mother called me on the phone and she said, 'You know, your dad died.' And this was exactly two months before a contest. 'Are you coming home for the funeral?' she said. I said: 'No it's too late. He's dead and nothing can be done. I'm sorry, I can't come.' And I didn't explain the reasons why, because how do you explain to a mother whose husband died that you just can't be bothered now because of a contest?

This little monologue precipitated the largest counter-inquisition in the history of Arnold's relationship with media. In 1985 he told *Rolling Stone* magazine that he had borrowed the story from a French bodybuilder, agreeing to deliver it, in his capacity as *Pumping Iron*'s star, as a representative tale of the muscle-building mind-set.

The film's director George Butler agrees that it was a borrowed story, since Butler had borrowed it. He heard it from the lips of a boxer – 'one of the Spinks brothers' – in the 1972 Montreal Olympics. 'When we were shooting *Pumping Iron* I discussed this story casually with Arnold the night before we filmed his interview. The next day he delivered it to camera, word-perfect, as if it was his own story about him not attending his father's funeral.' Butler let it pass since *Pumping Iron* had adopted a

New Journalism approach to documentary in which 'we took nonfiction material and gave it a dramatic structure'.

In the meantime, says Butler, Arnold vouchsafed to the director: 'What actually happened at the time of my father's death was that I was at a contest in Mexico giving an exhibition. Then I split for a vacation. No one could reach me, even by phone.' When he got back to Los Angeles, Franco Columbu met him at the airport to tell him his father had died and been buried. 'I immediately took the next flight to Austria to comfort my mother.'

In 1988 though, Arnold tells *Playboy* magazine that he was in an American hospital with a leg injury when he heard of Gustav's death. 'I couldn't go to the funeral because I was in the hospital. And I took it badly because I knew how much he had done for me.' 'Death,' he adds, 'never comes at the right time, no matter when it is.'

Death is indeed no respecter of people's convenience; the death of a famous man's father less so than most. The son cannot hide from the moral commentators. Every holier-than-thou hack looks to make capital out of observing the son's reaction. If the son opts for the gung-ho approach – a brusque but defendable 'he's dead, there is nothing we can do' – he is pilloried by the world's card-carrying Care Bears. If he offers up as excuse for non-attendance one of those harmless fictions that most of us, in the unexamined world of the non-famous, get away with every day, he volunteers for media crucifixion.

(ii) Weider Still and Weider

Two years after Gustav's death – if we follow the parricide-stained interpretational path of Wendy Leigh – Arnold attempted to knife his other father figure, Joe Weider. The broken heart and unattended funeral he had dealt out to Gustav were but rehearsals for the deadly tirade he published against Weider in a 1974 edition of *Sports Illustrated*. 'Rather like a rebellious son who is set on separating from his father once and for all.' writes Leigh, '. . . he launched an overt attack on Weider *relatively early in his career.*' (My italics.)

Early? By 1974 Arnold is already contemplating retirement as a bodybuilder, having been at the top for seven years. Leigh spoils a simple probable truth – that Arnold resents father figures – by going for a barnstorming 'true myth': that death hovers over every surrogate Dad in this young man's life almost before the dew has dried on their relationship.

The *Sports Illustrated* interview is, uncontestably, heady stuff:

> All of these magazines – Weider's, Hoffman's, Lurie's – I call them comic books, circus books! Those headlines! HOW ARNOLD TERRORIZED HIS THIGHS! Hah! THIS IS JOE'S BICEPS SPEAKING! Why are Joe's biceps talking to anybody? It is not that much of a biceps . . . None of these silly people are really interested in bodybuilding anymore. They are only interested in the money that can be made from it. Each of them says that he is for bodybuilding, but these men are not. They are knocking the sport down. I ask Joe why he prints such junk – why is everybody bombing and blasting and terrorizing, all these silly words?

This last outburst is rich coming from the future co-author of a book, *Arnold: The Education of a Bodybuilder* (published five years later in 1979), which is littered with those very locutions: 'blasting my muscles' (p. 22), 'bombing my muscles furiously' (p. 23) and so on. But that may only emphasise the gratuitous, storm-in-teacup nature of the tirade. Weider himself makes light of it today: 'We all make mistakes and at that time Arnold was moving up in life and I guess he wanted to "put down" his previous life.'

As Leigh herself points out anti-climactically, Arnold and Weider's relationship survived this and other spats: just as Arnold would later follow up his even wilder verbal onslaughts on Sylvester Stallone, a role model if not a mentor, by corralling him as a business partner in the 1990s. The biographer seeking dramatic punctuation points for his story needs to be patient. Sometimes what looks like a full stop is merely the first in a row of 'now read on' dots.

Besides, if Arnold was seeking a weapon with which to dispose of Weider, he would soon have the simplest, most bloodless one of all to hand.

Obsolescence. Where Arnold was going to next, Weider would have no place.

7

Earning Power

'I set out to be the best and I am'

(i) A Sport and its Psychobabble

As the Seventies marched on, Arnold the visionary developed double vision. One career dream, yet to be realised, got superimposed on another, all but fulfilled. Already the best bodybuilder in the world, he needed only a run of victories at the highest level to become the best bodybuilder in history. After that, what? Another goal was required to keep the achievement machine in order. Property millionaire? Sports mogul? Performance artist? Movie star?

Ideally the second career would be a natural offspring of the first, able to draw on similar attributes and aptitudes. But what *are* the essential components of the sport Arnold had selected?

Arnold himself once defined bodybuilding's appeal in terms as eloquent as any advocate could: 'We've always loved horse races because you can see the wonderful muscles in motion. People used to shy away from that with the human body, but now it's accepted. We like to see it function and move. And that only works if there are muscles there.'

But this is an aesthete's view of the sport. Why do most mortals who hump weights hour after hour on gravity-intensive terra firma do it?

Vince Gironda says that it 'started with people my height that lamented the fact they weren't six feet tall. So the only thing they could do was get a bigger body.' In Hollywood, he adds, they want to go on to be movie stars. 'Today in this town it's practically a necessity for people interested in motion pictures to get a good body.'

For Reg Park, a muscleman who did become a movie star, bodybuilding also began with the desire to crank himself up from insignificance to significance:

> I wanted to be the best physique in the world. It went back to my very early childhood days. I spent a lot of time with my grandparents, from about five to ten years old, and I remember they had prints of a wedding in Ancient Greece, when the guy had a kind of Greek skirt and scandals. And his physique was sensational, I always remember it. I wanted to be like that.

Set a psychologist loose on the bodybuilding phenomenon and you get a torrent of post-Freudian cerebration. Says New York practitioner Stanley Riklin:

> The man who engages in bodybuilding to make himself feel stronger, healthier and more confident so he'll be able to relate better to others is entirely different from the one who is preoccupied only with himself, with pumping his muscles up to an extraordinary size. But this second man, in my opinion, is usually quite insecure, and attempting to overcome deep anxieties – fears that he is small, damaged, inadequate. His energies are not going outward toward other people, but *inward*; he involves others only to obtain admiration and allay anxieties about himself.

The neurosis of self-display – is that what bodybuilding has in common with acting? Riklin again:

> There's a famous paper by Bertram Lewin called 'The Body as Phallus' that suggests that a person can sometimes treat his entire physique as if it were a penis. And indeed the bodybuilder who pumps himself up may be trying, on a fantasy level, to make up for his fear of a small penis.

But Arnold – let us call him back into the symposium – won't hear of this. 'Can you imagine, now, that a teenage boy stands naked in front of a mirror and says, "Hmhh. My damn weenie is so little. I better start building up my biceps instead."?' Arnold did not do forty tons of bench-presses per day, or lift in one year the equivalent of the QE2 in weight (as *Pumping Iron* director George Butler once estimated), to let this wacko notion grip humanity. 'Can you imagine the effort? Four hours of training a day for fifteen years because you have a short cock? It's so absurd.'

Yet compensation for some sense of lost or deficient masculinity, if not for the male member, seems as persuasive a theory as any other of bodybuilding's appeal. It also allows us to consider Arnold's 'clothing' of himself in muscle, and his later clothing of himself in macho movie roles, as a vocational extension of his clothing himself in his father's uniform. (Or his fantasy of doing so.)

Gustav loudhailed the 'Be macho' message to his son throughout his childhood. He wanted Arnold to be an army officer. Arnold, with his ambivalence about team spirit, was not about to do that. But bodybuilding may have been a sop to his father's virility propaganda combined with a parodic defiance. Arnold himself traces the choice of his sporting career to a sense of instability during boyhood: '. . . you have to be a little "off". Something has to happen in your childhood that you say, "I'm going to make up for this." You don't even know what it is. Maybe I was competitive with my brother or trying to prove something to my father. But it doesn't really matter. Something was there that made me hungry.'

(ii) *What the Butler Saw*

Success in bodybuilding may have satisfied the hunger for competitive manly achievement. It barely satisfied other hungers. The sport had little kudos outside its own circle of fans and flexers and offered scant reward to anyone whose dreams ran to money as well as fame. George Butler, the photographer and future film-maker of *Pumping Iron*, first met Arnold in September 1972. With writer Charles Gaines, Butler was on assignment from *Oui* magazine to cover the Mr America contest in New York.

> You have to think back and remember how primitive bodybuilding was in those days. Charles Gaines compared it to dwarf-tossing or midget-wrestling. The Mr America show took place at the Brooklyn Academy of Music in a small hall with an old Calliope organ. And here was Arnold, the biggest bodybuilder in history, the Muhammad Ali of his sport, being paid $500 to give an exhibition at the contest. Maybe he got ten other shows like this a year, in these primitive locations, with seedy changing rooms and paint peeling on the walls.

Wayne DeMilia, who has known Arnold for over twenty years and who today is International Chairman of Pro-Bodybuilding, endorses Butler's picture of the sport's lowly status; though he disputes that Arnold himself was a conspicuous victim. Many bodybuilders had to enhance their income, says DeMilia, by making themselves available – in all senses – to interested patrons.

> You can guess how they earned the money. They gravitated to California and some guys did things they'd probably regret now. But in Arnold's case there was no need. He was very well paid as a sportsman. By the early 1970s he was getting $300 a week from Weider – my pay was $140 (as a repairman for AT & T, the telephone company) – and he could command $1,000 to guest-pose. He did this almost every weekend at exhibitions, sometimes twice in one day. It starts to add up.

But it added up slowly, insists Butler. When he and Arnold met, the three-time Mr Olympia had a small condo flat in Santa Monica and was making extra money through 'How to' books on sport and bodybuilding. Butler visited Arnold's office with its pigeonhole system containing 'twelve different pamphlets some guy had written up for him. These were sold by mail order and publicised in Joe Weider's magazines. Weider allowed him a page per issue in which to sell his products.'

There was another dimension to Arnold's humble status at the time, says Butler: 'He had been Mr Universe for five years and

Mr Olympia for three years, and he had never been interviewed by anyone outside the bodybuilding press.'

A few years later Butler's film *Pumping Iron* would change that forever: ensuring Arnold a lifetime of assault by the media. Even early in their friendship Butler saw iconic possibilities in Arnold undreamt of by the man himself. 'I thought he could use his body like Fred Astaire. I saw a degree of sophistication in him which I still think is there.'

Eighteen months after the Brooklyn Mr America show, Butler filmed him in Holyoake, Massachusetts, where Arnold was giving a posing exhibition before three hundred people in the Forest Park Amusement Centre. Butler wove the footage, plus interview material with Arnold, into a sixteen-minute promo reel with which Butler hoped to snare prospective investors. (It was the acorn from which *Pumping Iron* grew.) Later still Butler would find other stunts and devices to push his belief that Arnold was not just a giant in a G-string but a highly-wrought human artwork. He would put him in a museum as performance art. He would persuade him to take ballet lessons. He would slap him, in a hundred black-and-white photographs, between the soft covers of magazines or the hard covers of sport-as-art coffee-table books. Finally he would immortalise him in *Pumping Iron*.

Arnold, though, co-operated at half-throttle. 'He had his own ideas, his own character and ambitions.' says Butler. One of these ambitions was to be a millionaire before he was thirty.

(iii) Pumping Money

Consider the extraordinary tale of Arnold the businessman. How does a humble Austrian policeman's son, carrying almost no disposable income when he leaves home at age eighteen, become a plutocrat after a mere six years in his adoptive country? All before he has secured a single one of his better-known, better-paid movie roles. Here is how.

By 1971, after two years of saving money from his Weider earnings and from *Hercules*, Arnold claims to have amassed $28,000. Borrowing $10,000 more from Weider, he bought a six-unit apartment as his first real estate venture. He had also become involved in a bricklaying and a mail-order business.

Arnold the entrepreneur had been born; though he had been conceived, we could say, twelve years before.

1. Pumping Ice Cream. It was high summer in Austria. Aged eleven, Arnold noticed that many people in the public park in Graz were walking about looking hot and sticky. He had his first business brainwave. He bought up a whole lot of ice-cream cones from a nearby vendor, for a shilling each, and sold them all for three shillings each. Two hundred percent profit. 'They were always thirsty and they were always sweating and they were always hot. I knew there was business there.' A few years later Arnold would take actual business classes at school. 'We had to go to a shop and be a salesman, writing out sales slips and orders . . . I did this from the time I was 15 until I was 18, so already that whetted my appetite for business.'

2. Pumping Bull's Balls. According to Arnold, he returned to Thal on a visit after winning his first world title and had to satisfy avid journalists in Graz and Vienna who asked him how he did it. Arnold's po-faced reply was: 'The secret source of my protein comes from eating bull's balls. Anyone can become champion if they just eat enough of them.' Before the newspapers could print the story (Arnold elaborates) he contacted the country's major meat suppliers and arranged to take a slice of the impending profit on Yaurine testicles. 'Very soon, of course,' he climatically embroiders, 'every high-school athlete in Austria was demanding to eat these things. No one had every eaten them before. They were cheap – the profit margin grew overnight. I made a small fortune!'

3. Pumping Mail Order. In America in the late 1960s Arnold bought a $3.75 business licence and set up a mail-order business. He sent out literature offering bodybuilding advice and correspondence courses – from that home-based office glimpsed by George Butler – plus a modest magazine. These were all published (post-*Hercules*) under the name 'Arnold Strong' and most of the material was written by Gene Mozee, an editor for Joe Weider. Arnold, as his bodybuilder friend Rick Wayne noted, had the habit of checking each newly arrived envelope

against the light and throwing away those that did not contain a cheque.

4. Pumping Bricks. During the same period of feet-finding in late 60s California, Arnold and Franco Columbu start up a bricklaying firm in Los Angeles. 'We had sixteen people working for us and we were all over town, building chimneys after the earthquake happened here,' Arnold told *Interview* magazine in 1983. Explains Columbu: 'We needed to eat lots of high-protein food – fish, meat and eggs – and what we earned from bodybuilding would hardly keep us for one day. I worked in construction back in Germany, so . . . I taught Arnold to mix cement and lay bricks and we did very well.' Arnold says he didn't do much cement-mixing. 'Franco did the bricklaying and I was the guy who went out nicely dressed, took the measurements and came up with the estimates. I bargained with the customers even though I knew all along what the price would be.' But he was not above mucking in when the need arose. One day they tore down Valentino's old home. Another day they did a Tarzan act atop a roof, undercutting another firm's $4,000 estimate for chimney-removal work by doing the job with their feet in ten minutes for $1,000. 'We laid on our backs and pushed the chimney over,' says Columbu. The grateful lady gave them the bricks, which Arnold promptly sold to a third party as antiques. Both men in after-years claimed that their firm was called 'Pumping Bricks'. But George Butler says this is impossible. 'Charles Gaines invented the term "Pumping Iron" in late 1974 . . . The term describes the sport beautifully. I don't believe Arnold when he claims to have used the phrase five or six years earlier.' Sure enough, in a more recent Arnie profile in *Hollywood Reporter*, Franco Columbu states that the firm's name was 'European Brick Works'.

5. Pumping Property. In 1986 Arnold told a British newspaper that money 'means nothing to me. If I make a film for $5m or $50m, it doesn't matter. I made enough money from real estate deals in 1975 to retire.' He started even earlier, encouraged by Joe Weider. 'He was gonna move to a new place [in Santa Monica],' Weider recalls, 'and I said, Why pay rent and end up with a lot of bills owning nothing? Put your money into property.' Arnold

was soon buying apartments, condominiums, office blocks. He bought a building in Santa Monica for $450,000 and sold it later for $2.3m. He bought an entire city block in Denver. He is said to have made $7m from selling a Nevada office building he had speculated on 'for peanuts'. Franco Columbu claims Arnold put virtually all his bodybuilding prize and exhibition money after 1972 into real estate. 'Once he did about five shows in South Africa and then I joined him and we did another five. He said, "I'm not going to touch any of this money; I'll put it all away." We came back and he put every penny of it into an apartment building.'

He scanned opportunities all across America. Sometimes the dreams or deals seem mildly demented: like the 15-acre site he bought in Palmdale, sixty miles outside Los Angeles, in anticipation of a supersonic landing strip being built in California for Concorde. (It never came.) In 1977 he was reported to be buying a coal mine in West Virginia soon after hearing of President Carter's new energy plan. But pouncing on property at such political moments was an Arnold credo. 'Whenever a Democratic administration is in power, we in the real estate industry make more money. Real estate goes with inflation.' Nor did Arnold the auto-didact depend on anything so wimpish as a business manager. 'I invest the money myself . . . I have been doing it ever since my first hour in this country.' In fact he now had a business degree to his name, obtained, mostly by correspondence course, from Wisconsin University.

6. Pumping Sport. In 1975 Arnold formed a business partnership with the Columbus-based bodybuilding promoter and Nationwide Insurance Company executive Jim Lorimer. He had first met Lorimer in 1970 while competing in a Columbus-held Mr World contest. Impressed by the way the show was run, he promised Lorimer that when he gave up bodybuilding he would return to Ohio to become his partner. In the six years between 1975 and 1981, during which they co-staged the Mr Olympia contest, the two men would boost the cash prize money per competition from $1,000 to $100,000.

By the mid-70's Arnold himself could earn up to $10,000 apiece for giving fitness seminars. He was sounding off on well-paid chat shows about his personal philosophies on politics, athletics and culture. And he joined the actor Burt Reynolds in a venture to extract more money from the TV and video screening rights to bodybuilding contests. Outlining his campaign to raise public consciousness about the sport during the 1970s, Arnold said:

> I mapped out how to travel from town to town and capture the local press. Then I used that to help secure national magazine covers. I systematically developed a personality that became saleable on television. I never went on and said, 'You must eat 200 liver pills to look like this.' I talked about fun in the gym. That you eat cheesecake and ice cream. That your sex life will improve. Well, people began to take notice of Arnold. It was brilliant.

8

The Long Hello

'I knew that in the past some people made it into films because of their builds. The question was, how to do it again? It's not exactly the "in" time to make Hercules films.'

In 1973 Arnold played a tiny role in Robert Altman's *The Long Goodbye*. He clumped onto the screen as one of the 'heavies' employed by gangster Mark Rydell to terrorise Elliott Gould's Philip Marlowe. Wearing a light moustache, a short-sleeved bicep-displaying red shirt and a look of tough-guy suavity – with a hint of 'Am I doing this okay?' diffidence – Arnold does everything right within the confines of a role that allows him to do nothing interesting. Correction: he strips down to his underpants at one point – Rydell has told his minions to do so as part of the bizarre psychological war he is waging against Gould – during which we see the muscleman cast a brief downward glance at his pectorals as if to check (a) that they are still there in this company of Hollywood cissies and (b) that they are jiggling to order.

Arnold, whether or not he had the talent, had no great encouragement for a movie career. His then girlfriend Barbara Outland, a San Diego teaching student he met while she was jobbing as a waitress at Zuckie's restaurant in Santa Monica, did not want Arnold to be an actor: which may explain why the couple finally split up in late 1974.

According to Arnold, Barbara had not been crazy for his muscleman celebrity either and when she saw him moving away from bodybuilding into another field, acting, 'I think she realised we could not go on together'. Arnold was distraught: 'A part of me had been ripped right out of my body. I had lost something good, something that had helped hold me together emotionally.'

According to George Butler, Barbara Outland's qualities were as a nestmaker. 'She was very level-headed, very loyal to Arnold. Almost a kind of earth mother. She gave him a very good home life.' But if it was a choice between cosiness in a condo and vanquishing the world as a high achiever, there was no contest. Arnold was not a well-balanced man, he confessed in his autobiography. He hated the very idea of ordinary life. 'The meaning of life is not simply to exist, to survive, but to move ahead, to go up, to achieve, to conquer.'

'Barbara had taught me how to appreciate a woman,' he declared. Now he was about to teach the world how to appreciate a man.

The Altman role had not worked wonders in Hollywood. Producers were not kicking Arnold's door down demanding that he sign six-picture deals. He was having trouble even finding an agent. What kind of a name is this for a movie marquee, they would cry, Schwarzenschnitzel . . . Shwarzenigger . . . '"Forget it,"' Arnold recalls them saying, '"You've got a weird-looking body and you've got a weird-sounding accent and you'll never make it."'

'"Look, Arnold,"' they would go on. '"You have very little chance in this profession because there is no one we know that has come from Europe – you know, from a German-speaking country or Italy or wherever – that has really gone through the roof, that has made it huge in this country."' (True of men, less true of women – *vide* Garbo, Dietrich, Bergman.)

But they were reckoning without Arnold and his vision and hunger. 'I stopped bodybuilding internationally,' Arnold would later state, 'to create the hunger for acting. That created the need to get attention somewhere else. I love it when the camera is on.' Later too he would claim he had always wanted to act, that bodybuilding was a stepping stone to movie stardom.

Yet if Robert Altman, then at the height of his darlingness with the critics, could not pull the sword of Arnold's screen potential from the stone of Arnold's brute geology as a physical presence, then who could? Fate finally made the inevitable choice: Lucille Ball.

Altman was too intellectual, arty. Miss Ball was a violent, determined trouper. She glimpsed Arnold one day in late 1974 on TV's Merv Griffin Show and liked what she saw. Her own TV special was coming up soon: 'Happy Anniversary and Goodbye'. And this man with the funny accent, goofy-sexy smile and body like a rock avalanche would be ideal for the role of the Italian masseur in one of the sketches.

So Arnold came to the audition. Or rather to the reading. And he thought this meant 'reading.' 'I sat there and literally read like I was in grammar school – word for word, with no emphasis on anything . . . I don't know why I was ever hired for the job.'

In the same year a screen-hungry Arnold could be seen as a guest victim on TV's 'The Dating Game' (America's answer to Britain's 'Blind Date'). He has now perfected his patter as the innocent abroad. 'I've only been in dis country five years,' he tells one girl, 'and dere are certain expressions I still don't understand. What means 'hanky-panky?' 'Playing around,' comes the answer. Arnold puts on a 'foxed' expression. 'Playing around with what?'

The big screen finally discerned the potential in this man with the untutored-hulk persona. Director Bob Rafelson, who had demonstrated his star-making skills with Jack Nicholson in *Five Easy Pieces*, was casting a story about bodybuilding called *Stay Hungry*. Screenwriter Charles Gaines, who had based his script on his own life as a well-born Southerner and fringe aficionado of the sport, proposed Arnold for the second-lead male role of Joe Santo: the European bodybuilder who befriends the hero (Jeff Bridges) and competes with him for the heroine (Sally Field). Gaines knew Arnold personally since he was in the midst of setting up *Pumping Iron* with George Butler.

Rafelson, who looked at over two hundred weight-lifters for the role, reluctantly agreed to see Arnold. He approved the build but was worried about the acting ability. Jack Nicholson suggested sending Arnold to Nicholson's own acting teacher Eric

Morris. This could have been a teacher-student marriage made in hell. Morris is the wild man of Los Angeles acting schools. He believes in digging deep into personal pasts and childhood traumas and that takes a long time. But when Hollywood wants action, it digs deep itself, into the money bags. Morris would have twelve well-paid weeks to turn Arnold into Marlon Brando, starting now.

'I said, well, Bob, I may confuse him in twelve weeks,' recalls Morris. 'He said, Will you meet him? I said, Sure, how will I recognize him? There was dead silence at the other end of the phone. Then Bob said, You'll recognize him!'

Arnold arrived in a Silver BMW and in no time, primed by the guru, he was blurting about his parents, upbringing, boyhood joys and agonies. In the last three weeks of this crash Hollywood gestalt, Morris went through the script with Arnold and each time they did a scene, the teacher would say: 'Remember that thing we talked about, I want you to talk to me about it now. I want you to have an imaginary monologue with your mother . . .' And Arnold would monologue, and laugh and cry, and Arnold would reach for those 'impacting impetuses' that would help him with his role.

'I don't think Arnold is a blocked person at all,' says Morris. 'I think he's very open and affectible. I've seen the man cry – oh yeah, yeah, I've seen him talk about his father, his early life, his frustrations. I've seen the man be everything you want an actor to be. If he wanted to play King Lear, he could do it.'

Morris toiled and spun for his appointed three months and at the end – startling but true – Arnold won a Golden Globe Award for Most Promising Newcomer. *Stay Hungry* gave him his first and only acting prize to date. As Milton Berle would say twelve years later, 'Waiting for Arnold to win an Oscar is like leaving the porch light on for Jimmy Hoffa'.

Arnold *is* extraordinary in *Stay Hungry*. He plays in essence himself: a reigning Mr Austria and former ice-curling champion working out in America and anxiously looking for the capital to pay off his gym-owning mentor. (R.G. Armstrong's grizzled performance suggests a mix of Joe Weider and Vince Gironda.) But the kinship of Santo and Schwarzenegger only highlights the honesty and clarity with which Arnold exposes his emotions.

Look at the big speech in the gym, which the actor-athlete aims through a nimbus of post-workout sweat-vapour at his new friend Jeff Bridges, and marvel at the fact that it does not *seem* a big speech. The lines themselves are plainspun, except dor the sonic baroque provided by Arnold's accent: 'I can't wait till all dis is over, man. If I win dis one, I can make enough money to repay Thor all de debts I owe him . . . he's de one who brought me over here from Austria . . . he got me voorking permit, helped we wid visa, tings like dat . . . I could pay *him* beck from de money I make from endoorsements.' But there is a 'thinking' process here, or the illusion of one, in the way Arnold pauses, searches for words, lets his gaze ricochet around the room, punctuates his phrases with nervous, weary towel-wipes.

In the scenes that might have been stuck in the movie with the sole design of making a fool of him, Arnold is just as human and warmly idiomatic. Santo is an amateur fiddler, so Arnold has to make with his rustic instrument at an open-air 'hoe-down'. What makes this scene work is not the specious expertise provided by two months' coaching from the film's music director Byron Berline and fiddle veteran Benny Thomasson. It is Arnold's look of gregarious bliss as the air squeaks and saws around him, alive with his and his pals' music-making.

Though Arnold is not a noted screen romancer ('I have a love interest in every one of my films – a gun') he makes a fair show of sweeping the admittedly portable Sally Field off her feet. 'I tapped a well that I'd never tapped before, I mean, when Sally Field grabs you and holds you and looks in your eyes and gives you that last hug before she leaves you, you believe her. And this shows in your face.'

'Acting was an enormous challenge for me.' he would later pronounce, looking back from the heights of *Conan*. 'In physical competition I'd had to learn to keep my emotions under control. To discipline myself against my emotions. You almost have to build a wall around yourself, guard against your own feelings and the feelings of those around you, too, because lows or highs, coming at the wrong times, can negatively influence how you perform. I trained myself that way for a long time. Well, – of course in acting it's exactly the opposite. You have to be sensitive to yourself and to those you're working with. Stay *open*. Keep your defences down.'

Stay Hungry is no more than a curio, but it offers a rare – even unique – sight of Arnold using the 'dig-down' approach. Nearly all his philosophisings to the press about acting versus bodybuilding, and their antithetical demands, date from his apprentice acting years between *Stay Hungry* and *Conan the Barbarian* (1976–1982). After that Arnold decided that he was better off being an icon.

Eric Morris remembers the break when it came. Arnold continued his acting classes with the guru of West Hollywood for a year after *Stay Hungry*. But then he drifted off. And in 1982 he drifted back to attend an acting class and to go to a Mexican restaurant with Morris afterwards.

What happened was – and very few people know this – that he said to me: 'You know, Eric, I don't really want to be the kind of actor you train people to be. I'm interested in action, adventure; I'm not interested in digging down that deep or taking that route.' The fact is, Arnold looks at acting as something that should be fun and exciting and fulfilling on a lot of different levels and really doesn't want to go through the darkest part of the forest.

9

Pumping Icon

'I'm coming day and night, I mean it's terrific, right? – so I'm in Heaven.'

Stay Hungry showed that Arnold Schwarzenegger could act. But acting, as Hollywood has taught us, has nothing to do with stardom. To achieve that, a man must process himself into a myth. For Arnold the campaign began in earnest with *Pumping Iron*. Before the movie, everyone who knew about bodybuilding had heard of this oversize chunk from Austria who chutzpah'd his way to one world title after another. After the movie every one, period, had heard of him: assuming that they were equipped with the muscles to pick up a newspaper or turn on a TV.

Pumping Iron was my own first glimpse of Arnold on screen. Opening in a small cinema in London, it threatened to be the stamina test of the week. But the first entertaining shock comes even before the opening credits roll: two bionic-looking men, Arnold and Franco Columbu, stand at the 'bar' in a ballet-training room, practising graceful curves of the leg and arm. (This scene was shot and added, at Arnold's insistence, after the end of principal photography.)

Soon we have moved from ballet to blarney. Arnold is delivering, at first in teasing voice-over, his famous philosophy of sex and exercise. 'Blood is rushing into your muscles, that's what we call the pump. Your muscles get a really tight feeling, like you're going to explode . . . It's as satisfying to me as

71

coming is; you know, as having sex with a woman and coming.'

After that it is open day for Arnold's transcendentally perverse charm. He speaks in a thick accent with a clotted bass-baritone voice, but is more articulate than anyone else. He is built like a truck but moves like a panther. He makes a big show of 'confiding' to the camera – i.e. the audience – yet we suspect he is mocking us as much as his poor, loaf-brained competitors. I and fellow film critics, back at that London press show, realised we were not watching some grim jock-umentary in which dimwit sportsmen grunt and thump. We were eavesdropping on the mewlings of an infant star.

The film's great moments are the psych-out set pieces involving Arnold and Lou Ferrigno, a two-time Mr Universe now competing for his first Mr Olympia in Pretoria, South Africa. The nervous Ferrigno is shepherded through the pre-contest days by his savvier father, a Brooklyn cop turned Lou's personal trainer. Neither man, though, is a match for Arnold, especially at the breakfast table. Chuckling and cooing with what seems genuine warmth for the newcomers, Arnie delivers the lethal throwaways. 'It's too bad for you the contest had to be now, Lou' – looking Lou over – 'Another month . . .' The sentence hangs there, deadly with mischief. Later, in the workout room, Arnold continues his game-plan. Lou, who has suffered from boyhood with partial deafness, is making loud grunting noises as he humps his barbells.

> Lou: Urrrhhh!!
> Arnold (across the room, all innocent enquiry): What did you say, Louis?
> Lou: I'm training, Arnold.
> Arnold (gently): You're making too much noise. You're supposed to be very quiet, like in a church. (To Lou's dad). Tell him . . .

This is inspired schtick. Poor Lou carries on humping and grunting, but he is no longer involved in training, he is involved in Arnold-defiance, a dire user-up of energy. When the big moment arrives, Lou duly trails third in the Mr Olympia contest, behind Arnold and second-placed Frenchman Serge Nubret.

In the wake of *Pumping Iron*, debate rumbled over how much the film was a fly-on-wall documentary, passively observing an unmediated reality, and how much it was 'rigged'. Were a hidden camera and microphone used to record Ferrigno's discomfiture in the workout scene, as one report claims? Butler, without denying it, says: 'When you make a film of this nature, you want to make sure the action is moving forward so fast the participants forget the cameras. They all frequently did forget them.'

Much of the film is shamelessly loaded in Arnold's favour. Lighting and camera angles give him the star treatment, while Ferrigno is shot in the dowdy setting of his parents' Brooklyn home or marooned in shadowy corridors in South Africa. Arnold too gets the largest share of the monologues-to-camera, including his radiantly cynical account of his psyching philosophy. All he needs, he explains, is one night in a hotel room with an opponent to thoroughly 'mix him up'. 'I go to book us a room together to "help" him in tomorrow's contest. And that night he will never forget!'

Several of Arnold's peers find the glimpses of gamesmanship in *Pumping Iron* more frightening than amusing. Vince Gironda knew this side of Arnold from of old. 'He had a Satanic ability to psych out poor big lummoxes like Lou Ferrigno and do a number on him.

Butler hints at the Satanic side of Arnold in *Pumping Iron* but drew the line at one potentially damaging utterance by the star. 'Arnold said at one point in the film that he had always admired people who had enormous power, like Hitler and John F Kennedy.' Butler cut it, though he still doesn't think it was anything Arnold needed to be embarrassed about. 'You have to understand the context in which it was said – it was not a damning statement as Arnold made it.'

Clearly, though, if Butler wanted *Pumping Iron* to sound a Messianic note for bodybuilding, he did not want *that* kind of Messianic. His own mystical attitude to the sport is apparent from the Biblical quotation printed on the pre-title page of his later book *Arnold Schwarzenegger: A Portrait* (1990). This consists of thirty-four verses from the book of Job hymning the divine power of Leviathan. ('When he raiseth up himself, the mighty are afraid . . . He esteemeth iron as straw . . .')

Pumping Iron the title also began its life by gracing a book: a photographic paean to Arnold and other Adonises with text by Gaines and Butler. Butler says that initial resistance to hymning the hulk fraternity, on either page or screen, was huge. An editor at Doubleday wrote to him: 'No one in America will buy a book of pictures of these half-unclothed men of dubious sexual purposes.' And when the book was published, by Simon and Schuster, the *New York Times* called it 'fag bait' and declined to review it.

Butler, undaunted, continued his campaign to polish up the image of bodybuilding. His finest coup was to persuade New York's prestigious Whitney Museum of American Art to host a live exhibition called Articulate Muscle: The Body as Art. On February 25th 1976 Arnold and two fellow flexers, Frank Zane and Ed Corney, posed on a revolving dais to the visual accompaniment of slide-projected sculptures by Rodin and Michelangelo, while three thousand ticket-holders gawped in the gallery. The exhibition was the best-attended event the museum had ever staged. Candice Bergen took photographs. The *New York Times* waxed enthusiastic. And further funds for *Pumping Iron* the movie, now in post-production, flowed in.

The film's overall cost was a modest $400,000. Contributions included $110,000 from Butler's then wife Victoria Leiter Mele, a department store heiress, and $25,000 from the man who came in as producer, Jerome Gary. Central to their willingness to donate had been Arnold's participation. He had wanted to retire from competitive bodybuilding in 1974, but agreed to stay on one more year to keep in shape for the film and the Pretoria Mr Olympia in 1975.

Any last popular resistance to Arnold – or to the bodybuilding phenomenon as acceptable screen subject matter – faded when high-profile American TV interviewer Barbara Walters had all three men on her show at the time of the film's opening: Butler, Gaines, Arnold. The star did his Mr Charm act. He merchandised his Styrian smile and answered questions on subjects from sex to steroids.

But then probably all resistance to Arnold crumbled anyway

among *Pumping Iron's* late 70s viewers when the man was seen
smoking a joint in the last scene of the movie. Imagine the
collective sigh of adoring approval – in a culture still hung-over
from Flower Power – when the leader of a community of
thick-eared health-and-power freaks is seen publicly endorsing
the peace-love culture. A few macho Republicans might huff:
but they would be consoled years later by having the muscled
millionaire on their hustings. For now – for most of America –
all it will take for Arnold to seem truly a demi-god made human
is for him to fall in love with a beautiful earthling and to think
of starting a perfect free-range family, with kids of all sexes.

10

Sex and Superman

'Sure I get treated like a male Raquel Welch. I love it.'

(i) Arnold on Love

Everyone agrees that Arnold was keen on women. We learned
of his abilities as a charm artist in British bars and nightclubs.
We know he picked up women on Venice beach so they could
watch him work out. We are told he would 'flex a tricep' at
girls in passing cars. And even on the set of *Hercules in New
York* fellow actor James Karen remembers that Arnold had 'an
eye for the ladies'.

In later years Arnold would claim that not only did the ladies
have an eye for him – rich ladies, poor ladies, young ladies, older
ladies – they on occasion almost raped him. There was the woman
at the San Francisco party (early 70s) who wanted to pour hot
chocolate over him and lick it off in public. There was the woman
who 'ripped her clothes off for me during an autographing session
and stood there naked. She said, "Can you train this body for me?"'
(She was removed by security guards.) There was the chambermaid
who would accost him in the lift of a hotel on the Cote d'Azur, 'She
became very excited and grabbed me by my pectoralis major. I
had a hell of a job getting it back.' And Joe Weider remembers
a female fan who confronted him once in a restaurant:

People were bugging him for autographs and when he was

76

all through and ready to get up, this woman walked through and wanted another autograph. Arnold sighed – 'Oh God' – and said jokingly, 'I'll sign you an autograph if you let me touch your breast.' And so she takes his hand and moves it all over her breast and gives him the paper to sign.

In addition there were the women who offered him one thousand dollars to spend a 'discreet night' with them. Perhaps it was in terror of this escalating demand for him as a toyboy that Arnold vetoed the publication of a set of nude photographs taken of him in 1976 by Francesco Scavullo. They were intended for *Cosmopolitan* and showed, says Scavullo, the full Schwarzenegger works. 'He stayed here the whole day, we did tons of pictures – absolutely nude – and he was very co-operative, easy and charming.' But a few weeks later, says Scavullo, *Cosmopolitan* contacted him to say Arnold did not want them published.

Obviously so much willed and unwilled sexual attention *could* turn a man into a 'male Raquel Welch' (Arnold's words); and the concept of a male Raquel Welch raises the issue of sexual ambivalence that is never far from the world of male body culture. It is not an issue Arnold himself wished to skirt. Indeed it is hard to shut him up about it in the statements he gave to the media just before and just after the release of *Pumping Iron*.

> When you train and deal with your body, it doesn't mean you are a homosexual. Straight guys can . . . look in a mirror and say, 'I look like shit and want to do something about it.' I try to be very careful when I talk about this. I don't want anybody to get the impression that I'm knocking homosexuality.

Arnold has caught Political Correctness fifteen years ahead of its time. In 1976 he tells the *New York Times*, 'When it comes to sex, I don't give a shit what anyone's trip is. Two of the last five Mr Americas [unspecified] were gay.' And asked later in *Cosmopolitan* whether he minds about all the gays who hang out in the bodybuilding world, he declaims: 'Why should I mind? I have no sexual standards in my head that say this is good or this is bad. "Homosexual" – that only means to me that he enjoys sex with a man and I enjoy sex with a woman . . . it's all legitimate to me.'

'I've spent so much time fighting inaccurate stereotypes about bodybuilding,' he goes on, 'that I can see the harm stereotypes do in other areas – and that includes anti-gay stereotypes.'

For a famous sportsman and future grandstanding Republican, Arnold seemed relaxed about moving in recherché circles in the 1970s. He was helped perhaps by Butler's role as pygmalion and mentor, pushing him into the demi-monde of painters, ballet and performance art. Arthur Seidelman recalls an incident four or five years after he had directed the Austrian newcomer in *Hercules*.

I was up at Andy Warhol's loft one day, and I was walking across the floor, and out of the corner of my eye I thought I saw Arnold posing naked for someone. It didn't seem an appropriate moment to stop and say 'Hi!', so I kept walking. But a moment later behind me I heard '*Seidelman!!*' and there came Arnold bounding after me without a stitch of clothing on, rather upset that I hadn't stopped for a chat.

Though clearly not gay himself, Arnold at this time seems startlingly bi-functional as a spiritual and ideological animal: a plutocrat and pot-smoker, a conservative and liberal, an athlete and aesthete, an icon of manliness and an outspoken gay sympathiser.

In later years movie appearances would push him towards an ever more hyperbolised maleness. But in those same movies – as if this early open-spiritedness demands to be shown the more it is repressed – the opposite keeps coming in like a demon. There is something mesmerically androgynous about Arnold in *Pumping Iron*: a sly, tousle-haired, bedroom-eyed charmer amid the surrounding cast of dumb puddingheads delivering Stone Age monosyllables. There will be something both funny and apt about Arnold smuggling himself onto Mars in *Total Recall* disguised as a large woman who looks as if she's about to create hell in a Christmas sales queue; and something both *touching* and apt in Arnold playing surrogate-hausfrau to Danny DeVito's hellraising petty crook in *Twins*. Later still, in his bravest bow to sexual ambidextrousness, *Junior*, Arnold will become pregnant. Like many female divinities of the screen, who caused most havoc and heart-racing when they dressed up as men (Dietrich in *Morocco*, Garbo in *Queen Christina*), part of Arnold's charisma as a male superstar lies in his ability to summon up – at will, or despite his will – a dormant other-sex self.

(ii) Arnold In Love

On August 28th 1977, at the Robert F. Kennedy tennis tournament in Forest Hills, New York, Arnold was introduced to Maria Owings Shriver. Maria's brother Bobby had invited Arnold to the celebrity-packed event after seeing him in *Pumping Iron*, aware that the Shrivers and Kennedys – two families related by marriage and Democratic impulse – would be keen to cram one more off-the-headlines VIP into the tennis contest cum meeting of the clans.

As the daughter of Eunice Shriver, nee Kennedy, Maria was the niece of John F. Kennedy. As the daughter of Sargent Shriver, a former vice-presidential nominee (McGovern campaign, 1972). Maria was born to the sound of political table talk and high-level Washington gossip. When she and Arnold met a second time, after their brief introduction, at a later Kennedy thrash in Hyannis Port, the amorous rumours began to whir and so did the surreal tales of rapprochement between the Republican-minded Arnold and the country's great Democratic dynasty.

Could Capulets embrace Montagues? Could Guelphs lie down with Ghibellines? Yes, given the political will. For if the Schwarzeneggers and Shriver-Kennedys were separated by politics, they had a surprise kinship in language. Arnold could speak in his native tongue to Sargent Shriver, who was descended from German stock, and he could also practise Teutonic badinage with Rose Kennedy, the German-fluent matriarch.

Arnold, who enjoyed a gauntlet flung down to his intellect, also duelled with the famous Senator from Massachusetts – 'My biggest challenge is turning Teddy around!' he quipped. Maria wryly assured her uncle that he was not obliged to accept her suitor's political views. "Don't look at him as a Republican," she said, "look at him as the man I love. And if that doesn't work, look at him as someone who can squash you."

Jackie Kennedy Onassis more than once engaged the muscle-man, as they threaded among party guests by the pool or strolled amid the rosebeds, in discussions about Greek sculpture. All this was most welcome to the Austrian auto-didact: 'I like hanging around successful people. If you hang around low foreheads, it means you are a low forehead.'

According to reports from the Hyannis Port drawing room, as Arnold became a more and more regular guest, 'a typical evening's conversation veers from sober economics to Soviet premiers, European law, the Iranian revolution, dog psychiatrists and women's breasts'. Nor is Arnold's contribution confined to bemused monosyllables. With Rose, for instance, as the relationship deepens, he will go for long walks answering questions on German grammar and Vienna operas. And with Maria herself – as if love alone were not conversation enough – he strives for that magical entente between liberal humanism (hers) and cutting-edge entrepreneurialism (his).

'I can make her understand big business and big corporations,' explains Arnold, 'while she makes me understand the importance of dealing with poor people, unemployment, stuff like that.'

The mutually enlightening effect of this friendship between a competitive athlete-actor from Europe and a family of high-thinking, high-society American liberals is well summed up by Arnold in a later interview he gave to Britain's *Sunday Express*:

> They think so much about serving the public, about social work and being involved in politics and charitable activities. So much of their dialogue [*sic*] at home deals with 'What can we do for others?', and eventually this has an effect on you. Sports are a very selfish activity because you think only about yourself. Even in team sports you are trying to make that score, and thinking about yourself as an athlete. You have to. In acting it is even more exaggerated. So it was ideal for me to be exposed to that other side where no one talks about 'me,' they talk about 'you'.

As for his romance with Maria, Arnold assesses its trajectory thus. 'She always says that the first time she met me she really liked me and it was like love at first sight. I'm slower about these things, I don't jump . . . As time went on, the more I talked to her and the more I saw her, I started to love her.'

Maria – love at first sight or not – approached the new man in her life with caution as well as enthusiasm. 'Dad said to pay attention to how Arnold treats the dog, because that way I'll know how he'll treat the children.' Sargent Shriver was obviously smoothing the way for his later gift to the couple of a labrador puppy called Conan.

But the woman called Maria seemed designed by destiny to be Arnold's partner. Smaller than him, her round characterful face with the tumble of dark brown hair, sparkling green Irish eyes and toothsome Kennedy smile was an ideal match for his monolithic Easter Island features. And Arnold responded approvingly to Maria's tough, sassy, grown-up manner. 'Girls giggle,' he elucidated to one reporter, 'while women enjoy their feminity, are proud of their intelligence and evoke a self-confidence without having to challenge a man that they are the man's equals. A true woman feels equal, just the way she is.'

Unfortunately, one woman who was not made to feel equal was Arnold's then current girlfriend. She was Sue Moray, who had replaced Barbara Outland in his affections. But love, like death, has a bad sense of timing. Arnold had known Sue only a month – they met on Venice beach in July 1977 – when he met Maria. And though Sue testifies in Wendy Leigh's biography to the force of her and Arnold's romance – 'Ours was a lusty encounter' – the 25-year-old Beverly Hills hairdresser's assistant with the blonde hair and cornflower-blue eyes was served the dish of jealousy at an unfairly early stage in that relationship. Arnold, it seems, did his best to keep both liaisons going for a while, until Sue was finally back-burnered in August 1978.

Ben Weider, Joe's brother and the president and co-founder of the International Federation of Bodybuilders, claims: 'Arnold said at the beginning of his time in America that he was going to fulfil certain goals, one of which was to marry into a leading American family.'

Joe Weider, though, says, 'I don't think he planned to marry a rich girl. I never heard him say that. He met Maria and they got along good, and I guess Maria understood his animalistic passions. I guess everybody else, all these Harvard guys, were being coy with her and Arnold swept her off her feet. There's an old joke. A woman is like linoleum; if you lay it good you can walk on it for years.'

Then again maybe the Arnold–Maria combination had a romantic inevitability from the start: especially if we believe in Plato's fable about love being one incomplete soul's search for its wandering other half.

He was intelligent – or smart – as well as muscly. She was a tough cookie brimming with physical stamina who would habitually beat Arnold at tennis and would soon develop an exhausting bicoastal routine of weekending with him in California while spending the week in New York pursuing her $500,000-a-year job as anchorperson on CBS TV's 'Morning News'. Maria was becoming a media meteor just like Arnold. They not only loved each other. They deserved each other.

11

Arniemania

'I've been round the world twenty times, all free. I've got real estate worth a million dollars. I've met all the best people and now I've got into movies.'

1977 was Arnold's *annus mirabilis*. He hustled the TV and film studios, especially after the success of *Pumping Iron*. He paid his first visit to the Cannes Film Festival, epicentre of razzmatazz. Most spectacularly, he signed a five-picture deal with Paramount to do a series of costume epics featuring the warrior-hero Conan, though it would be six years before the first of these hit the screen. 'If the first picture is successful they have an option for another four,' he tells British interviewer Scott Meek in October '77. 'But if it does turn into a series, I have a clause that lets me make other kinds of films between Conans.'

The cultural cloud formations were in Arnold's favour. In the mid-1970s Macho Man came to power. Robert De Niro skipped rope, pushed weights and ate pasta to turn himself into boxer Jake La Motta in *Raging Bull*. Dustin Hoffman pushed the pain barrier and the movie credulity threshold as a runner in *Marathon Man*. Before either of these, a plug-ugly Italian with an adenoidal Brooklyn accent, one Sylvester Stallone, carried out an astonishing raid on the 1977 Oscars after writing and starring in that hit film from nowhere, *Rocky*. The magazines knew a good cult when they saw one. Stallone immortalised his muscles in *Vogue*. Schwarzenegger bandied a bionic bicep in *Esquire*.

Arnold the would-be actor, though, still trailed behind Arnold the one-man publicity industry. The only role that fashion's new hunk got to play in 1977 was a don't-blink-or-you'll-miss-it cameo on TV's *The Streets of San Francisco*. He was cast, imaginatively, as a European bodybuilder. Suspected of murder, his character runs amok and wrecks a studio set. 'All I had was one take,' rued Arnie. 'Just smash up the room, and if you do it wrong, tough. That's it.'

The star of the series, Karl Malden, barely remembers the Austrian newcomer's acting contribution. But he does recall that Arnold was taking retirement from bodybuilding seriously at that time. 'He was beginning to take off weight. He said, "I work harder now to come down than I did to build up: because I can't become flabby, but at the same time I can't stay this size anymore."'

In '77 he found ways to push his weight around even as it was diminishing. He posed for photographer Annie Leibowitz in a well publicised photo-session with Dolly Parton, during which the two helped to down six bottles of champagne. 'The nicest weight I have lifted in a long time,' quipped Arnold, referring to DP 1 (Dolly Parton) not DP2 (Dom Perignon). He sat, or rather stood, for painter Jamie Wyeth. 'He's terribly articulate and can stand there for hours,' commented Wyeth. 'I started collapsing on the floor.' He dialogued with Natalie Wood in a long, bizarre tete-a-tete in a *Hollywood Reporter* anniversary issue. (Arnold: 'Do you sleep in the nude?' Natalie: 'No.' Etc.) And at the start of the year he met the man of the hour and the star destined to be his own rival counterpart doppelganger, Sylvester Stallone. This was at the Golden Globe Awards held in the Beverly Hills Hotel, where with Arnold holding one Globe aloft for *Stay Hungry*, Stallone another for *Rocky*, it looked like a get-together of tuxedo'd Atlas wannabees.

Arnold also published a book: *Arnold: Education of a Bodybuilder*. His fierce publicity drive pushed the illustrated autobiography to the number one bestseller slot. Asked to visit seven cities, he insisted on twenty-seven and boasted he could sign four hundred books in an hour. 'I just do Arnold and then "S" and a line and two "g"s.'

Marketing himself was becoming a major skill and obsession.

The boyhood home at 145 Thal-Linak. Open window-shutters mark Arnold's bedroom.

The castle ruins viewed from Arnold's room.

Gustav Schwarzenegger, (second from the left) blows his Flugelhorn for the Graz Gendarmerie Musik.

Teenage Arnold, growing his first muscles.

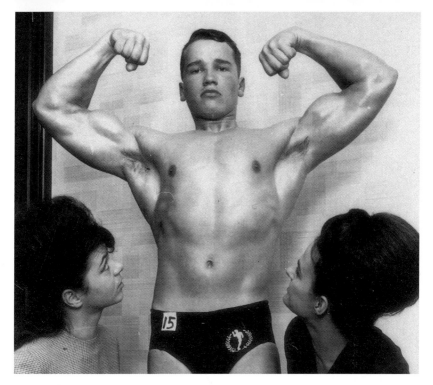

An early bodybuilding jury.

Mr Olympia in his prime.

Negotiating the Fifth Avenue rush hour in *Hercules In New York*.

Kirk Douglas, Ann-Margret and Arnold in an offguard moment on *The Villain*

Pumping literature: Arnold signs his 1979 autobiography.

Hollywood's first couple, off duty.

Celebrating *Conan:* from left, Arnold, Conan, Aurelia
Schwarzenegger, Sandahl Bergman.

Conan the Destroyer relaxes with co-star Olivia d'Abo and director Richard
Fleischer.

On the rampage: Arnold as the Terminator.

Pre-ecological Arnold, declaring war on the rain forest in *Predator*.

Arnold and Maria get hitched (1986).

Caroline Kennedy's wedding (1986). Bobby, Arnold, Eunice and Sargent Shriver.

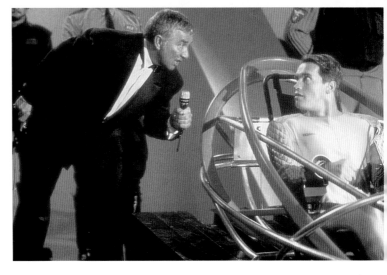

The Running Man: death-or-glory gameshow host Richard Dawson insists that Arnold *won't* be back.

On one promotional tour for the book, Arnold found himself on a plane from Atlanta to Birmingham, Alabama. Also aboard was a gaggle of authors heading for a literary seminar at the University of Alabama. Among them was Charles Gaines. When Arnold asked him what they would be talking about, Gaines burbled appropriately about literature, art, politics . . . 'You mean they're not going to discuss how to sell their books?' asked the shocked Arnold.

When the plane landed, Arnold stepped into his black limo, the humble scribes into their minibus; but not before Arnold had asked Gaines how many copies of these writers' books had been sold. Gaines said, about 15,000. Arnold quickly computed that his book had sold more than all theirs put together. 'They ought to invite me to that seminar,' he summed up for Gaines. 'I'll teach those guys how to sell their books.'

In the same busy year Arnold reached that El Dorado for the self-promoter, the Cannes Film Festival. Touring the western world for *Pumping Iron*, he created ripples of super-hype at the Cote d'Azur movie spree, where this writer first encountered him in person.

Arnold at Cannes was a phenomenon. He arrived with Franco Columbu, to whom he instantly issued the social pack drill: 'We're only here four or five days, no sleeping!' After that it was Arnold-a-gogo, as any journalist present could have testified – not least this one, from my vantage point on a celebrity beach.

After I had dispatched the medium-famous director I was interviewing, I studied the Austrian weight-pusher and his method. There he was, a living Ozymandias on his patch of sand, complete with look of warm command and lordly-hilarious sneer. Surrounding him was a hired cast of lovelies from Le Crazy Horse bar, all wearing ribboned straw hats and Laura Ashley-style dresses, making the event seem like a garden party that had been gatecrashed by some large, well-bred troglodyte. Arnold gave pec jiggles for the girls. And the girls in turn were encouraged to feel his muscles and give giggling, conspiratorial looks at the press cameras. Arnold himself tried on a girl's hat, primped coquettishly and gave a laugh like escaping hydrogen.

Beauty and the Beast was obviously the high concept behind

this stunt. Yet Arnold turned it upside down. He was wittier, suaver and more charismatic – in some monstrous way more beautiful – than all the rent-a-bimbos put together. You felt that if the surrounding crowd of Cannes journos and gogglers had been offered 'a night out with' the beach specimen of their choice, they would have pounced, man and woman alike, on Arnold.

He was giving them what they wanted. Photos, jokes, great copy. Even, to a degree, candour. When quizzed in Cannes and elsewhere during that year's blithe PR jaunts about his more controversial deeds and words in *Pumping Iron*, he said: 'When you saw me getting stoned, it was all designed very thoroughly, to sell the idea of bodybuilding.' Likewise when he said that pumping was like coming: 'To sell something on TV and stand out, I knew I'd have to do something spectacular, so I came up with comments like pumping up the muscles is much better than having sex.' 'If you tell people that pumping up feels as good as sex,' he elaborates, 'that you can eat all the cake you want, get stoned, have a good time, and everybody will love you – well, those are "sell" statements.'

But all this marketing of oneself puts a strain on a man. A few months later, arriving in London, an Arnold in publicity overdrive was starting to sound as if his engine was boiling a little.

'America is so money-oriented,' he tells *Time Out* magazine's Scott Meek, in a peculiar, free-association interview, when quizzed about how he is acclimatising to his new country.

Thank God! It has always helped me! But it has its disadvantages, because the psychiatrists know that their business doesn't mean a thing if there are no sick people around, and so they make everyone feel guilty. You know, all New York city is running to a psychiatrist. All America thinks it has sexual hang-ups. Everybody's running to shrinks. Nixon was always being attacked sexually. It was always said that he was a fag and that he had no sexual relations with his wife for 15 years and that was why he liked power. And Hitler had only one ball and that was why he wanted to conquer the world . . .

What I want to do is to make Americans aware that they're

fucked up when they equate everything a person does with some sexual trip. You know – if you hold a pencil in your hand it's a phallic symbol, and you really want to hold a cock in your hand. And a football coach doesn't really want to be a coach, he likes to slap football players' asses. And it goes on and on and on, all the fucking time.

The attack on Americans is all the more peculiar since Arnold was being hosted through his London press bash by two Americans: Barbara and David Stone, a British-based cinema-owning couple from New York who had bought *Pumping Iron* for UK distribution. Perhaps they were exempt from criticism, having had the wisdom to settle in England.

For the Stones the man was a high-performance charm machine: he did everything he was asked in terms of meeting the press and posing for publicity photos. 'He had a real serious personal drive about him,' says David. 'He said, I'm gonna be bigger than Sylvester Stallone,' remembers Barbara. In the meantime the machine needed fuel. David would go jogging with him every morning round Hyde Park and Kensington Gardens, after which they would stop off for breakfast at the Royal Lancaster Hotel. 'He'd have a dozen scrambled eggs,' remembers Stone, 'some bacon, ham, toast, a steak . . .' Then the couple might have him over to their flat – Arnold was staying round the corner from them in Kensington – where a large bowl of fruit had been put out for the general delectation of guests. 'It was gone in two hours,' says David. 'I don't think anyone else touched it.'

The Stones also got a glimpse one night of Arniemania. They drove their captive VIP to a bodybuilding show in North London, where he had been asked to present prizes. 1,500 people packed the large movie theatre. The Stones stood with Arnold backstage at the climax to the show and were surprised when he turned and said, 'Now I'm going to give the award. As soon as I give it, I'm gonna leave. We're gonna walk towards the door, and when I say "Run," run!'

'Arnold, whaddayou talking about?'

'I'll tell you later. Just run to the car.'

And when he went on stage, say the Stones, 'the applause was wild. Everyone just went apeshit. And we ran to the car, which was parked away from the building, and hundreds – hundreds – of people were following us. We had no idea where they came from.'

For Arnold the adulation of a live audience, let alone a runaway one, was becoming part of the tiresome past – and part of the reason for his move to films. 'The rush one gets standing in front of 10,000 people, and they're screaming and chanting, and there are trumpets in the balconies and banners. It was terrific. But after ten years of it, I felt, "So what?"'

Enter the new celluloid Arnold: a man who could move in a world where adoration from afar – much more controllable – was replacing live exposure and the laying on of hands. You couldn't schmooze or outwit some screaming groupie determined to paw you to pulp. But you *could* manipulate those distant filmgoers on the other side of the cinematic looking-glass – and beguile their representatives, the movie press.

Arnold set forth his principles in interviews. Do plenty of publicity, but on your own terms. When necessary, ask the interviewer himself/herself informed questions. Summing up his 1977 promo-travels, Arnold says:

A lot of actors don't understand why it's important to spend a week in Europe and travel around and make a name for yourself. They don't understand why it's important to get a little background on France and its current situation, so when you do interviews you can talk about their country, let them feel you have an interest in them.

Sometimes, though, you must put the hack in his place.

If you do those press junkets, you give an interview of only three, four minutes. Then it's clear that you don't want to get into talking about your baby, or your wife, or this or that, because you're wasting your time. I mean this guy is only there for one thing and this is to sell your tickets. Right? So you don't want to waste time with the baby talk because it's not going to sell the tickets.

ARNIEMANIA

Sell, sell, sell. Is there anything at which Arnold would draw the line vis-à-vis selling? Yes. He would never, he firmly tells the *Chicago Tribune*, take the low road to limelight preservation by endorsing other people or other people's products:

> I don't want to be another Mark Spitz or Joe Namath, where you go in and sell milk or peddle pantyhose, and the next thing you know, you're sitting around with your millions and asking, 'Where do I go from here?' You know where you go? Nowhere.

12

Two Beginnings
and a Comeback

'When you have a unique look and a unique body like mine, you have to ask yourself, is this a role that anybody else could play? I don't want to fill in for Joe Blow.'

During the next year the movie career still failed to blast off, though there was increased activity around the rocket base. Arnold allowed himself the luxury of turning down a movie role, as one of Mae West's toyboys in *Sextette*; and he publicly spurned the idea of playing TV's Incredible Hulk. 'I'm much too pretty to play the Hulk. He's supposed to be ugly. How can this face play the Hulk?' The role was passed to Arnold's old sparring victim Lou Ferrigno.

Arnold also came close to being cast as Superman before Christopher Reeve took the part. Apparently the problem for the film's makers was that, dressed in a suit as Clark Kent, Arnold still looked like Superman. When the film was released, an unfazed Arnold went to the premiere and announced, 'They did a good job of telling my life story.'

It was late 1978 before he finally faced a movie camera again. Director Hal Needham cast Arnold in his spoof Western *The Villain*. He plays one 'Handsome Stranger' – no other name for character supplied – in a movie that set out to bring cartoon conventions to the live-action cowboy film. 'A Road Runner done with live people' is how Needham explained it to me, fifteen years later, from under a size-umpteen stetson in a Los Angeles hotel lobby. Handsome Stranger is a young innocent:

a freelance he-man with an unexplained German accent who spends the film rescuing Ann-Margret's Charming Jones, the town whore, from pursuing psychopath Kirk Douglas. While Ann and Arnold thunder over prairies in a bouncing buckboard, Douglas's Cactus Jack plays Wile E. Coyote to their Road Runner, executing a series of 'hilarious' self-defeating traps and ambushes.

Seen today, the film is about as funny as a punch on the nose: or as 89 minutes of punches on the nose. The Arnold who won a Golden Globe for *Stay Hungry* and the world's hurrahs for *Pumping Iron* is nowhere in sight. We see an embarrassed actor in a powder-blue cowboy suit, delivering lines with all the enthusiasm of a postman delivering mail on a wet day. We recognize the worst from his opening sallies to the town telegraph man. 'Pardon me, soor. Uh'm Handsome Stranger'; 'Wad about ma' telegram?'

Later, the sound and spectacle of an Arnold lost deep in the wild West takes on a more hypnotic absurdity. 'We gaht to be keerful from here on,' he warns Ann-Margret, 'dis is Indian country.' But no one is careful in this film, least of all the director. Needham's experience as a top Hollywood stuntman – who would later direct the superior action caper *Smokey and the Bandit* – should have taught him greater caution when it comes to hurling objects human, vegetable and mineral around a notionally comical landscape. Robert E. Kane's script has one half-charming leitmotif, and that is the byplay between sexy Ann-Margret, trailing clouds of U-certificate lasciviousness, and baby-faced Arnold, playing the 'innocent' with reasonable conviction. 'I play the most naive guy of all time,' he said on location. 'My character has absolutely no interest in women – a serious acting challenge for me.'

For Needham, achieving total recall fifteen years later in his strong Texas accent, this plot gimmick 'worked out perfect; 'cos all the way through the movie Ann-Margret's tryin' to get in his jeans, and he doesn't understand at all'.

Why did the director pick Arnold in the first place? 'We looked at him 'n' we looked at the part 'n' we said, Y'know what? It doesn't matter if he's really bad or not, 'cos it'll fit right in.' As for the accent, 'In the film he was just called Handsome

Stranger and nobody knew where the hell he came from or who he was.'

This is a prophetic glimpse of future Hollywood casting policy concerning Schwarzenegger. The unexplained provenance of this man in film after film gives him his mythic radiance. He can be a cowboy in *The Villain* or a modern-day Florida sheriff in *Raw Deal* or an amateur astronaut in *Total Recall* or a Hyborian hero in the *Conan* films. What matters is the man playing him and the loony authority he lends each role: that of a cracked demigod flexing his power and charisma on the turntables of earthly cyclical storytelling. For as we shall discover later, virtually every Schwarzenegger big-screen plot is the same as every other, though some are more cleverly *disguised* than others.

Arnold's next screen role, apart from a delible cameo as a Nordic gym instructor in the almost straight-to-video chase comedy *Scavenger Hunt* (1979), was more challenging. He had to don a suit and play a real-life character. In the CBS made-for-television film *The Jayne Mansfield Story* he was cast as Mickey Hargitay, the bodybuilder and former Mr Universe whose other claim to fame was marrying film star Jayne Mansfield.

It was an error on the makers' part to use Arnold's voice for the off-screen narration. Giving us the staging posts of 'Chayne's' career at 20th Century Fox, he is about as lucid as a subway tannoy announcer speaking through a sandwich. ('She still hed de kahntract wid Fucks.') Arnold the on-screen actor, though, gets his best workout since *Stay Hungry*. He laughs, jokes, flirts, frowns, 'thinks.' He even has a dramatic bedroom scene when the full gamut must be run from anger at Jayne posing for photographers on their balcony – 'Well den, sell tickets, why don't you, de whole voorks!' – to emotional collapse ('I luff you, don't you understand that, I luff you') on the industrial-strength double bed.

Played in the film by Loni Anderson, Mansfield was a 1950s sexbomb condemned to be adored for her body even though she had an IQ of 162. Instead of being allowed to use her brain, she was expected like Arnold to go round the world jiggling parts of her anatomy whose dimensions other beauty-seekers could not match. Finally, in one of those fate-sealing denouements beloved by TV bio-pics, she died in a car crash in 1967.

Arnold saw the film as a fable about sexism and bodyism. 'Studios can't do what they did to Marilyn Monroe and Jayne Mansfield and all those girls years ago. "If we can't get one, we'll get the other. She's blonde, she has tits, she has an ass, she has a good body." If one didn't want to do a script, they'd get the other. That's what *The Jayne Mansfield Story . . .* was all about.'

'I learned that you have to establish yourself in an area where there is no one else,' he goes on. 'Then you have to create a need for yourself, build yourself up. While their empire goes on, slowly, without their realising it, build your own little fortress. And all of a sudden it's too late for them to do anything about it. And *they* have to come to *you* because you have what they want.'

At the moment, though, few people thought Arnold had what they wanted – or few were offering him what *he* wanted. The delayed *Conan* had forced him to take bit parts, unsuitable parts, TV parts. If his ambitions for big-screen stardom were locked up in this tardy epic it was surely possible to use the interval more productively, for both publicity and training. To play a semi-naked hero-warrior who went around conquering everything in sight, Arnold had better look in his prime.

Conan had at last been given a belated start date: January 1981. Then the date was brought forward unexpectedly, bouncing Arnold into action. His first scenes would be shot in August 1980. In addition, he recalls, 'Universal, the distributor of the film, was going to use this footage as a promo along with its Christmas release of *Flash Gordon*. All of a sudden I had no time at all, I had to get big, and fast.'

The best way to get big – and to get attention doing so – was to attempt the unthinkable: to make a comeback as a top international bodybuilder. Arnold pondered the thought of competing in the 1980 Mr Olympia contest, scheduled to take place in Sydney, Australia. Friends put on the pressure. Franco said he should go, so did Joe Weider. Finally, 'One day just a few weeks before the contest I woke up with the idea fixed firmly in my mind . . . "you must compete."'

This time, though, the spotlights would turn into something more akin to a show trial. Arnold's friend George Butler stumbled on the closely guarded secret of Arnold's comeback when he visited the ex-champ during training days in Santa Monica. Could he possibly win after a five-year layoff? Arnold was 'very close to a majority of the judges', volunteered one of his gym cronies. Arnold himself was standing nearby, reports Butler, and grinned.

When he arrived in Sydney, the ex-champion was attending, so far as most people knew, only as a TV commentator. But also in town was his friend Reg Park, who suspected that Arnold might spring a surprise. Park had a triple-threat job at the event as Master of Ceremonies, halcyon body beautiful in a one-man guest display spot, and one of the panel of seven judges. The day before the contest – no sooner – Arnold rang Park in his hotel.

> He said to me, 'Reg, I'm competing' [Park recalls]. And I think I remember saying, Well, look, you've put me on the spot, Arnold, because everybody knows we're buddies. But I'm going to judge it the way I see it. And I spoke to the promoter and said, Listen, people know that Arnold and I are friends, but if I don't think he rates it I won't give it to him. So that's the way I went into it.

Protests were lodged by fellow contestants at Arnold's late registration. But rules were bent or waived. In any case, most people believed the favourite would triumph anyway: America's Mike Mentzer. Arnold lost little time in dealing with Mentzer. Ben Weider, as long-reigning head of the IFBB the sport's chief eminence at the Sydney contest, was there when the two men squared off in the wings beforehand.

> I think Arnold was psyching out Mike Mentzer, and Mike was a very hyperactive guy and didn't like it. Arnold said to him something like, 'With your belly I think you'll be giving birth next week. What are you doing here?' I stepped in. I didn't want to see the both of them get into a fight.

Boyer Coe, a fellow competitor, remembers a different flare-up – or perhaps the same one differently. Coe had been instrumental in getting IFBB contest rules changed for the 1980 Mr Olympia, so that instead of the winner being chosen from the best of two weight classes he would emerge from six all-comer finalists. 'Arnold was the only one who objected to this', says Coe, 'He wanted to go back to two weight classes. That way there was only one man to beat. So he said to me, 'Boyer, you're acting like a baby.' And Mike jumps in and says, 'Arnold, *you're* acting like a baby!' Ben Weider had to come between them and cool things down.'

Arnold's gamesmanship, if such it was, was understandable. It seemed inconceivable to his competitors that he would win by physique and talent alone. 'He was not anywhere near to his former competition shape, we sort of felt sorry for him,' says Coe. He also recalls that Arnold was 'extremely nervous'.

Arnold corroborates this in a forty-minute documentary produced by the Sydney contest's promoter Paul Graham. (His old buddy from California days was then, and still is, the IFBB's man in Oceania.) The film, titled *The Comeback*, is shamelessly biased towards Arnold. Only one other relatively obscure contestant, Tom Platz, is mentioned by name, let alone interviewed. Graham says this was because 'we didn't have enough footage of other bodybuilders to play them up'. Boyer Coe says it was because no one else signed releases.

Arnold takes advantage of his screen sovereignty to admit that coming back into the limelight has been difficult. 'I'm the kind of character who doesn't like to expose myself', says the ex-champion and budding movie star; 'I didn't like it at all.'

It seems more probable he didn't like his own ill-preparedness. As well as the handicap of a truncated training schedule, he came to Sydney with an injury and associated ailments. After harming his shoulder during bench-presses, he had taken a shot of cortisone, one side-effect of which is water retention. 'On the plane to Australia I kept drinking and drinking gallons of water and juice. Finally Maria stepped in and told me: "Arnold, you have to stop drinking so much. You're going to be all puffy onstage!"'

George Butler, who was on the same plane, confirms that Arnold looked tired and strained. Judging by film and photographs of the Mr Olympia contest, the look never left him.

After a day's heavy training in Sydney with Franco Columbu, to try and get rid of the water and free up leg muscles that were stiff and swollen, Arnold admits that he was 'exhausted' by contest day.

During the climactic evening he was almost back to full-throttle. By then, however, by any normal reckoning it was too late. He was battling his own stamina, not to mention some *commedia dell'arte* happenings on the stage. No one was sure if it was an example of high-concept psyching or high farce when Franco Columbu started yelling to his man to move into a better-lit part of the stage and then, when Arnold failed to respond, rushed onto the platform and spoke rapidly in his ear in German. Complaints at this unseemly intervention were deflected when Arnold raised high Columbu's arm, as if taking time out to pay tribute to a great Sardinian bodybuilder. Order was restored, during which Arnold slipped over to the better-lit part of the stage.

Finally the judges totted up their score cards and the winner of the 1980 Mr Olympia title was – Arnold Schwarzenegger! The Sydney Opera House, where the show was held, erupted. Not with applause, but with boos, whistles and catcalls. Seat-arm covers and other missiles were thrown at the stage.

Arnold struggled through a loudly heckled acceptance speech. (Even *The Comeback* cannot disguise this, although earlier the documentary manages to cut short the victory moment just before the yells begin.) Then the conqueror lost little time in storming from the building, redfaced with anger or embarrassment and yelling at Maria, who was with him, to follow him away from the mobbing reporters.

Few of those present, least of all the contest's one-time favourite Mike Mentzer, believed that justice had been done. As British bodybuilder John Citrone recalls: 'I met up with Mentzer some time after, when he came back from the competition, and he said quite categorically that Arnold shouldn't have won. He said it was just ridiculous. He wasn't fit. He wasn't anywhere near the top line.' Boyer Coe agrees. 'A fair placing for Arnold in that competition would have been eighth or ninth.'

Mentzer himself, pressed today for a reluctant comment, says: 'What happened fourteen years ago is over. Arnold may be a different type of person these days. I hope so. Hopefully he's grown to become a mature human being.'

The Arnold camp, though, is still willing to defend its verdict. Reg Park, representing a judging panel accused of stark favouritism, says:

I didn't think Mentzer was in the same league quite frankly. There's a certain amount of 'presence' on stage which counts – call it charisma, call it showmanship – and I don't think Mentzer had that appeal to the public. Arnold had that appeal even five years after 'retiring'. He wasn't the Arnold of '75, but to my mind he was good enough to win the contest.'

Paul Graham says the furore was just sour grapes from Arnold's fellow competitors. 'They couldn't take the fact that Arnold could come back and do about three months' training and be able to beat them.'

George Butler also gives Arnold the vote. 'I know a lot of bodybuilding officials and camp followers disagree with me, but in looking at photos I took and films, I think Arnold won as squarely as he could.' Butler is also a lone voice in disputing Mentzer's place in the supposed pecking order. 'Chris Dickerson was the man who could have beaten Arnold. Mentzer never could have. It's like suggesting Lou Ferrigno could have beaten Arnold in South Africa in 1975 [the *Pumping Iron* contest]. Mentzer didn't have the muscles or basic body frame to beat Arnold.'

Any suspicion of retrospective Arnie-cronyism on Butler's part has to contend with what happened to the champion's friend in the wake of the Sydney victory. Two days after the contest the two men had agreed to meet for a photo-session. 'Arnold just didn't show.' says Butler. 'He had left for L.A. It's the first time I'd ever known him fly the coop without any phone call or explanation.'

For months the spectre of Sydney followed Arnold about. At his own Pro-Mr Universe contest, held a month later in Columbus, Ohio, his earlier promise that the new Mr Olympia would guest-pose at the event was broken when Arnold refused to go on stage. Later there were rows with journalists who refused to perpetuate the Arnie view of history by trumpeting the Sydney win as a deserved triumph. Arnold finally took refuge in a lofty stoicism. He said to Rick Wayne: 'I know I am getting a hard time for this now, but give me a year – six months to a year – they will all have forgotten all the fuss. And I will still have won the Olympia seven times.'

Fifteen years later, no one connected with the event seems to have forgotten it. The problem with hoping you can command fame and destiny at will is that you need a pliant army of chroniclers. But history is not always written by the victors. Sometimes it is written by those who demur at the cult of the unconquerable.

13

The Austro-Hyborian Empire

'It's a big picture, a violent picture, fighting against thousands of skeletons in the desert and all those crazy things.'

(i) Introducing Conan

Some time in the late 1970s – the exact date is lost in the mists of Hollywood apocrypha – Arnold Schwarzenegger met big-time producer Dino De Laurentiis. Then at the height of his involvement in American folklore epics, De Laurentiis was considering Arnold for the role of Flash Gordon. Trying a little badinage, Arnold said to the Italian mogul marooned behind his office's giant power-base: 'Why does a little man like you need a big desk like that?'

The meeting is said to have lasted one minute forty seconds. Arnold's agent later commented: 'That was the worst thing I ever heard anybody say when he's trying to get a job.' According to Arnold himself, Dino had time only to comment, 'You have an accent! I cannot use you for Flash-a Gordon! Nah! Flash-a Gordon has no accent!' Arnold retorted, 'I have an accent? I can't even *understand* you!'

Tempers mend. Soon after that, Dino cast Arnold in the role that would make him a star, Conan the Barbarian – or more exactly Dino *acquiesced* in the casting when he was approached as prospective partner by the producer-director team of Edward R. Pressman and John Milius. A thinking person's macho-man among US film-makers, Milius had made *The Wind and the*

Lion (Sean Connery and Candice Bergen in the desert) and *Big Wednesday* (surfing and buddyism) as well as writing *Apocalypse Now*. Pressman was a high-rolling independent producer who had brought forward directors like Brian De Palma and Terrence *Badlands* Malick.

Both Pressman and Milius had been attracted to the legendary hero created by author Robert E. Howard in the 1930s. Conan was a warrior-primitive who lived and fought in the carnage-prone land of Hyboria 12,000 years ago. He proved so popular with Depression-battered western readers – their own land strewn with bodies fallen from high office buildings – that he swashbuckled through twenty-one Howard-authored stories and also leapt into the form-fitting format of the comic strip.

Howard was an amateur bodybuilder. He turned himself from a skin-and-bone child into a two-hundred-pounder, before deciding that life even at that physical apogee was not worth living. In 1936 he told his beloved Ma he was about to die and blew his brains out with a Colt .38 automatic, secreted in the glove compartment of his car. He was thirty.

Howard's hero, as limned in purple prose by the writer and illustrated in high-camp macho contours by artist Frank Frazetta, is a hypnotic hybrid: part Tarzan, part Superman, part Thief of Baghdad. A freelance robber, Conan was also a freelance anarchist and primitive. Through his hero's actions and appetites – which included a primal instinct for wrong-righting – Howard could tell inter-war, post-Crash Americans that if systems of civilisation and economic laws broke down, never mind. There was always Square One to go back to: the wonderful world of social non-development and virtuous savagery; a world so rugged and visceral that it made life in the rootin' tootin' Old West seem like a tea-dance at the Algonquin.

Forty years on, this was perfect stuff for a nation suspicious of Carterian wimpishness and soon to move into Reaganite gung-ho. And who better to play Conan than the man from the Austro-Hyborian empire. Arnold certainly looked the role. And if it turned out that audiences did not understand a word he said, it could be put down to the complicated phonemes and diphthongs prevailing in 10,000 BC Hyboria.

According to legend – or, interchangeably, to Arnold –

producer Pressman approached the aspiring movie star at a restaurant on Sunset Boulevard. 'It's one of the typical things that happens to me every day,' explains the Austrian. 'Someone comes over and says, "Hi, I'm a producer, I want to make a movie and I want you to be the star." I never, of course, pay attention to this, but Pressman talked in such a low-key fashion that I took him seriously. He is a man who has a kind of weak appearance but has a very great inner strength.'

Pressman has no memory of this meeting. Far from having to introduce himself to Arnold in Hollywood as a producer, he says he had known Arnold for some time in New York. Admittedly, when I first ask him if he remembers his debut encounter, he pauses for half a minute as if reviewing the file 'Official first meetings with A.S.' Finally, in his low-key voice he says he probably first met his future star at Arnold's Santa Monica home but later lunched several times at Arnold's place on 36th St in Manhattan. Back in 1976/77, after first being shown *Pumping Iron* by his friend Jerome Gary, *Iron*'s producer, Pressman says he was 'very taken with Arnold's charismatic personality and thought right then about the right movie vehicle'. A friend who owned a New York comic-book store introduced him to Conan, and 'it was such an automatic fit that from then on it was always my notion that Arnold would be Conan'.

'Even then Arnold drew crowds,' says Pressman. 'People treated him as a movie star long before he was one.' So the producer signed him to a Conan contract at $250,000 for the first film and the same for each sequel, with a retainer while he waited. And he did wait. First there was a period of directors' musical chairs. Milius had to go off and make *Big Wednesday*, so he was replaced first by Oliver Stone, *Conan*'s screenwriter, who would co-direct the movie with *Jaws* second-unit man Joe Alves: then by animator Ralph 'Fritz The Cat' Bakshi. But Arnold and Ralph had a row in a restaurant and that was the end of that. So Pressman thought about Ridley Scott, then about Alan Parker. Even Hal Needham, who had steered Arnold to disaster in *The Villain*, claims he was asked to take on the Barbarian franchise.

Probably the biggest mistake of my life was: we finished

Villain and he got ready to do a film called *Conan* and he wanted me to direct it. I read the script and really and truly I didn't understand it. 'Shit, Arnold, I can't do this,' I said. Probably big mistake, 'cos I haven't been asked back to do anything else.

By the end of all this Milius had finished *Big Wednesday* and could resume the *Conan* hot seat. Four years after the project had first been mooted, on January 7th 1981, principal photography began in Spain. Arnold got into final shape by running, cycling and reducing his weight-training to an hour a day – to make the muscle tone seem as if it had been acquired by hard work rather than through organised exercise. He practised samurai sword fighting, broadsword fighting and kendo. He even threw away his eating cutlery. 'I had to practise to get rid of things we have learned up to now – how to take a fork and knife and eat the proper way. They just take the food and stuff it in their face.'

Under Eric Morris's influence, Arnold also delved among the history books to research 'a time that had no religion, no morals. You could kill anybody you wanted, and take what you wanted.' In such a society, 'It was an honour to die in battle rather than of natural causes, so that had to be brought into the acting.'

Arnold praised the film's mountainous, inspirational Spanish locations. 'You're not going to find a nice Holiday Inn or a Sheraton Plaza; you'll find a tent and you'll freeze your ass off and that's good too. It's hard to play a primitive at 9 am when you're taking a jacuzzi at six.'

Although the film was to be a savage study in primitive living and fighting, Milius also wanted Arnold to show some serenity under pressure. 'I said to him, "Whenever you kill somebody, I want your face to have a Zen-like grace, always the hint of a smile."' Arnold took this on and added his own refinements. When a sword skims his face, he trained himself not to flinch: just as he would later train himself to be robotically impassive in the midst of mayhem in the *Terminator* films. 'If it was an honour to die in battle, someone would not be afraid of a sword.'

When the twenty-week shoot began, the new movie star found help and inspiration from distinguished veteran co-stars

James Earl Jones and Max Von Sydow. 'Hollywood is filled with sick people,' he explained, 'but these guys behave like human beings.' He even had occasional acting advice sessions in Jones's trailer.

But nothing could have prepared him for the assault course to come. 'On the first day I had to be attacked by wolves and fall from a high rock. I landed on my back and had to have stitches. On the second day I had to fall into a cave. This time I hit my head and began bleeding. The director was delighted.' In addition he was 'kicked by a camel, thrown over an elephant, cut by swords, run over by horses.' From his director's motorbike, Milius comforted his star by saying: 'Pain is temporary, but a movie is permanent.'

Our truth-and-myth swingometer begins to twitch again here. Did our hero really do all this? In another interview he says that he used a double twice: 'once when I had to climb a mountain that was too steep, and then when I had to fall twenty feet in a cave.'

The film must have been hard work even if Arnold didn't perform every feat of gymnastic masochism. We know he rode a horse – we see him do it. We know he gets into some blistering fight scenes – we see the fists and swords flail. And he makes passionate love to Sandahl Bergman as his warrior girlfriend; and to a Hyborian whore who glad-eyes him into her hut in one scene, only to turn post-coitally into a witch, whereupon Arnie throws her with memorable lack of ceremony onto the fire.

Meanwhile there were the special effects and extra-special gewgaws to contend with. Conan has to fight a 34-foot giant snake in one scene. It was constructed by effects supervisor Nick Allder as a cantilevered skeleton animated by internal mechanisms, with a hydraulic ram at the front so that the snake's head could lift our hero off the ground. The creature was also fitted with a retractable forked tongue and saliva pumps. And there was another monument to make-believe ingenuity. The 'wheel of pain' at which the grown-up Conan is first discovered toiling Samson-like in the middle of the desert was built over a pit that had been jackhammered out of bedrock. When Arnold first pushed against his giant spoke, the wheel revolved too easily; so an offscreen crew was deputed to push like mad in the opposite direction.

Then there was the vulture they mocked up for Arnold to bite to death while he is nailed to his crucifixion tree in the desert; the abandoned convent they turned into a barbarians' saloon; the camel they arranged to have knocked out by a blow from Arnold's fist. . . .

All this labour-intensive make-believe prompts us to ask: What is the real adventure, the true myth being enacted here? Perhaps the challenge to God and nature in a movie like *Conan the Barbarian* lies less in the film itself than in the story of the film's making. In 1982 Werner Herzog directed the jungle epic *Fitzcarraldo*, another semi-mad movie enterprise involving a self-willed Teuton in an inhospitable location. The interest that greeted the film itself was as nothing to the interest greeting the movie that followed about the production travails on *Fitzcarraldo*. Les Blank's feature-length documentary *Burden of Dreams* – a precursor and role model for Eleanor Coppola's *Hearts of Darkness*, which documentarised and almost upstaged *Apocalypse Now* – was a wonderful peer behind the veil of make-believe and moonshine that went into the Herzog opus. Suddenly the metaphors and mythic overreachings of *Fitzcarraldo* itself paled beside the True Myth of this bizarre Bavarian hacking out, in deepest nowhere, his self-image as an explorer-artist.

Every time I look at Arnold Schwarzenegger on screen, or attend to his garrulous chutzpah off screen, I keep thinking of Herzog. They are both joined at the hip in the great tradition of German fabulism. They come down from the Grimm Brothers and *Der Freischutz* and the tales of the Black Forest. And though Arnold did not direct *Conan*, his utterances about the movie before, during and since its shooting, combined with the peculiarly demented charm of his 'acting', give this project its reach and campy resonance. Like *Fitzcarraldo*, *Conan the Barbarian* is not a good film and is prone to longueurs. But its making is a wonderful tale of the genesis of a sub-genre – sword and sorcery movies would now fly forth like bats from a belfry at the first toll of cracked bells – and the genesis of a movie star who could always talk a great film even when he didn't make one.

(ii) Langue and Parole

It seems appropriate that the adult Conan makes his first bow looking like Victor Mature in DeMille's *Samson and Delilah*. *Conan the Barbarian* is a mish-mash of old myths and legends, from Samson (wheel of pain) to Christ (crucifixion), whirred around in the Moulinex of John Milius's brain. No wonder what emerges is two hours of inflated pap fiction; nor that Arnold himself at this stage in his career seems to be getting his legends in a twist. 'If somebody would've asked me to play Hercules, I wouldn't have done it. Anyone who can push columns apart – you can't sympathise with a guy like that in a fight. Anyone who wipes out a temple, how can he have any trouble?'

It is all grist to the movie. *Conan the Barbarian* is a hotch-potch of the sublime and the ridiculous, of folklore and fairy tale. There are only two effective ways to approach the film while preserving some sanity of perspective. (Neither of these, we add, is the mystical-supremacist avenue recommended by Milius. He puts a Nietzsche quotation on screen at the film's beginning: 'That which does not destroy us makes us strong.' And a prowl through the *Conan* research documents held at the University of Southern California reveals that much delving was done into Macchiavelli's *The Prince*. A dossier of one-liners from that work was prepared by a Milius researcher, though their intended use is not clear. Perhaps apophthegms like 'Cruelty, by accomplishing the ends of peace and order, may be mercy' and 'There can be no good laws where there are not good armies' and 'Men must be animals, be like all else in nature, and not try to be human beings' were meant to be pasted above everyone's shaving mirrors on those harsh location days.)

No, the two ways to address *Conan* are as an allegory of Arnold's rise to fame in Hollywood and as a first serious flexing-ground for his jabberwock charm. At the heart of *Conan* is a snake cult. Slippery acolytes, led by the wicked Thulsa Doom (James Earl Jones), worship the serpent species and in some cases try to turn into them. This is clearly a symbol for the metamorphic bad faith that has encouraged the growth of second-generation Method acting in Hollywood: the tradition of shape-changing 'anti-stars' like Hoffman, Streep and De Niro.

Farfetched? Then listen to Milius himself talking about acting and Arnold. 'He's not a natural. He'll learn and he'll improve, but he's not an actor. It's demeaning to a man. From the point of view of someone who is displaying himself, it is not pure. It's not an occupation for a superhero.' The slimy proteanism of the 'actor' is invidiously compared to the immutability of the hero/icon. Clearly Arnold-Conan's duty, egged on by a Milius who has never had truck with the fluidities of realism as against the monolithic grandeur of myth, is to destroy the snake cult. In the film's finale – by far its most resonant sequence – he must track his way to Thulsa's hilltop lair and exterminate this high priest of herpetolatry.

Soon he is *mano a mano*, or eyeball to eyeball, with Thulsa at the top of the temple steps – give or take some halfhearted interception work by Thulsa's guards. Far below, the darkening, light-winking valley bears a startling resemblance to Los Angeles seen at nightfall from the Hollywood Hills. And we are left with the growling high priest of changeability, Jones, as he awaits the *coup de grâce* from the champion of constancy: he with the interestingly stricken eyes, the head up-tilting with broody expectation, and the large sword.

If you want to know what made Arnold a star, look at this scene. His presence is magnificent. Surrounded by the reverberant career symbolism – the Tinseltown lights below, the old actor above, the new actor with chopping instrument in hand – Arnold senses that this is crunch time. Thulsa Earl Jones burbles out his Laius-like final lines to this waiting Oedipus – 'Who is your father if it is not me? Who gave you the will to live? I am the wellspring from which you flow . . .' – and then, hiss-kthunk, down comes the blade. Thulsa's head flies into eternity, Arnold's look of boyish-innocent triumph, perfected over a hundred bodybuilding pose-offs, seals the sequence.

Thus Arnold is crowned the new king of Hollywood's castle. But what also helps him to stardom in *Conan* is the very thing he had been told would *stop* him becoming a star. The accent. No one can listen to this man mangle the English language without falling in love with those discombobulating cadences. Any other actor might have sunk without trace beneath the cod-Hyborian dialogue. Add Arnold's own accent and the mixture becomes an inspired sonic catfight. Straight into movie legend went his enunciation of Conan's conquering creed: 'To crush your enemies, to see dem driven before you and to hear de lamentation of de vimmin!'

Universal Pictures were unhappy about the accent, fearing it would scupper the film's box-office hopes. They lopped much of Arnold's dialogue to the floor, and in one scene we can detect another actor's voice used to post-dub an Arnie line. (It is Conan's first utterance in the campfire scene, 'What gods do you pray to?')

He was trying, though. For weeks before *Conan* he toiled with voice coach Robert Easton, who has ministered to the tongues and palates of the famous. He taught Bob Hoskins to talk Brooklyn and Rutger Hauer to de-Dutch himself. The first voice exercise Easton gave Arnold was, 'Queen Victoria wore violet velvet woollies.' Arnold tried it: 'Queen Wictoria vore wiolet welwet voollies.' 'No, no,' said Easton, and explained that what they had here was a problem of the voiced bilabial split fricative. 'Ja, ja,' said Arnold, and tried again.

When that got better or was put aside, other problems reared up. 'We are going into the willage looting and blundering,' Arnold would declaim as Conan. 'Looting and *plundering*,' insisted Easton. 'Ja, ja', said Arnold, 'looting and blundering.' Ps and Bs continued to perplex. When coach and pupil went to lunch together, the waiter would ask what they would like as a starter. Arnold: 'Crap cocktail.' Easton: 'No, no, Arnold, that is *scheisse*. No. You want *crab* cocktail!' 'Ja, ja, crap cocktail.'

It was Arnold's life story in miniature. Easton remembers him saying that 'He was raised in a rural community, and so when he went into Graz they would laugh at his accent because he had this rural hillbilly dialect. Then he went to Vienna, and everyone there laughed hysterically because he had the Graz dialect. So then he went to Munich, and all the sophisticated Bavarians laughed hysterically at his Viennese dialect. Finally he told me, "I came heeah and effrybody laughed!"'

More and more, though, as Easton realises, Arnold's accent has become part of his charisma. 'I always said to him, the most important thing is clarity. If it comes out as a different *word* in English and changes the meaning of the line, you have to get it right. But I never worried about totally "de-Austrianising" him.'

Once on location, without Easton, Arnold availed himself of Milius's acoustical patience. 'I have problems with long speeches,' the actor admitted. 'And John Milius is one of those writers who love long speeches . . . I went to his trailer every day before lunch and practised my long monologue for him. We rehearsed it fifty times.'

By the time Universal were through with the dialogue scissors, there was no long monologue left. Presumably Arnold refers to the 'De Hell wid you' speech to the gods. Even short, this retains an epic splendour. It announces a new actor-icon with presence and self-spoofing potential. As the helmeted hero stands there, clasping an axe while hewing the English language into unrecognized shapes, he competes for numinous monumentality with the landscape around him. The voice has such a siren absurdism. The frown is so massive and endearingly mannerist. It is clear that unlike Norris, Lundgren, Van Damme and the rest of those interchangeable action dullards, Arnold Schwarzenegger is his own man. Nothing and nobody, not even the finest accent coach in the world, can iron the Arnold abnormalities into routine talent.

(ii) Reintroducing Conan

Many people were upset by the violence in *Conan the Barbarian*. The media crackled with controversy as the film bounded towards its $100m worldwide take. There were too many slayings in the film, too many burnings, lootings, gratuitous beheadings. '*Conan* is a sort of psychopathic *Star Wars*, stupid and stupefying,' said *Time*. 'Brutal "realism" . . . cruddy oracular pomp,' pronounced *New York* magazine. Even Schwarzenegger's mother put in her two schillings' worth. 'I hope it doesn't show in our village, the priest will be shocked.'

Yet the film had not always been planned thus. Back in 1977, when Arnold first mentioned the project in interviews, he had talked of a 'serious type of science fiction, as serious as *Star Wars*'. 'Milius wants to tone down the violence,' he went on, 'because it's supposed to be a film also for kids. So there won't be any close-ups of a guy's stomach falling out when it gets cut with a sword.'

When shooting began, though, Milius reverted to type. Soon the PR line on *Conan the Barbarian* was how very violent it was: but violent, we should understand, in a way that was faithful to the society depicted, even though that society never existed. As Arnold pointed out, 'There is no way to make a movie about barbarianism [*sic*] and not show violence.' For the more militant Milius, 'With any luck Conan toys could be voted the most dangerous of the year.'

After shooting ended Arnold was clearly upset at studio attempts to damp down the mayhem. This, after all, was a man who had seen Peckinpah's blood-boltered *The Wild Bunch* thirteen times. 'Originally when Conan's mother was killed, they showed a close-up of the sword going through her neck, a shot of her head flying through the air, and then a shot of her head on the ground with the eyes closing and blood spurting from the neck. Now all you see is the head flying through the air.'

Sic transit gloria movie. Later, Arnold would react tetchily when French film critics complained that Conan the character was a vicious fascist. 'You deserve Mitterrand!' he snapped. He was determined – mark of a true star – to define and outline the zeitgeist for everyone else. 'Fantasy is definitely the thing now, because they [the audience] can get off on the killing on screen. They can get off on seeing someone get killed without feeling guilty.'

But in America we were entering the age of the Moral Majority, under Arnold's new hero Ronald Reagan, and bloodletting on screen was as bad as other forms of carnal excess. So with *Conan the Destroyer*, the actor's next project, it was decided to moderate the violence. Dino De Laurentiis now had control of the *Conan* franchise and an option on three more Schwarzenegger films. His daughter Raffaella, put in charge of production on *Conan 2*, said the sequel would be less bloody and more children-friendly in order to secure a PG certificate.

Into the director's chair, in place of the violent Milius, came the veteran Richard Fleischer. He had made such family entertainment as *The Vikings* (one blinding, one hand lopping), *Barabbas* (one suicide, three crucifixions) and *10 Rillington Place* (half-a-dozen murders, necrophilia, a hanging). Fleischer played along, though, with the notion of a squeaky-clean *Conan*. That way they could lighten the whole thing up. 'The first film took itself too seriously,' he says. 'After all, you're dealing with a comic strip and how serious can you become? I thought it would be better to have some fun with it and do a bit of tongue-in-cheek.'

Not all Fleischer's ideas pointed in a 'U' certificate direction. He thought Milius had overdressed Conan in the first film. 'The thing you've got to play for with Arnold – or had to then at least – was his body. He was no Olivier. He was just barely getting along as an actor. So I decided to take the clothes off and show the physique.' Fleischer boned up on bodybuilding terminology before meeting Arnold. He went to the star's house and told him he wanted Conan to have a more 'cut' look. 'Better cut?' gurgled Arnold. 'You're the first director who ever asked me to have more muscles!'

Arnold obediently pumped up as well as practising his martial arts. 'For two hours every day for three months I trained with samurai swords, broad swords and did stick fighting.' And once they were filming – locations in Mexico, studio work in Mexico City – he had weights and equipment always available. De Laurentiis had given him a $40,000 portable gymnasium as a gift for *Conan 1*, which he could take with him to remote shooting venues. And in Mexico City Arnold and his stuntmen training friends set up their barbells on an indoor gallery overlooking a fashionable restaurant in the Zona Rosa district. 'It was like a kind of floor show.' recalls Fleischer. 'The customers would look up from their tables while eating and see these straining, sweating, grunting supermen.'

After Arnold's strange amorous wrestlings, half chaste, half kinky, in the first *Conan*, the new director and his screenwriter (Stanley Mann) had to decide what kind of women to throw at their hero. So they gave him one chaste woman and one kinky. The blonde Princess with the English accent (Olivia d'Abo) would provide the ideal of virginal womanhood – and motivate the gimcrack plot about a symbolic gemstone being rescued from a fairy-tale castle – while the darkhaired Queen Taramis (Sarah Douglas) would do duty as saucy sorceress. She would give Arnold, censors willing, a few adult moments in bed. But the censors – or the studio's scissors-wielders – were not willing. The Conan-Taramis love bout fell to the cutting-room floor, to Douglas's regret: 'There was a lot of grease and sweat and flailing legs. It was a good raunchy scene.'

The third woman in the film transcended sexuality altogether. Grace Jones, later an Arnold friend, played his fellow warrior Zula. Between them, Conan and Zula provide a startling acreage of muscled flesh, perfunctorily held in by leather loincloths or cleavaged breastplates. Zula also sports a straight-up hairdo, like a paintbrush sticking out of her head, and makes play with the 10,000 BC weapons. Arnold commented: 'Any time you deal with swords, the danger of getting your eye poked out is high, especially when you deal with people like Grace Jones, who has no feeling of anything, and she just whacks you over the head with a stick. After a while, any normal person starts worrying about these things.'

It was too late to worry. By November 1983 the film was under way and its lunacies were in overdrive. The plot consists of Arnold riding or romping about the landscape, uttering emergency directions to his band of allies. 'Into de boat!' 'Back to de crypt!' 'Into de tunnel!' And summoning up his full eloquence for the final menacing appearance of Dagoth, a horned stuntman dressed in what appears to be melting PVC: 'Save de girl!'

One well-executed drunk scene is all that he salvages from the film's scanty acting challenges. Fleischer praises, none the less, his star's perseverance and good humour. Arnold kept cast and crew happy by doing bits of schtick between takes – spoof TV commercials were a favourite – and when a scene went well he would do a little dance, a soft-shoe shuffle, in mock-triumph. The voice, though, was an uphill struggle. Every line of dialogue was done over in the Mexico City dubbing studio, and the sessions could be a nightmare. 'He had to cope with three things simultaneously,' says Fleischer. 'Lip-synching, getting the pronunciation right, and changing some of the "readings". It was like rubbing your stomach while patting your head.'

The completed film was like shooting yourself in the foot. It made a drab $30m in America. The *Conan* saga, which Arnold had hoped would keep him in cash and kudos for years, fizzled out with part two. What he now needed was to find a film or series of films in which he could say, with resonance and credibility, 'I'll be back.'

14

Citizen Arnold

'Americans are very positive thinkers and achievers, always shooting from the top.'

On September 17th 1983 Arnold Schwarzenegger became a US citizen. For the ceremony he wore a blue-and-white striped suit with a red tie and a stars-and-stripes-pattern handkerchief in his top pocket. Two thousand fellow immigrants joined him at Hollywood's Shrine Auditorium to be inducted into the American way of life.

A special dispensation from the Austrian government had allowed Arnold to take out dual citizenship. But there was no doubt which country was now home; nor which city. 'When East coast snobs complain there isn't any culture here,' asserts Arnold from Tinseltown, 'it shows that they don't know the area. Not only is there culture and intellect, but Hollywood has creative geniuses who make fantastic movies that every country in the world enjoys.'

At the same time as championing his adoptive home in America-Hollywood. Arnold is aware of the privileges and motivating power of his foreign origins.

> I wouldn't be where I am if I hadn't been born in Austria.
> I was lucky to grow up in a country where I had to fight obstacles; I was hungry and determined. In America there are no obstacles, no rules, and I might not have gone so far if I had been born here.

113

'We Europeans went to the gym twice a day when the others went only once,' he expands.

> We just had this drive . . . Any European gets to think like that . . . The guys who own the most real estate in Los Angeles are Europeans . . . a friend of mine came over from Czechoslovakia in '68 and now owns four apartment buildings. Americans are still sitting on their asses waiting for it. Europeans are hungry because we don't have that much.

But what is Arnold hungry for? Perhaps, having fame and money, he already envisages that third member of the ambitious man's troika: power. Perhaps Arnie the politico is in pre-training, seven years before he would stomp around the hustings with George Bush while deflecting, Caesar-like, inquiries about his own ambitions for office.

At present he is content to throw out cooing remarks about the current Republican incumbent and the example he sets to all Americans, including himself. 'Look where Ronald Reagan is today. I call that achievement. There is a long, long way to go. I'm only at the beginning.' But he has a kind of end in sight. 'I wish I could experience the feeling President Kennedy had, speaking to 50,000 people at one time and having them scream and be in agreement with him.'

The scenario is alarming but plausible. Arnold has a flair for lobbying. 'When you're driving in California with him,' says Wag Bennett, 'every time he stops at a traffic light he's saying hello to people, ready for when he goes into an election.'

And when he does say hello, adds Bennett, there is this sense of a warming demotic rapport. 'With Sylvester Stallone they only want to beat him, like a gunman in the Old West. But with Arnold they know he's only taking the piss out of himself. And he's accepted as one of the boys. So he doesn't need bodyguards and the rest of it, because nobody tries to "call" him.'

But however good he is at gladhanding, Arnold, as a foreigner born outside America, still cannot get to be President according to the rules.

Bennett: 'He says he'll find a way round that. "We'll get the law changed."' Vince Gironda agrees. 'I think Arnold wants the world. I think he wants to be President. He'll find a way round the Constitution.'

If he did, what ideas and ideals would he foist on the American people? 'He's a conservative Republican,' says Jim Lorimer. 'He believes in keeping government off the backs of people and letting people make their own way, without being taxed to death.'

Arnold's economic views have been taking firm shape since 1980. That was the year he donned cap and gown to pick up his bachelor's degree in economics from the University of Wisconsin and also the year he fell in love with Milton Friedman's TV documentary series *Free to Choose*, all about the virtues of the free market. 'It expressed, validated and explained everything I ever thought or observed about the way the economy works,' said Arnold. He became, on his own admission, a 'pain in the neck' with friends, giving them tapes of the programmes for Christmas. 'Then, as the Eighties rolled on, I would call them up and say, "See, Milton was right!"'

'I am more comfortable with an Adam Smith philosophy than with Keynesian theory,' Arnold sums up. It is part of his budding high Republicanism as the Reagan years unfold and the new movie star with the magic ingredient – built-in political potential – sees a brother, or kindly godfather, in the old movie star who *made* it to the White House. 'A fine man you can talk to easily,' effuses Arnie. This, too, was the President famed for consulting Sylvester Stallone movies on matters of foreign policy, and for reinforcing Reagan-omic policies on the money front with Rambo-comic policies on the military front.

Arnold's rightward bias seems undisputed, and according to one friend there is a 'whiteward' bias too. Rick Wayne remembers forceful opinions expressed in debates about the race question. 'He told me a hundred times that the apartheid system was correct. He was deadly serious. We would have wars about this.'

When the two men were together with a Jewish buddy, the photographer Art Zeller, Wayne also recalls: 'He would reduce Zeller to tears with his anti-semitic jokes.'

Laughter or grief is not specified. Many of Arnold's remarks were no doubt made in jest. Perhaps they all were. But a nation's electorate may pause before entrusting the keys to Armageddon to a man with so incendiary a sense of fun.

After *Conan*, Arnold's informal constituency in America was growing fast. People already screamed at him across the land, even if it had nothing to do with his political views. By 1982 he had an army of potential yea-sayers, who might march with him on the White House as soon as he told them he was swapping muscles for mandates.

During a marathon race in Portland, Oregon, he created a mob scene merely by peeling off his shirt. 'I couldn't believe it,' cooed Arnold. 'I mean, there were more than 100,000 people chanting "Flex, flex, flex."'

Aware, however, that too big a show of delight in his own renown would be injudicious, he gratifies respectful interviewers with moments of self-deprecation. 'To me my fame is not a burden. Some people in my position are always hiding, putting on sunglasses and weird clothes to be incognito. When people stare at me, it's not something that brothers me.'

To keep that ordinary-guy quality, he hymns the simple life. 'I like running around like a bum all week and every so often getting dressed up and playing the serious businessman.'

As for showing off his body, he is trying to put all that behind him. When the Los Angeles *Times* reporter who caught the Portland muscle-flexing story asks him to remove his shirt and strike a double-biceps pose, he refuses. 'When pictures go out now, I'm usually in a suit. It will take a lot of time to convince the public and the industry that I am an actor. I have to prove myself.'

This image-monitoring can go to bizarre extremes. 'I do tests,' he divulges in 1982. This consists of walking down New York's Fifth Avenue and stopping strangers. 'I say to ten people, "What do you know me for?" and people will say, "I know you from Wide World Of Sports – Mr Olympia." I say, "Anything else?" And they say no. Then I go to the next guy . . .' Two years after that, he will try again. One person will say he knows Arnold from movies, another that Arnold wrote a book. 'It's not accurate information, but somehow I always know where I'm at.'

Arnold believes that such self-concern is no bad thing. Money and ego satisfaction are the two reasons he gives one interviewer for wanting to act. To another he states that 'ego is the thing that gives you will. Otherwise you're a vegetable.' It is all part of the 'Citizen, help thyself' creed he has inherited with his Americanisation. By the bootstraps thou shalt haul thyself up. And acting may be only one stage on that route. 'My goal is to stay with it until I'm forty and then get out. Then I'll do something else the next ten years. I may end up as a beach bum. Who knows?'

Or as Arnold the statesman. After *Conan* rumours began to whirl that the Governorship of California was a tempting prize, and that Arnold might make his friend John Milius head of state police. A joke? Many hoped so. If not, it would place Arnold firmly on the Great Right Way of American politics: in his view the healthiest highway to be on, as he explained to *Playboy* interviewer Joan Goodman:

My political point of view has been the same since I was eighteen. When I came to this country, I was in heaven, because Richard Nixon was President and Reagan was governor of California. I said, 'This is great. This is right up my alley.'

15

Arnold Cybernegger

'The Terminator . . . *it's some shit movie I'm doing. Take a couple of weeks.*'

The process by which a star perceives megastardom within reach is a mysterious one. Perhaps it happens on the movie set. Perhaps in the publicity department. Or perhaps it happens in his head when 'ordinary' incidents start – partly by his own will – to take on extraordinary resonance.

Shortly after midnight on December 29th 1983, Arnold was driving along Interstate 10 in the Palm Springs area ninety miles east of L.A. Wanting to stop and let Maria drive, he steered his jeep to the side of the road and slowed down. But instead of stopping, the jeep slid off the highway down a forty-foot embankment. Arnold, says the police report later, 'misjudged the width of the road's shoulder'. There was no evidence that he had been drinking. But he would be cited for driving without a licence.

Those are the bare facts. But ten months later Arnold tells the Los Angeles *Herald-Examiner* the 'Palm Springs Story' in fuller detail as it really – or surreally – happened. Jeep crashes. Arnold is badly bruised. Maria is bleeding. Nobody stops to help. They begin walking along the dark road. Then rescue arrives in the form of two policemen. 'One policeman looked me over and then began asking about how to improve his triceps. Maria couldn't believe what was going on. "I'm bleeding," she told him. The guy kept talking. Then his partner started asking me whether or not he should work out every day. It was unbelievable . . .'

No, Arnold. Not unbelievable. Congruous with the legend! Somewhere between the simple truth and the possible souping-up – or beyond them both – lies the wonderful zone of the True Myth. Either the incident went the way you say, in which case what sweeter illustration of the way your fame is bonded to your body in the public mind. (The Palm Springs P.D. can ignore a bleeding Kennedy princess in order to quiz a superhulk about achieving hulkdom.) Or the episode has been polished to provide copy for the media: in which case it still tells a tale, of a life indentured to fame as that fame is indentured to its proprietor's body.

By the time of that second jeep-crash recital Arnold was making a movie that might offer him a twofold escape: from the tyranny of the body and the tyranny of one-dimensional screen heroism. Given a choice between two flung-from-the-future action roles in a new sci-fi adventure called *The Terminator* – bad killer cyborg or good guerrilla fighter – Arnold picked the inhuman baddie.

The choice was inspired. 'Everyone around me said, Maybe you shouldn't play a villain. It might be bad for your career.' But Arnold thought of all the *Conan* baggage he could exultantly throw away. Instead of the bare-everything Mr Good Guy with the seething pectorals and long speeches, here was a robot, walled up behind black leather and shades, whose terse dialogue was composed like haikus from Hell. 'Fuck you, asshole' (or as enhanced by Arnoldspeak, 'Faak you, ess-hole'.) And the immortal, indelible 'I'll be back'.

The Terminator was an ambitious SF adventure being made for a modest $6.5m by a Canadian-born film-maker whose only previous directing credit was *Piranha 2*. James Cameron came up through the famous Roger Corman production stable: a stud farm for aspiring cineastes where men like Francis Coppola, Peter Bogdanovich and Martin Scorsese learned how to gallop in mini-budget movie-making courses. Inside and outside the Corman palings, Cameron dabbled in special effects and art direction (*Battle Beyond the Stars*, *Escape from New York*). Later still, after *The Terminator*, he would add further merit points to his hulk-wrangling diploma by co-scripting *Rambo* with its star Sylvester Stallone.

The 27-year-old Cameron and his producer wife Gale Ann Hurd wanted to make a film about 'the dark side of Superman'. Borrowing from diverse sources – Harlan Ellison (who threatened a lawsuit until the film gave him a credit), the Siegfried legend, earlier Hollywood cyborg lore – they hewed a story about an android assassin sent from the future to kill the mother-to-be (Linda Hamilton) of a prospective warrior-saviour. Only a rival, human commando (Michael Biehn), likewise dispatched from the next millennium, can kill Cyborg Arnie and save the woman who carries the last best hope for civilisation.

Cameron and Hurd submitted a 122-page treatment to the production company Hemdale, after the project had been turned down by all the major studios. To make Hemdale a sales presentation they wouldn't forget, Cameron got his actor friend Lance Henriksen to dress up and pay the company's boss John Daly a visit. 'I went to Hemdale with gold foil from a Vantage pack over my teeth and a cut on my head, and kicked the door open,' Henriksen says.

Daly chose the peaceful life. Hemdale linked up with Orion Pictures and Home Box Office to bankroll the project. The only stipulation was that plot and action effects must be slimmed down to keep the budget the right side of $4m. Once Cameron had Arnold on board, though, with the ex-Conan's now beefy asking fee, the director could argue successfully for $6m. (The first choice for the Terminator role – which for later viewers would have lent it a whole new resonance – was O.J. Simpson.)

Initially, Arnold thought the movie would be a minor chore, something to keep the pot bubbling. Rick Wayne, who doubled as a journalist when not heaving weights, went to interview him at the time of *Conan the Destroyer*.

As we sat there talking, he picked up the *Conan* sword, which weighed a ton, and went through all the movements he'd practised. Then he picked up a pair of shoes and I said 'What are those for?' And he said, 'Oh some shit movie I'm doing, take a couple of weeks.' And it was *The Terminator*! That was the movie that made Arnold! But he didn't want to talk about it, for him it was just some crap picture.

Joe Weider remembers: 'Arnold said to me, I don't know what kind of a crazy movie this is, they're from outer space, they're killing each other, they shoot each other. I told him, this movie's *made* for you. You don't have to act it!' Weider had long believed that Arnold was a superstar waiting to happen, and that otherworldly roles were ideal for him. 'His face was so powerful. Almost prehistoric in a good-looking way. Together with that massive body, he *looked* like someone who came from the mists and dawn of mankind.'

Perhaps Arnold was anxious, not just indifferent. 'The hardest part of the whole thing was trying to establish me as a villain,' he says. Because of *Conan*, and because the new improved public Arnold had also begun the health and fitness campaigning that would climax years later with his job as sports supremo under President Bush, it was going to be hard persuading others that he could be a screen demon. Or even persuading himself.

Arnold did it by a kind of existential regression. The emotional blinkers he had worn as a bodybuilder and then discarded for the self-revealing art of acting could now go back on again. *Reculer pour mieux reculer.* Nor was this just a philosophy of villainy. Arnold now fancied it as a philosophy of adventure movie acting at large:

In action films where you do the action yourself, you can't always show emotion. I think the majority of people out there appreciate that. They like to be able to disconnect emotions and go after what they want to go after, destroy what they want to destroy. That's why they go to see those films. It's a fantasy.

For Cameron, Arnold's Terminator role embodied a fantasy of anarchic power. 'I think people root for him because there's some little chittering demon down in the back of everyone's mind that would like to be him for about two minutes, to go in and talk to the boss without using the doorknob.'

Arnold's own perception, proved correct, was that *The Terminator*'s audiences would identify not with the handsome, loquaciously explanatory 'hero' (Michael Biehn) but with the strong silent villain. The movie cunningly swaps the old stereotypes. Heroes in traditional action lore are taciturn, high-minded men, getting on with the job of cleaning towns. Villains, by contrast, are often logorrhoeic dandies given to toying verbosely with their victims. Though *The Terminator* does not stand alone in post-1980 cinema in reversing this trend – mute psychopaths stomp through the *Halloween*s and *Friday the Thirteenth*s while the good guys (and girls) chatter out battle plans – it was the most high-profile trailblazer of its time. Biehn is the one given to long, un-charismatic burblings: notably in his speech to Hamilton's Sarah Connor which contains vital information about Android Arnie while being delivered so fast that it doesn't (hope the makers) have time to bore the audience. 'All right, listen. The Terminator's an infiltration unit, part man, part machine. Underneath it's a hyper-alloy combat chassis, microprocessor-controlled, fully armoured, very tough, but outside it's living human tissue . . .'

Meanwhile the combat chassis himself says next to nothing – under a hundred words in the whole film – while electrifying our attention. Everything Arnold would later say about the technique of playing an action hero would apply to playing this action villain.

There are a hundred rules for playing a hero. Never blink your eyes when you shoot – you look weak if the noise makes you blink. If you want to show power and anger convincingly, never move your head when you say your lines. John Wayne never moved his head. You can only move your lips; that shows you are ballsy. Show no emotions: You're above emotions. Never skip or hop; you must sprint or take powerful strides. When you are going up or down the stairs, never look at the stairs. When you are reloading a gun, do not look at the gun. Look at the victim. Practise a hundred times so you can reload without looking. Every gesture has to separate you from the rest of the bunch if you want to play a stud.

To prepare for his Terminator role Arnold spent three months training with machine-guns, submachine guns, rifles, shotguns, pistols, revolvers, grenades: not just so that he could use them, but so that he could become used to them. 'You didn't want to have the Terminator be scared of explosions or fires or shot.' Add to this unearthly impassivity the tombstone timbre of the Arnold voice and the brilliant body semiotics (which Arnold claims to have conceived) of a head-tilted-forward walk; and then submit the actor to three hours in the make-up room for his 'distressed of Silicon Valley' look – gashed metallic head, popping eyeball, spurting wires etc. – and you have a malevolent icon for the year of the Orwellian nightmare. 'Big Cyborg Is Watching You.'

Arnold spent the equivalent of six consecutive days in the make-up chair. Or so the promotional film *The Making of Terminators 1 and 2* assures us: though it injects humour into statistical overload with glimpses of an Arnold wryly insisting on star treatment as he settles into another putty-and-prosthesis session. 'I need my foot massages, my oatmeal and my Austrian Christmas music.'

'What it is,' he complains into the mirror. 'I'm too handsome. No camera can take all this good looks. So what they do . . . is put appliances on and put terrible make-up on to make me match up with the rest of the actors in the movie.'

This man could not match up – or down – if he tried. Michael Biehn and Linda Hamilton disappear into the scenery while Arnie barnstorms through, a human juggernaut topped by a face that could scuttle a thousand ships. Director of photography Adam Greenberg saw Arnold's mythic potential from the start. 'He has great cheekbones, very strong and powerful. I used harsh top lighting to pick up the highlights and to spread shadows beneath. I also wanted to make him bigger than life, more powerful; so I would shoot from below using wide-angle lenses to distort him'.

'We wanted a stylised, cold, metallic look for the film,' expands Greenberg. 'Nowadays more and more movies are done in that style, but in 1984 it was a very different approach.

We had to do it very simply, primitively, because of the budget.'

Cheap ways were found to achieve dramatic camera effects. Operating his own camera (against union rules), Greenberg improvised 'tracking shots' by having himself pushed at high speed in a wheelchair. And when time came to film the metal-skeleton android – the Terminator's final manifestation – 'We couldn't afford to build the whole thing, so four crewmen carried the top half around on two sticks of wood like a litter. I filmed with a handheld camera and tried to time my walk to the jerky motion.'

Everything memorable in *The Terminator* is memorably simple. Not least Arnold's own dialogue. When he said 'I'll be back' to the cop behind the counter, the three-word line stepped straight into immortality. The plain statement is coloured by the actor's clotted boom of a voice and the lethal wit of the context. He *is* back, almost instantly, driving an armoured jeep through the police station glass doors.

Among the actors getting hell on that precinct-shootout day was Lance Henriksen as Sergeant Vukovich. 'When he attacked the police station, that was a week's work,' says Henriksen. 'Hundreds of thousands of squibs going off as he shot everybody. They used big explosive charges planted on the body which went off like shotgun shells. I got several real burns.'

Arnold, says Henriksen, was a disciplined actor who would scrupulously obey General Cameron, not just here but in other sequences. 'He had to give up any ego at all.' In one scene designed to establish the cyborg's implacability, the Terminator has to rise like a hi-tech phoenix from a sidewalk after being blown through a saloon bar window by a shotgun. Cameron would direct his moves, explains Henriksen, second by robotic second as the camera rolled. 'Jim would say, "I want you to lay there, Arnold. Then when I tell you, I want you to start lifting up with your head. Then your shoulders. Then I want you to sit up. Then I want you to look straight ahead."'

Ego under control. Obey director. The Arnold Acting Programme.

Cameron was not a director you willingly disobeyed. 'He's not the kind of guy who will try to say things in a diplomatic way,' says Arnold. 'If you do something right, he'll say it was disastrous but probably a human being could do no better. If he was dealing with machines, *they* could do better. So you walk away going, "I guess he likes it."'

Cameron, could also lead from the front. 'He was like an encyclopaedia of technology,' says Arnold; 'if a shot was a half inch off the way he visualised it, he would go crazy.' And if a stunt needed demonstrating. 'he would show it to you himself without any padding. He was totally mad.'

With Arnold's ego under fire from one quarter – monomaniac director – it sought to reassert itself elsewhere. Linda Hamilton, asked today if Hollywood's action hunk had resented having a strong female co-lead, says: 'He was very frightened to share. And after the movie was over, he never mentioned my name in all the press interviews.' Her contribution was so under-puffed, she claims, both by the fellow star and the film's makers, that she was virtually jettisoned from the publicity campaign. 'There was a whole press junket that was planned in New York and they cancelled my part of it because nobody wanted to talk to me. Arnold never mentioned his co-star. He is the most shameless self-promoter – and very clever about it too.'

Arnold saw that *The Terminator* could be a blood transfusion for his career, and the more blood it involved the better. As a contribution to the zeitgeist, the film is two hours of crunching violence and bio-mechanical ingenuity that defines Homo Reaganus as a semi-berserk automaton warrior-visionary, trying to sort out the next millennium while the current one lies twitching for attention. (This was the era of that great pipe dream for future self-fortification: the Strategic Defence Initiative, or 'Star Wars'.)

As a contribution to Arnold's career, *The Terminator* is a masterpiece of lateral vitalisation. Don't move up the same ladder towards cliche'd apotheosis: by that method the next film after *Conan the Destroyer* should have had Arnold taking off yet more clothes, speaking more strenuously antiqued lines and homing in further on the family/fantasy market. Instead, *The Terminator* shuttles him supersonically from 10,000 BC to

2000 AD; sprays the screen with a mixture of blood and engine oil; and limbers Arnold up for a movie future in which heroic individualism is allied to advanced weapons technology, and in which our hero must sometimes be resourcefully nasty to be redeemingly nice.

16

Maria, Sonya and Brigitte

'Ten years ago a friend asked me what kind of woman I'd like for a wife. I said, "Dark-haired, pretty, intelligent, witty and very challenging." Otherwise I would walk all over her.'

In 1985 Arnold carried Maria's engagement ring around for half a year. Set on ending his bachelor days, the *Terminator* star could not terminate the long period of romantic suspense. More exactly, he could not find the place to pop the question. America? Too much like one's own backyard. Hawaii? Every celebrity does it there.

Finally, in the early summer, Arnold and Maria take a little, long-mooted trip to Austria. They go to Thal and visit the relatives. Smiles and hugs all round; then Arnold suggests to Maria that they go boating on the lake. It is the very lake he learned to swim in: that glimmering glass of Nature where he saw, like a reflection of his future, the bodies of the muscle-pumping local youth.

The couple rowed out to the middle of the Thalersee and Arnold took out the diamond ring and asked 'Will you . . .?', and Maria said 'Yes, Arnold'.

Years later Arnold would recall the moment. 'I can use that in movies,' he enthused. 'If a big muscular guy is sentimental, it's a big surprise for audiences.'

How, though, had he decided to marry Maria in the first place? Jim Lorimer believes it happened at Arnold's home in Santa Monica.

He and I were sitting in the hot tub together one evening around midnight. I said, 'Arnold, you have just about everything a person could want. You don't have to work again ever if you don't want. But it's essential that you experience all of life's processes. One of the great, great pleasures is parenthood, marriage, grandchildren. You've been going with this woman [Maria] eight years now. You've both got career challenges and pressures, but your love has continued to grow. So it's time you thought about marrying her.'

About eight weeks later I got a telegram from Graz, Austria, from Maria and Arnold saying 'We did it, we're engaged. See you when we get back.' I don't think he's ever regretted that hot tub.

The engagement was announced in late summer. But before the romance goes any further – certainly before marriage – it is time for us to find out more about Maria herself.

She was brought up in a family rife with Kennedy values of self-help and pioneering community spirit. Her father Sargent Shriver married John F. Kennedy's sister Eunice and was the first director of Kennedy's Peace Corps, created in 1961. At age fifteen, while still a pupil at the Stone Ridge Country Day School of the Sacred Heart, Bethesda, Maria wanted to join the Corps and was sent to Tunisia for the summer by her father. She found herself in a house with no running water and an open outside toilet. She slept in a bed with five members of a Tunisian family. 'I stayed there two days and knew there must be some mistake. I knew my father wouldn't send me directly from the convent to this place.'

Hitching to the American Embassy, she sobbed out her feelings to her father on the phone. 'Maria, you've been living like that for just two days,' said Shriver. 'Peace Corps volunteers have to live under those conditions for two years.'

'But there are men in the room! There are men in the room!'

'That's okay. Just don't tell your mother.'

Maria went back to the Tunisian house.

Later, at Georgetown University where she majored in Ameri-can studies, she was still intent on imbibing Kennedy values: she wrote her thesis on JFK's 1960 West Virginia primary campaign. She graduated in May 1977, three months before first meeting Arnold. Her ambition to become a TV anchorwoman sent her to apprentice reporting jobs at KYW-TV in Philadelphia and as a writer-producer with WJZ-TV in Baltimore.

Throughout the late Seventies and early Eighties, though based on opposite coasts, Arnold and Maria would get together for weekends and he would escort her to occasional high-profile public do's such as 'The Event'. This New Age conference held in New York and masterminded by that mover and shaker of the post-hippie era, Jerry Rubin, featured a wall-to-wall gathering of fashionable gurus, from architect-thinker Buckminster Fuller to sex therapists Masters and Johnson.

In 1981 Maria became a correspondent for *PM* magazine. In this year she also did sports specials for Ted Turner's Cable Network and hosted a syndicated ABC TV show for Tony Scotti called Portrait of a Legend': a series of bio-features on famous music stars. In 1983 – the anchoring dream approaches! – she was named West Coast reporter for CBS 'Morning News.' And two years later it happened. She became the programme's co-anchor and was up and running on a salary of $500,000.

Soon she would say, from the security of her own office: 'It's real important for me to know that I deserve to be here at CBS, that I worked hard to be here and that it's understood I didn't drop from the sky.' Or, by dynastic parachute, from the dizzy heights of the Kennedy clan. 'People say, "Oh she's rich, she's pretty and she's marrying Arnold." Well, every day I have to get through the day wondering if I'm going to eat five muffins and gain ten pounds.'

Maria didn't get a lot of distracting blandishment from Arnold. While her mother called several times a day and her brothers and friends were in constant touch with suggestions for the programme, 'Arnold never calls with story ideas,' she said. 'That's nice since everybody else does.'

To see how single-minded Maria was about her job at this time – and how ironically aware of her own ambitiousness – we need only look at the wall above her typewriter. There is a cartoon of a young woman crying, and the speech balloon coming from her mouth says, 'Nuclear war? What will happen to my career?' Arnold approved of this Maria. 'It makes me respect her tremendously because she's very successful, because she's very bright, because she's a go-getter, because she's very hungry for knowledge all the time.'

Arnold's next film project would whet that hunger. In 1985 he pushed off to Italy to make a sword-and-sauciness epic called *Red Sonja*. He claims to have signed on out of loyalty to producer Dino De Laurentiis – 'He asked me, he begged me to do him a favour because he didn't have a name in the movie.' According to the director Richard Fleischer, though, the star had no choice about the film: it was part of a multi-movie deal he had with De Laurentiis after *Conan the Barbarian*. 'Dino could get him at what was then a bargain price for Arnold. It was good business sense. Arnold had a lot of other commitments at the time, so since he didn't have the main role in *Sonja* he came and went during the shooting.'

That main role went to Danish model Brigitte Nielsen, making her first movie appearance. She plays the warrior-beauty of the title, complete with cascading red hair, metal skirt and decolleté snakeskin blouse. We are still in Hyboria, more or less, though Arnold plays not Conan but Kalidor, a freelance righter of wrongs on permanent emergency call-out. Whenever Sonja is in trouble – a band of thugs, a rock-pool monster, anything else that screenwriters Clive Exton and George Macdonald Fraser can dream up – enter Kalidor.

Raiding the lesser-known stories of *Conan* writer Robert E. Howard, Exton and Fraser also put together the plot about a green talisman which can destroy the world. This is held by an evil queen (*Conan*'s Sandahl Bergman) who dislikes Red Sonja because the girl once spurned her lesbian advances. Can our outcast heroine get her act together, with the help of Kalidor and other cronies, and march on Gedren and destroy the talisman?

Arnold is mostly on point duty again: 'You go dat way, I'll go dis way.' He does, though, have one startling scene in a forest glade. Expounding the plot's prehistory to a raptly attentive Sonja/Nielsen, glad no doubt of a break from trying to hew recognizable sounds from her own accent, he delivers the longest speech yet entrusted to him in a movie. 'Centuries ago,' begins Arnold, 'de high lords of Hircania had entrusted de talisman to de priestesses because only vimmin could touch it . . .' And so it goes on, this long, wonderful wrestling match between an unarmed man and the English language, until we reach the point where *Red Sonja* started and we viewers came in. 'I found yer sister dying and loorned dat de talisman had been stolen.'

The dying sister episode begins the main action. Having ridden over most of Italy during the credit titles – Dino would get his money's worth from Arnold even if it meant filming his riding practice – Kalidor pulls up in the giant training arena where Red Sonja has been taking martial arts lessons.

'I'm looking for Red Son-ya,' he asks a tall, fetching girl in designer battle-dress.

'I am Sonja,' replies the girl.

Pause and snort from Kalidor's horse.

'Yer sister's dying, I'll take you to her.'

And out rides Kalidor, with Sonya following, through the legs of the giant stone statue serving as arena gateway. (The production design, wilful and wondrous, is by ex-Fellini collaborator Danilo Donati.)

After that it is open day for inanity. Incoherent fight scenes and action set pieces are hung from the quest plot like washing from a line. Arnold's own role as a pop-up rescue specialist shows the problem Fleischer and his writers had in creating a role for a main-attraction star who thought his deal was for a cameo.

'We looked for places where we could bring Arnold into the action where it would logically fit, and not be too arbitrary,' says Fleischer. 'We had the problem of how to work him into the scenes without weakening the character of Red Sonja, so it didn't look like she always had to be rescued. She was supposed to be this big superwoman.'

Nielsen's vapidly acted heroine needs all the rescuing she can get. The completed *Red Sonja* came out, was crucified, and went away again. Finally it found an indigent's resting-place on the video shelves.

What sort of relationship, though, did Brigitte and Arnold have off screen? Maria Shriver, clairvoyantly, had tried to discourage Arnold from making the film. She was not happy when rumours flew back from the locations in Celano and Abruzzi, near Rome, that a romantic flame had been ignited under the film's two European stars. Wendy Leigh insists that by November 1985 a 'torrid liaison' had begun with the 'Danish bombshell'. According to Leigh, Arnold's mother, arriving in Rome for a visit, 'took one look at the adventuress who had bewitched her son and was dismayed'.

Jim Lorimer, who visited Rome and went sightseeing with Arnold and Brigitte, thought it was all 'a tempest in a teacup'. 'People imposed a much more meaningful relationship than actually existed,' he says.

Richard Fleischer, asked if tales of Hyborian hanky-panky are true, composes a wryly evasive smile: 'I'm very naive about these things. Affairs can go on on the set and I never know. I hear of it later and I say "No kidding? Really? That was happening?"'

Around the insouciant director, the scandal mill whirred. During shooting there were rumours that Maria had despatched spies. After shooting Arnold and Brigitte were said to have gallivanted over Europe, enjoying parties in Vienna and skiing holidays near Innsbruck, before the Danish bombshell arrived in America. Here it seems she was keen to continue the liaison even though Arnold had given her a watch as an emotional retirement gift. He, with only months or weeks to go to the day when he would solemnise his vows to Maria, took the only course possible to extricate himself from a 'bewitching adventuress'. He stepped aside while she went on to meet to Sylvester Stallone.

17

Arnie and Sly

'*Le narcissisme post-écologique laissé partiellement de côté par son prédecesseur* [Stallone], *lié a l'engouement occidental soudain pour la bonne forme et le bon* look, *consecutif au developpement intensif du darwinisme économique et l'egocentrisme de l'ère* yuppie.' French film magazine *Positif* on the qualities distinguishing Arnold Schwarzenegger's screen persona from Sylvester Stallone's.

'The difference between Sly Stallone and me is I am me and he is him.' Arnold Schwarzenegger

For nearly twenty years the careers of Stallone and Schwarzenegger have run in close parallel: so close that like two chariots in a *Ben-Hur* movie they have sometimes collided. Whenever they do, the world clutches its ears, aghast that two grown men – overgrown men – could make so many screechy noises about each other.

To be fair to Stallone, Arnold did most of the screeching. He obviously felt that the man who started the machismo craze in 1976 with *Rocky*, and then took it to heights of swollen-muscled inspirationalism in the Rambo films, was a dangerous rival: even – yes – another of those father figures whom Arnold has dedicated his life to terminating.

The Austrian Oak openly acknowledged his debt to the Italian Stallion. 'I think Stallone did a big service to my career, because he opened a whole new type of movie where you get a *body* accepted; go see the *body*. That would never have happened ten years ago.'

Arnold also paid tribute to Stallone's determination. 'He didn't have that much natural potential. He had to work hard to gain size, but he has a tremendous amount of willpower.'

Yet between 1985 and 1986 – *anni mirabiles* of this rivalry between brothers in butchdom, and the period in which the Brigitte's new romantic interest in Sly led to their marriage – Arnold's tune changed from piping flattery to strident mockery.

Stallone takes himself too seriously, he tells *GQ*'s Jean Vallely. Arnold knows because the two men have spent years pumping at the same gyms.

> If you're doing 120-pound curls, he [Stallone] will say, I can do 130. He's obsessed, and that carries through in the way he dresses, how hard he tries to belong to a charity organisation. It's all Rocky, It doesn't come from, you know . . . [Arnold points to his heart] There's no love there. And people see that. You can fake your way through for a year, but for ten years, that's hard. Eventually, it catches up with you. I think that's the difference between him and me.

This in Arnold is mild mood. When he lets rip, one is astonished that Stallone does not come back with a libel suit or a challenge to a duel. 'I'd be angry at hearing my name mentioned in the same breath as Stallone's,' Arnold states in a 1985 interview.

> Stallone uses body doubles for some of the close-ups in his movies. I don't. One, my ego wouldn't let me. And two, I don't need a stand-in because there's nobody around with a better body than mine. We probably kill more people in *Commando* [Arnold's then upcoming film] than Stallone did in *Rambo*, but the difference is that we don't pretend the violence is justified by patriotic pride. All that flag-waving is a lot of bull – we're all in the entertainment business. And if killing is done with good taste, it can be very entertaining indeed.

The final onslaught comes in a *Playboy* interview in January 1988. This time Sly is taken apart for his lack of political correctness.

'I make every effort that is humanly possible to be friendly to the guy, but he just gives off the wrong vibrations. Whatever he does, it always comes out wrong.' Arnold gives as an example Stallone's invitation to his fellow actor to join a new club he is forming:

I said, 'What club?' He said, 'It's going to be an all-male club with no women allowed. Just like in the old days. Only men. And we sit around and smoke stogies and pipes and have a good time.' I told him it was the worst thing he could do. That we're living in a very sensitive time period when women are struggling for equality. I said that I didn't agree with half the stuff they were talking about, but a club like that would offend every smart woman in the country. I said to stay away from it.

But Stallone must have good points, as a man or an actor film-maker.

Listen, he hired the best publicity agents in the world and they couldn't straighten out his act. There's nothing that anyone can do out there to save his ass and his image. Just the way he dresses. Seeing him dressed in his white suit, trying to look slick and hip – that already annoys people. And the gold ring and the gold chains that say, 'Look how rich I am' – all that annoys people. It's a shame no one taught him to be cool. He should have L.L. Bean shoes and corduroy pants with a plaid shirt. That's cool; that's how a director should look, rather than have that fucking fur coat when he directs.

Stallone must have been bewildered, caught in the eye of this obscurely-motivated defamation hurricane. He uttered a brief, well-behaved response in December 1987: 'There's enough competition in life without one actor trying so actively to compete against another. This kind of thing can only end in bitterness, and unfortunately there can never be any real winner.' There was also a reported phone call from Stallone to Arnold after the GQ interview, in which Arnold told Sly he had been misquoted.

On only one occasion did the victim act out his annoyance in public. In September 1988, reports the New York *Post*, Stallone and his bodyguards walked into a nightclub, noticed Arnold's picture on the wall and told the owner that if he did not remove it Stallone would leave and never come back. The photo was surrendered to Sly's minders, who promptly destroyed it.

Ultimately, though, the spat may have suited both men. Feeling sympathy for Stallone goes with his screen image – the bruised punchball who keeps rebounding – while love-hate emotions about Arnold's ego-supremacism on screen go with the image of Superman Schwarzenegger.

While Stallone thrives on a macho masochism Arnold the movie star comes up with the transcendent brutalism and outrageous soundbites ('Killing with good taste'). His extra comic and cosmic nerve explains why the Austrian moved up on the Italian and overtook him. The Stallone movies moralise; the Schwarzenegger movies have a sardonic anarchism. The Stallone movies are all about anguish, worn on the sleeve like *Rocky* or internalised in militaristic anomie like *Rambo*; the Schwarzenegger movies are about the wry, affectless dispensing of rough justice. The Stallone movies are humourless; the Schwarzenegger movies have a powerful sense of the ridiculous.

If the hour brings forth the man, then Stallone was a creature of the 1970s – Carterite dove in hawk's clothing – while Schwarzenegger was the distillation of battle-glamour Reaganism. Stallone's militarism carries its own deconstruction programme. We *know* this man wants to get out of these war situations, because he wears his misery in that gaunt face with the dragged-down cheeks and in those near-feminine lips and eyelashes that seem to plead for peace even when they're clenched for battle.

Where Stallone's is the last face you would put in a recruitment commercial – and the last voice, with that funereal, lispy croak – Schwarzenegger's handsome mug and warmer monotone would do wonders in a conscription drive. This man thinks meting out punishment is fun. He is built as a justice machine who dispenses wisecracks on the side.

In response a hemisphere of indignant commentators has emerged over the years, from anti-violence film critic Michael Medved, stringing up Arnold as offender number one in his book *Hollywood vs America*, to psychiatrist Carole Lieberman, chairwoman of the National Coalition on TV Violence.

Medved's distaste is for the Arnold hero as moral lobotomy specimen. 'Even on those occasions when he isn't *supposed* to be playing killer robots, the Big Guy deals death with mechanical, deadpan precision; in many instances, the only twinges of humanity allowed to creep into his characterisations are those murderous *bons mots* with which he rids the world of the human rubbish around him.' The Schwarzenegger canon has just one retrograde message: 'Deadly and unreflecting efficiency as the ultimate standard of manliness.'

Lieberman ups the 'anti'. Summarising her film-by-film analysis of violent acts – *The Terminator* has eighty-four violent acts per hour, *Raw Deal* one hundred and forty four, *Commando* one hundred and sixty five – she pronounced: 'Arnold Schwarzenegger has become an American icon, worshipped as the god of violent power by the disenfranchised and powerless masses.'

Other Savonarolas have risen up over the years in other countries, hurling their lexicons of distaste at Arnold's screen persona. 'He is American fascist art exemplified, embodied,' wrote British journalist Ian Penman. 'Repellent to the last degree,' pronounced his compatriot critic and author Gilbert Adair of *The Terminator* and *Total Recall*; going on to charge 'insidious Nazification' and an 'appeal rooted in an unholy compound of fascism, fashion and fascination'.

The writers' vatic overreaction and politicised thesauri tell us more about their own critical preciosity than about any plausible social menace in Arnold's screen persona. Commentators who condemn screen mayhem do so because they believe cinema is about behavioural prescripts: if a film's actions are not fit to be mimicked they are not fit to be seen. Art's freedom and privilege, though, are to stretch, titillate, provoke, shock, deconsecrate. 'Do you think before movies there was no violence?', Arnold himself snaps. 'Have you read the Bible? If I were to make that book into a movie, it would be the most violent show around.'

There are more up-to-date parallels. If you mimicked the actions of the average Buñuel film – murder, disfigurement, blasphemy, obsession, revenge – you would be out of social circulation for life. While Arnold is not Buñuel, his screen personality is the best that modern popular American cinema has offered in the Buñuel sphere of moral disorientation. In the Spanish film-maker's world, acts of violence are redeemed by the surreal insouciance and sense of higher justice with which they are committed. 'Civilisation' is often a synonym for hypocrisy and duplicity: 'brutality' can be the brave or witty man's short cut to radical moral rearrangement.

This is the world according to Cinema Arnold. What a twinning the Spaniard and the Austrian would make in an ideal afterworld. We somehow picture a celestial, heretical movie dimension in which these two artists of the Anarchic Ideal dwell in perfect and eternal cinesthesia. *Arnold of the Desert. Los Arnoldados. Un Chien Arnoldou. The Terminating Angel.*

18

Taking out the Trash

'The guy was in shock. He said it was a sick, stupid idea, that no one's ever done it before. I told him that was precisely the point to do something that hadn't been done before.'

(i) From Val Verde with Love

'I saw it as a James Bond kind of film, where Sean Connery used to deliver those one-line quips at the end of a big action sequence,' says Mark L. Lester, the director of Arnold's next film, *Commando*.

Lester, a young film-maker who had presented his mayhem credentials in the Stephen King thriller *Firestarter*, had learned of the existence of a new Arnold-tailored action script during a pyjama party at Hugh *Playboy* Hefner's mansion.

Lester found himself talking to producer Joel Silver, a man with his hand on the pulse of high-fever pop culture ever since making that essay in comic-strip neo-realism *The Warriors*. Silver described a screenplay about a retired army man called into action to rescue his daughter, when she is kidnapped by counter-revolutionaries from the South American country of 'Val Verde'. The original script by two Columbia University film school students, Joseph Loeb II and Matthew Weisman, had been smartened with one-liners by seasoned scenarist Steven De Souza. Later a fourth writer, Richard Tuggle (who scripted and directed Clint Eastwood's *Tightrope*) was brought in to re-darken the script.

Tuggle's omission from the credits points to Lester's own eventual preference for the jokier De Souza version. 'I felt I had to utilise that humour, because I'd met Arnold socially and I knew he was funny in real life, and because the big lines in *The Terminator* got such a laugh.'

As a longtime James Bond fan, Arnold was all for turning himself into Sean Connery. He liked too the plot's emotional underpinning. 'He responded to' the relationship with the daughter,' says Lester. 'You build that up so that later when he's rescuing her the audience really cares about what he's doing. You're on his side even though he's killing all these people. You're rooting for him.'

Keen to make the psychology of this loving father and war veteran convincing. Arnold hired famous acting teacher Jeff Corey. Corey, also a well-known movie character actor who has specialised in gaunt hobos or eccentrics (*Lady in the Cage*, *Little Big Man*), coached Kirk Douglas for *Spartacus* and Jane Fonda for *They Shoot Horses, Don't They*? Now he would tell Arnold how to play John Matrix, the man who turns himself into a war machine after a visit from his old General.

'We sat across from each other at this desk,' says Corey in his rambling cabin-style home on a Malibu cape.

I told Arnold, you're a retired army Lieutenant-Colonel, and you don't want any part of war any longer, but these guys won't let you be. Get as much *polarity* as you can. What this guy wants is to cultivate his own garden, smell the lilacs and plant radishes. 'Go away, you guys! I want to be back with my little kid in this idyllic pastoral enclave I've established on top of this hill! Take your goddam helicopters away!'

We did many hours of work on that. He [Matrix] dreads becoming a robot, he doesn't want it to happen. It's all in Shakespeare, you know. 'The time is out of joint! O cursed spite, that ever I was born to set it right.'

Arnold makes the most of these scenes; though he seems to prefer uprooting and carrying entire trees to smelling lilacs and planting radishes. He affectionately joshes his daughter (Alyssa Milano) about her taste in music – 'Why don't dey just call him Girl George. It would cut down on all de confusion' – and nurtures his vertical bristle-cut hairstyle.

Arnold liked the parent-child content, but 'of course the film has action. I have the physical presence for action and I think it will always have a place in my films – though hopefully to a lesser extent. But, for now, there still remains a body count.' Pressed to specify: 'I destroy an entire army. I think it will be a new record.'

One journalist, Stu Schreiberg of the San Francisco *Chronicle*, estimates *Commando*'s corpse tally at over a hundred, putting it confidently ahead of *Conan* (fifty) and Stallone's *Rambo* (seventy). Meanwhile *Premiere* magazine put *Commando* at the top of its list when it did an all-time cinema slaughter survey. In 1992, to clinch the film's reputation, America's National Coalition against Television Violence put it at number one in their roll-call of Arnold movies to date.

The star himself was anxious that the violence not be confined to routine fisticuffs. 'You're always trying to think of unique ways of wiping out guys,' he explained. He had one idea that became, in all senses, a *casus belli*.

> In one scene I chop a guy's arm off. So, when we're filming it, the stunt man does something not in the script – he starts to scream. Well, I got the idea to tell him to shut up and slap his face with the arm I just took off. They thought it was too much. I thought it would be fun.

He thought it would be *such* fun that he took the idea all the way to 20th Century Fox's Lawrence Gordon. 'I went to the studio head to argue over including the scene in the film. The guy was in shock. He said it was a sick, stupid idea, that no one's ever done it before. I told him that was precisely the point: to do something that hadn't been done before.'

When Arnold proposed the idea on the set, Lester replied, 'No, no, it's too campy, too silly.'

The incident suggests, nonetheless, a growing confidence. The deferential robot-thespian of *The Terminator* was getting a taste for authorial input, and that taste ran to comedy.

Commando's strength is the throwaway wit that Lester had wanted to encourage from the start.

The film's spoken gags range from one-liners to one-worders. During a car chase, as Arnold screeches impassively through the streets with heroine Rae Dawn Chong at his side, she asks him, much as Linda Hamilton had asked Michael Biehn in *The Terminator*, if he could please explain what is going on. Unlike Biehn, who had launched into his big speech of the movie. Arnold simply replies, 'No.'

This hero is a man of few words, but most of them have a satisfying pulp-fiction wit, delivered in a voice at once sepulchral and as rich as a *sachertorte*. Holding the villain's henchman by one ankle over a cliff-edge, he says: 'You remember, Sully, I promised to kill you last?'

'Yes,' says Sully.

'I lied,' says Arnold, in a *sotto* boom.

Sully falls to his death. Back at the car Rae Dawn asks him what he did with the man. 'I let him go.'

With this monosyllabic magic, there is little that fellow actors can do but gesticulate at the edges. Chong's performance takes the skittery approach, dancing about the foothills, and becomes the lithest heroine in all Arnold's movies. Her funniest lines seem designed to deconstruct the movie as we watch. 'I don't *believe* this macho bullshit!' she squeaks from the back of a sofa as Arnold lays into another henchman in a motel room; and moments later, 'These guys eat too much red meat!'

Australian actor Vernon Wells played the baddies' chief hit-man who gets impaled with a heating pipe in the climactic boiler-room fight (Arnold: 'Let off some steam, Bennett'). Wells says:

Let's be logical. If Arnold's in a scene with you, you either better pick your nose and fall over and die or have someone shoot you to get attention. Even if he stands there doing nothing, he's three quarters of the frame because of his size. You could have walked up his back and beaten him on the head with a baseball bat, he would still have dominated that scene.

The film's tongue-in-cheek detailing – note the Wagnerian

mist that suddenly appears on a sunny deserted beach when
Arnie is dressing for battle ('I thought of it as fog off the water,'
Lester airily volunteers) – gives *Commando* some of the tailored
wryness, James Bond-style, that the director had hoped for. We
wonder, though, not for the first time in an Arnold product,
how far that whimsical persiflage spread beyond the camera.
According to one promo tale, the star claimed to have dislocated
an arm while performing the dangerous stunt of jumping from a
plane's nosegear during take-off. 'Arnold didn't do that stunt,'
Lester reveals to me. But he did do one stunt, more bathetically,
that ended in mishap. For the sequence of cut-up shots which
shows Matrix dressing for battle on the beach, Arnold insisted
on doing the close-up in which the hero's hand is seen sheathing
his commando knife. The double was going to do it, Lester
relates, but 'Arnold said, "His hand doesn't look like mine". So
Arnold got the knife and went – boom! – like that' – Lester
mimes knife being sheathed – 'and it went right into his hand.
He had to go to hospital and get stitches and we had to close
down for a couple of hours.'

When the film came out, it had enough recorded and advertent
carnage to satisfy redblooded critics everywhere. Not least San
Francisco's famous Joe Bob Briggs, who gleefully counted
the enormities: 'Two exploding jeeps. Exploding boat. Five
gratuitous farm-implement deaths. Knives thrown into seventeen
different body parts. Arm rolls. Kung Fu. Cadillac Fu. Shopping
Mall Fu. Bulldozer Fu. Coffee Table Fu.'

And on the campaign trail, Arnold Fu. 'He'd sit for days
and days in a hotel room,' says Lester, recalling the publicity
labours, 'and no matter who came into him, if it was the smallest
newspaper, he'd do it as if it was the *New York Times*. It was
quite amazing. He should teach classes in promotion to other
actors.'

Arnold's own judgment: 'I am a publicity genius. I could be
the head of any studio publicity department.'

(ii) New Look Arnie

During the filming of *Commando* Joel Silver had quipped, 'What's
a bunch of Jewish guys doing trying to make this big Teutonic guy

look good?' Rival producer Dino De Laurentiis must have asked himself the same question in 1985, changing 'Jewish' for 'Italian.' Although the years had rolled by since *Conan*, the mogul was *still* waving the old multi-picture contract under the Fliegende Osterreicher's nose.

The new Schwarzenegger vehicle was *Raw Deal*. Arnold would play Mark Kaminsky, a Southern sheriff of East German extraction with an alcoholic wife and a dossier besmirched by dismissal from the FBI. He had used excessive force on a suspect who had, as Arnold articulates it on screen, 'muhlested, moordered and middlated' a little girl.

He was keen on the script, written by Norman Wexler from an original story by two Italians Luciano Vincenzoni and Sergio Donati, because it was full of 'shootouts, fights in the alley, general kicking of ass.' The death count was respectable, if short of *Commando*. 'Maybe we reach fifty or sixty people. That sounds about right. Whenever you work with Uzis or submachine guns, you have massive destruction.'

British director John Irvin, lauded for his TV John Le Carré series *Tinker Tailor Soldier Spy* and for gritty action movies like *Dogs of War* and *Hamburger Hill*, was picked by Dino and approved by Arnold. Irvin found the actor 'very self-aware, as you can imagine any man would be who stands in front of a mirror building muscles. And he has a very clear understanding of what he's selling. He's not a great actor, he's a commodity star.' Arnold in turn applauded the director's focus on histrionics rather than hardware. 'John is an actor's director and he concentrated on the acting. He works on your neuroses, trying to get the most out of you.'

Another attraction of *Raw Deal* was that it would allow Arnold to wear suits. With that glistening mountain range of a body concealed under several metres of quality worsted, he would be encouraged to develop his communication skills. 'Things are changing slowly,' he would explain. 'For instance my wardrobe in *Conan* cost $4, while for *Raw Deal* I got twenty expensive suits made in Beverly Hills. The bill for the baby oil in that film was very low, while in *Conan* it was very high.'

The director agreed to the cosmetic changes to Arnold's image, nodding as the star stipulated his concern with varying his hair-style from film to film. 'After *Commando*, which was that rather odd straight-up look,' says Irvin, 'he wanted something more slicked back. And he was also concerned with the right hair colour for the role.' This ended up a rich, somewhat shoe-polishy, russet-brown.

Occasionally the director had to take time off from discussing Arnold's look to cast the supporting roles and re-cast the screenplay. Irivin brought in *Dogs of War* scenarist Gary Devore, to freshen up the material, particularly the Mafia shenanigans which the director found 'old hat'. (The story has Arnold re-drafted by the FBI to infiltrate an Italian-American crime clan, headed by Sam Wanamaker.) Devore also contributed several one-liners because, says Irvin, 'Arnold always wanted more jokes'. Meanwhile the casting policy was to 'throw good actors at him'. Doughty and durable character players were drafted in, such as Wanamaker, Darren McGavin, Steven Hill and Ed Lauter.

Despite the competent cast and direction, *Raw Deal* ends up overblown and underconceived. There are too many shoot-outs, with too little in between them. A hybrid of Coppola's *The Godfather* and Eastwood's rebel sheriff films, it has one other rogue antecedent near the close. Arnold decided that the ending, in which he and girlfriend Kathryn Herrold, an ex-Mafia moll, were to have flown off together into the sunset, should be more in the style of *Casablanca*. So the lovers part on the tarmac, mumbling their equivalent of Bogart's and Bergman's farewell speeches, and shortly afterwards our hero returns to his presumably now dried-out wife.

The wife, played by Blanche Baker (daughter of Fifties film star Carroll 'Baby Doll' Baker), is the film's one electrifyingly off-kilter character. She also inspires Arnold's finest utterance. Returning from a hard day's mobster-chasing early in the film, the sheriff is shocked to discover Blanche inebriated. She is smearing the chocolate topping onto a freshly-baked cake as she yearns aloud for a return to the gregarious years they enjoyed before being banished to the boondocks. Suddenly, her patience shredded, she picks up the cake – revealed to have 'Shit' scrawled in the topping – and hurls it at Arnold who moves his head just in time to watch the whistling item hit the wall. Pause. Withering look at wife. Then: 'You should naht drink and bake.'

This moment is known to break audiences up. All else apart, the idea that this machismo machine knows enough about kitchen activities to choose the precise word 'bake' – in the heat of a conjugal quarrel – is somehow deeply, endearingly deranged.

But *Raw Deal*'s whole charm – the charm of a good-bad movie – is built around mismatch and anomaly. What *is* this Austrian-accented Mr Mega-Muscle doing, pretending to blend in unnoticed in a backwoods southern town? Reviewing the film, *New Yorker* critic Pauline Kael mused on the surreal Arnold persona. 'He's a puzzling cartoon phenomenon, like a walking brick wall . . . How can you make a hero out of a man who seems likably, harmlessly gaga and who appears to have hams implanted above his elbows?' Clive James would later cap that image with his memorable summary of the Arnold physique: 'a condom filled with walnuts.'

Even that, though, suggests a kind of unity. *Raw Deal* shows there are anomalies within the anomaly. Artist Jamie Wyeth, who had painted Arnold's portrait in 1977, observed: 'He's got a sensitive, classic head which, visually, doesn't go with his body.' Nor do the legs go with the torso. We see this in *Raw Deal*, where the star is not distracting us with costumes either ancient-fantastical (*Conan*) or demented-supertech (*Commando*). The knees buckle slightly when Arnold walks, creating a Groucho Marx-style incongruity between the upright upper half and the low-loping support structure. Arnold looks like two characters – three with the 'classic' head – in search of architectural synthesis.

The mismatch body, just like *Raw Deal*'s cake-thowing scene, hints at the tension between strength and weakness, machismo and quasi-feminity, that will enfranchise Arnold's comic persona in *Twins* and his Goliath vincibility in *Kindergarten Cop*. One early moment in *Raw Deal* catches the tension in a single 'gesture'. When his telephone rings at home – the call that will summon our hero back to FBI duty – Arnold goes over and sits down to pick up the receiver. The movement seems strangely awkward. The body is fussed into a sitting position side-on to the phone, while the arm and hand grasping the receiver are held fastidiously away from the body. I re-ran the scene on my video. Then I realised what it showed. This man cannot handle a light weight naturally!

'He couldn't do it,' John Irvin remembers. 'I think it was because he was so used to a similar movement in picking up weights that when he picks up the phone it's like "Hmmm, how disappointing!" But you're right, it did look very unnatural, very uncomfortable. We had a lot of trouble with it.'

19

Announceable Love

'My wife – I think she is my greatest accomplishment.'

Another kind of acting Arnold had difficulty with, apart from the picking up of telephones, was love scenes. They 'embarrass the life out of me,' he said. 'Somehow I feel I'm giving away the secrets of my own bedroom.'

John Irvin remembers Arnold's less than eager approach to the romantic interlude with Kathryn Herrold in *Raw Deal*. His character is already drunk when they reach the bedroom and falls asleep shortly after the unfastening of the first shirt button. 'Violence is good fun as long as it's comic-strip,' says Irvin, 'and it is comic-strip in Arnold's firms. But love-making is not comic-strip and you can't do it as comic-strip. If you do it seriously, it calls for a physical and emotional exposure that he's not prepared to give; because it takes away from the mystery and the magic of what he does so well.'

In *Commando* an entire love scene between Arnold and Rae Dawn Chong was cut because it was unconvincing. Nothing resembling a conventional clinch occurs either – only a series of strange, wild wrestlings – between Arnold and his women in *Conan the Barbarian*.

Sex as emotional surrender, as opposed to sex as macho assertion, can be dangerous to the screen he-man. He must not soften or be vitiated. He must remain vigilant, battle-hardened. There was, after all, the example of Samson: a warrior-hero who

148

paid the penalty for falling asleep by having his 'hair' snipped off by his beloved.

We should not be surprised that Arnold has spent his movie career playing opposite tough heroines: from *Conan*'s Sandahl Bergman via *Terminator*'s Linda Hamilton to *Total Recall*'s Rachel Ticotin. Their combat-geared asexuality lets him off the amorous hook. They are there for danger not dalliance. They can be comrades in arms, but not in his arms.

Real romance was different. There no one gets paying spectators following him into the bedroom. The furthest that scrutineers come is to the church door, through which love's initiate will process, before and after the fastening of the holy knot. He will be wearing, if he is Arnold, a size-48 rented morning coat with a wide tie, cut-back collar and spray-like boutonniere. His bride Maria will be dressed in a white muslin Dior gown with an eleven-foot train, designed by Marc Bohan.

So it happened on the day of April 26th 1986. But the day, and the hum of public expectation, began long before the wedding doors opened. At 6 am the streets around the pretty white clapboard church of St Francis Xavier, Hyannis Port, began to fill with people. The driveway in front of one Eleanor Siscoe's house became a holding area for reporters and photographers. The skies were leaden and threatening, but that did not stop the athletic from climbing trees to secure a sightline. They were in no danger from low-flying aircraft because such traffic has been banned during the day, or at least between 10 am and 6 pm, from cruising below 2,000 feet.

In order that the list of five hundred guests be kept secret, Provincetown-Boston Airline had been persuaded to lock up its computers on the day before the wedding, in case passenger details gave the game away. One hundred rooms had been set aside at the Dunfey Hyannis Hotel, which had hired twenty extra security guards. To enter the church where Jack Kennedy and Bobby Kennedy had once served as altar boys, guests needed a gold button as 'laissez-passer'. The notable absentee from the ceremony was Rose Kennedy. At ninety-five she was not strong enough to attend, but watched it instead on television. As for Ronald Reagan, Kurt Waldheim and the Pope, all were invited but none could come. Reagan and Waldheim sent congratulatory telegrams. The Pope sent a blessing.

At 9.30, in buses and limousines, the guests and family members started to arrive. The Kennedys, the Shrivers; Arnold's mother Aurelia, wearing violet under a mink coat; Maria's mother Eunice, in green silk Dior. The loudest cheer was for Jackie Kennedy Onassis, sporting a smart navy suit with white triangular inset. Then came the officiators: among the ushers, Arnold's longtime friend and stuntman Sven Ole Thorsen (size-54 morning coat); maid of honour, Caroline Kennedy; best man, the faithful Franco Columbu.

Arnold cunningly cheated the crowds and photographers by debouching straight from a limo into the church's back door. The bride herself arrived fifteen minutes late in a $60,000 limousine. And last of all – the ceremony was all but beginning – came Andy Warhol and Grace Jones. The famous artist had travelled up with the famous actress-model, having been refused permission to bring a male friend of his own. Jones was wearing a skin-tight emerald green evening gown with a black mink stole. Warhol wore white hair, black leather and black Reeboks. The pair slipped into the church to sit on the last pew.

Inside the church, draped with roses, lilies and flowering branches of plum, pear and cherry, the Reverend John Baptist Riordan conducted the ninety-minute service, assisted by the pastor of St Francis Church, the Reverend Edward Duffy. Maria walked down the aisle to the strains of the Lohengrin wedding march. Edward Kennedy, Eunice Shriver, Sargent Shriver and Arnold's business friend Jim Lorimer all read passages from the Bible. The Shriver parents and son Bobby offered prayers for an end to violence and terrorism, for Jewish friends celebrating Passover, and for family members who had died. The service came to a climax emotionally with Oprah Winfrey reading Elizabeth Barrett Browning's poem 'How do I love thee?' Finally, as the happy couple processed down the church after being pronounced 'husband and wife' – Maria's preference over 'man and wife' – the aisles came alive to *The Sound of Music*. The song 'Maria' accompanied the leaving of the church and the cheering of the crowds.

Before and after the wedding, there was much opulent and

well-planned celebrating. On the Friday evening before, Aurelia Schwarzenegger presided over the 'rehearsal dinner'. This took the form of an Austrian clambake and set the table richly groaning with wiener schnitzel, lobster, strawberry shortcake and *sachertorte*. The guests laughed when six bridesmaids performed a skit to the tune of 'Old MacDonald had a farm,' renaming the protagonist McArnold.

That evening also saw the presentation of a valuable gift. Arnold gave his parents-in-law the silk-screen portrait of Maria he had commissioned from Andy Warhol, who had worked on it since early April after a photo-session with the bride-to-be. ('She's really pretty and she took good pictures,' he noted in his diary. 'She's a little heavy on the bottom. She was cute, she talked a lot.') Arnold handed over the picture to the Shrivers with the words, 'I'm gaining a wife and you're gaining a painting.'

One person not gaining a great deal that evening was Arnold's old friend and the man who had made him a movie star, George Butler. The director of *Pumping Iron* had brought his Leica and a roll of film, hoping to eternalise a few blithe pre-nuptial moments. He walked to the dinner with Franco Columbu and was stopped at the bar by 'one of Arnold's secretaries, whom I had known for years'. 'No cameras,' she said. A startled Butler protested that he had no professional assignment, the photos would be purely for his own pleasure. Besides, he always cleared such matters with Arnold. 'I've been asked to impound all cameras,' persisted the functionary. Butler records that at that moment he 'felt my whole experience with Arnold opening and closing like a book'. In his mind, he says, he screamed 'That's the fucking German camera that made Arnold famous!' Outwardly he pasted on a smile and joined the crowd.

The next day came the après-wedding festivity. Guests repaired to two tents in the Kennedy compound, where oysters, cold lobsters and chicken breasts in champagne competed for their attention. At cake-cutting time, everyone turned to the seven-foot-high, eight-tier wedding cake weighing 425 pounds. 'Not good for the waistline!' quipped Arnold. When the band struck up merrily for the dancing, Arnold and Maria took the floor, she first lacing on two white running shoes, the better to protect a pair of broken toes incurred during a fall in her New York flat.

Also on show were the wedding gifts. In addition to the usual dinner sets and finest crystalware, interspersed with Warhol silk-screens, there were two large pieces of sculpture. One, called 'The Futility of War,' had been donated by Bill Fischler, owner of Patrick's Roadhouse, Arnold's favourite eatery on the Pacific Coast Highway. 'I hope Maria likes it!' Fischler had exclaimed on handing it to Arnold during a visit to the Roadhouse by the prospective groom and his mother. Arnold is said to have replied in German, 'I like what I like and what Maria likes doesn't matter. In my house I am king.'

The other piece of sculpture was unnamed. Donated by Kurt Waldheim, it took the form of two papier-maché replicas of Arnold and Maria, she dressed in an Austrian-style dirndl, he hoisting her on high as if over the threshold of married bliss. At that time Waldheim had come under scrutiny for his wartime past, and had been banned from entering the United States. The previous evening Arnold had reportedly made a short speech thanking the man he called a friend and whose Austrian presidential campaign he was then supporting. 'My friends don't want me to mention Kurt's name because of all the recent Nazi stuff and the UN controversy. But I love him and Maria does too and so thank you, Kurt.'

This provocative oration was largely forgotten by the following night. Andy Warhol witnessed the glamour, the warmth, the interlacing of unlikely celebrities. Grace Jones danced with Ted Kennedy. Arnold and Maria danced with everyone they could. Food was eaten. Vegetables were steamed while you watched. At a climactic point, the bridegroom rapped for attention.

'Arnold gave a speech,' writes Warhol, 'and was saying wonderful love things like that he'd always make her happy. It was the first time I'd seen really announceable love, saying everything out loud.

20

Jungle Politics

'The first half I have clothes. In the last quarter, I'm in the mud.
In the middle, we all take off our shirts.'

(i) The Forest is our Home

The marriage ceremony interrupted filming on Arnold's new
action adventure *Predator*. Shot in Mexico, this was the tale of a
group of American commandos who make the forest their home
while pursuing a semi-invisible monster who has slaughtered a
previous battalion of US soldiers and is about to kill all but one
(guess whom) of them.

This creature from another planet – an 'armour-clad reptilian
biomechanoid' – has thermal vision and delights in flaying its
victims and hanging them upside down from trees. When the
movie came out, it was seen as *Alien* in the jungle. To director
John McTiernan, as well as being his first big-budget step on
a career that would lead to *The Hunt for Red October* and other
mega-movies (including Arnold's ill-fated *Last Action Hero*),
Predator was 'in essence a battle of Titans . . . a classic hero
story and a horror story, like the Norse myths, where heroes
battle against supernatural beings'.

It is also, by chance or supernatural design, an allegory of
Arnold's relationship to his own new-budding belief in group
endeavour at this time. 'I am part of a team,' he explained. 'It
was one of the reasons I took the script. I like to be part of
a team.'

This is an odd warp in Arnold's ideological development. Back in his youth, we recall, he was almost allergic to team activities: hence his mania for muscle-pumping. 'The worst thing I can be is the same as everyone else,' he had said, 'I hate that. That's why I went into bodybuilding in the first place. It was the idea of taking the risk by yourself rather than with a whole team'.

We know that movie stars adapt their PR tunes to the latest films they are shooting. However, there is something strikingly cumulative in the manifestations of team-spiritedness in Arnold's life at this time. He has just formalised his union with his life partner. In several interviews since *Raw Deal* he has waxed garrulous about the virtues of traditional menswear – 'team' clothes. In his new film he is playing Major Dutch Schaefer, one of a cadre of guerrillas fighting an extraterrestrial shape-changer. And in his next film – the futuristic *The Running Man* – he will be part of a band of fighters all near-wearing identical costumes and pitching for survival in a death-or-glory TV game show.

McTiernan himself insisted that the comradeship motif be as realistic as possible. 'Even though many of the cast had military backgrounds,' he says, 'I wanted them all to get a chance to know each other, develop a sense of something as a group. The idea was to endure something rough and conquer it together.'

Down there on location, miles from civilisation around Puerto Vallarta, Arnold and his army obliged. 'In Mexico we'd get up at 6 am for breakfast,' the actor recalls 'and then run four or five miles to get into condition. After that we worked five or six hours in the jungle on skills training – everything from climbing trees to rappelling down ropes to handling the weaponry. We had to learn how to move silently through the jungle and communicate with hand signals and deploy for specific manoeuvres. By that time we were exhausted. Then we went back to the weight room in the hotel and trained for two hours, and then the director called us and said, "OK, now we rehearse!"'

Team spirit taken to the brink of insanity. In the event, though, the platoon in *Predator* falls apart – and a more interesting movie emerges. The men are picked off one by one by the creature, until only Major Schwarzenegger is left. He has to go 'back to nature' and bring primitive know-how to the fiend's destruction. The jungle's weapons – sticks, stones, mud – are harnessed in the fight to the death with the hero's few remaining tools of his own trade: a couple of flares, a knife and the ultimate death-dealer, the Arnold one-liner. 'You are one ugly motherfucker', growls the Tacitus of modern cinema, to a creature that removes its helmet to reveal a hideously squashed face with snaggled tusks.

Dutch survives by completing the submersion of his identity. He becomes a driven shape-changer like the Predator – who with his distinctive rasp-gurgle says to him at the end, 'I am what you are' – and he is made one with that ultimate team leader and overseer, Nature. The sacrificial heroism of Dutch's men made the survival of the one, and the destruction of the enemy, possible. But the true victor in *Predator* is metamorphic but all-dominant Ma Nature who – yes! – has all the answers if only man will see and honour them and blend himself into her will.

Seen in this perspective, *Predator* is a film ideally suited to the mid-1980s, when the world was experiencing that outbreak of team ideology called the Green movement. (Soon, we shall see, the offscreen Arnold too would be getting into ecology, recycling, whole-earthism and the rest.)

There is another, more anarchic movie, though, inside the green one. Arnold is the beast-battler but also the beast. The invisibility of the monster is a mirror to his own 'invisibility' as a camouflage-smeared platoon leader and the laconic spokesman for military homogeneity. When the monster is finally made visible so – abracadabra! – is Arnold the resourceful individualist. Hurled into that vortex common to all Arnold action films, where time is rewound so our hero can reinvent himself as a primal warrior, bare of civilised values even when bristling with hi-tech weaponry, Avant-Garde Arnie proves that time is curved by becoming superperson and caveperson at the same time.

Predator turned one way to the light is a dream of men united by, and surviving through, the flame of eternal battle-readiness. Turned the other way, it shows the agenda of individualism emerging late, in the apocalyptic presentation of Arnold as a kind of Last Man on Earth.

Even the make-up and lighting hint at this notion of a rebel icon. Every soldier character has camouflage markings on his face; only Arnold has his main smear carefully placed so it highlights and strengthens his cheekbone, while the smears on his forehead are designer-positioned to give his brow the right vengeful, numinous frown. Meanwhile director McTiernan and cameraman Don McAlpine make a leitmotif from the shots of the star slowly turning his head from a face-away position towards the camera, like some primeval sculpture being revolved towards the light. Each device assists Arnold's transformation from actor into icon: into a moving statue wired for ceremonial one-liners.

(ii) Der Wald Ist Unser Heim

The tension, and sometimes overlap, between team-playing and self-assertion, on and off screen, is the signature trope of Arnold's life at this time. What on earth was he doing hobnobbing that summer with Kurt Waldheim? Was this a natural maverick's one-finger gesture at world opinion, or was it an unguarded doffing of the cap to his own roots, and his own patrimony of discipline and *kameradschaft*.

The two men met at Waldheim's villa at Lake Attersee near Salzburg on August 29th 1986. Years later Arnold tried to put the event behind him in an interview with Britain's *Sunday Times*. 'All these claims that I am a friend of Waldheim's are nonsense. I have only met him once in my entire life, when I was vacationing in Munich and I got a call from his office saying he was in Salzburg and did I want to come down for an afternoon. I said I was coming down anyway to show my friends around the city and so we visited him for an hour and had a lot of fun talking about his career in the UN and all that and that was it. We took some photographs and that made me a "best friend of Waldheim".'

Waldheim was sufficiently sensitive to the delicacy of the meeting to ask Arnold if he would mind it being reported in the press. Arnold said no. 'He is my president. I have both US and Austrian citizenships.' he later commented. Surely he knew of Waldheim's controversial war record? 'No. We don't even know about it now. There is a debate going on.' (This in 1989.)

Quizzed in the *Sunday Times* interview about his father Gustav,

Arnold went on to broaden the question of the Schwarzeneggers and their politics. 'As to my father, it's irrelevant because I know nothing about his past, nor was it ever explained to us. I myself did research with the Simon Wiesenthal Center to find out if it is true because when I heard about it I thought, Hmmm, maybe there is some truth to it, what do I know? No one ever talked about it in our house.'

Aurelia Schwarzenegger reportedly confirmed that the subject did not come up much at home. She met Gustav in 1945 after the war had ended. 'I don't suppose he ever said more than a few words to me about the war or what he did in it in the 27 years that we were married.'

21

The Public and Private Lives
of King Arnold

*'I love the world of business; I also like paintings, sculpture,
lithographs and skiing, and horse riding and skeet and trapshooting
and motorcycle riding. And sometimes I have to spend time with
my wife.'*

A man who shakes hands with a demonised statesman may
have, among many motives, this one: he wants to get near
the rushing sound of power. He wants to feel its contrary
thrusts of responsibility and freedom to be irresponsible. For
he feels he is fast entering that mad, fascinating, schizophrenic
slipstream himself.

(i) The Two Arnolds

Arnold and Maria honeymooned in Antigua, after which Arnold
returned to Mexico to complete *Predator*. Once the newlyweds
were back together in America, the bicoastal routine resumed,
although in 1986 the couple traded in their $300,000 Spanish-style
home in Santa Monica, with its 800-pound double bed made from
the wood of a crashed pier, for a $2.8m home in Pacific Palisades
just up the coast.

Their near neighbours now included Walter Matthau, John
Forsythe, Milton Berle and Sylvester Stallone. The move reflects
Arnold's increased earning power. 'Ninety percent of my invest-
ments have been very, very profitable,' he tells a reporter over a

158

three-egg omelette at Patrick's Roadhouse. He is building Oak Plaza, his own $10m development on Santa Monica's Main Street, which includes three separate multi-storey buildings and six boutique-style shops, built over three levels of underground parking. This red-brick *massif* will also house Arnold's own office and the HQ of his Oak Productions (to which only those with a special elevator key can gain access), as well as his restaurant Schatzi's.

Arnold does all this wheeling and dealing, dreaming and achieving, himself. He still refuses to have a business manager, unlike most actors who dabble in the business world. 'He [the manager] presents them with a weekly cheque,' expostulates the star. 'It's like a kid getting spending money from a parent. The actor has to beg for money to buy a car, only to be told, "No, don't get a Porsche, the insurance is too high. I think you'd be better off with a Volvo!" When I ask actors if they are investing in stocks, bonds or real estate, they look at me as though I'm mad!'

There is something surreally forward-marching about this man, off-screen as well as on. What is this non-American doing telling Americans how to be entrepreneurial? Perhaps he is reflecting the paradoxes of his own film persona, part maverick, part martinet. He is an individualist who makes his own rules; at the same time he uses the megaphone of his fame and power to tell people to get in line according to a collective ideal. Make yourself rich, be part of the American Dream.

Arnold *could* be frustrated by a financial minder; he is his own mobile, one-man advertising system for that Dream. He likes swish cars, such as the Cadillac El Dorado Biarritz Convertible he drove in 1985 or the Red Porsche 911 he is driving in 1987. He enjoys tooling around the Los Angeles canyons on his Harley-Davidson motorcycle, which he has had painted purple, his favourite colour. He smokes expensive cigars. As a plutocrat he has achieved lift-off. He is becoming a public mascot for the ideals of New World self-fulfilment.

The mascot, though, also needs times to let his hair down. Arnold only got to be part of the establishment by being anti-establishment: the bodybuilder who trampled on the sport's traditions and niceties and then chutzpah'd his way into follow-up careers he had no business in.

The hoaxster-jokester of old still likes to *épater* anyone available. In 1985 he was interviewed by Lynn Darling for *Esquire* in the Los Angeles Sports Arena. As they left, a shy young security guard approached the star, offering to escort him back to his limousine. Arnold started quizzing him about his life and learned that he was going to night school to study business, with the hope of starting up his own shop.

'You should sell dildoes,' Arnold told him.

'I beg your pardon, sir?' replied the taken-aback guard.

'Sure. People buy them for presents, they like to be funny at parties. They really sell.'

The future of the unnamed security guard, after this interface with an idol, is not recorded.

Another form of comic relaxation for Arnold is the physical prank. If you are eating with him in a restaurant he will order you a coffee; when it arrives he will warn you that the milk is sour; and when you lean over to sniff the cup, he will push your head in it.

An ambitious variant on the joke was played on Maria in New Orleans. In the Caribbean Room of the Pontchartrain Hotel in 1978, Arnold pushed her face into a monster concoction of meringue, cream and chocolate sauce called a Mile High Pie. The room was mesmerised; Maria was speechless.

We could see this Arnold as a joker jumping out of the pack to goose the rest of the cards, including the royal suit. Or we could see him as King Arnold himself, proving his omnipotence by showing what he can get away with under the banner of regal impunity. For Arnold *is* now a king. To discover that, we need only visit a famous diner on the Pacific Coast Highway, as I did on my first field trip to Los Angeles. It contains Arnold's throne, Maria's matching throne and the special shrine dedicated to the star's life and career.

(ii) In the World of Patrick's Roadhouse

'It started by his coming here with his brother-in-law – or his now brother-in-law – Bobby Shriver', rasps Bill Fischler, as I am ushered into the small, two-level greasy spoon with wooden floors and walls. It is early in the morning; I am trailing clouds of jet lag; and I am carrying a small BBC tape-recorder as part of my alternative and *bona fide* guise as a radio writer-presenter from 'London, England'.

The German-extracted proprietor, wearing shorts and a form-fitting black T-shirt over a pot belly, sits me down at Arnold's special table. Patrick's Roadhouse, a shamrock-and-white-painted shack sitting opposite the ocean on Pacific Coast Highway, was for years Arnold's favourite breakfast place and has become – such is the power of kings – a mecca for Hollywood's and America's high-rollers.

'They used to come together,' says Fischler of Arnold and Bobby Shriver. 'Then Arnold started coming on his own. After *Conan* I put a chair here for him, and then a larger and larger chair, until this throne he sits in now, which cost me a fortune to buy at an antiques show. Then Maria said, wouldn't it be nice if she as queen consort could have a chair of her own. So I bought this one I'm sitting in.'

'Nobody sits here without his permission,' declaims Fischler. 'Only when Arnold is out of town can certain people sit here, like Jeff Katzenberg the President of Disney [as he then was] or Jeff Berg [head of super-agency ICM].'

Emma Thompson had been to the Roadhouse recently, but had had to sit outside because her friends smoked. Prince Andrew had visited. And photographs showed Bill Clinton stopping by during a power jog. In this august company Arnold *still* had the top table

'Everyone loves Arnold. As a person he is outstanding.' Bill Fischler gears up for further superlatives, but a train whistle suddenly goes 'Whoo-whoo'. He picks up the private Arnie-phone on the table, shaped like a locomotive, and takes a breakfast reservation.

Arnold used to eat a five or six-egg omelette [continues Fischler] 'Now he's cut down and has a special dish of sautee'd onions and sautee'd tomatoes, mixed with scrambled eggs. No bread, just English muffins. No butter, sugar, jams or citrus juices. A pot of black coffee, not decaffeinated. Arnold himself doesn't care for potatoes, but he makes sure Maria has them. And she has fresh fruit. But no eggs.

He's a very handsome man, his wife is a very beautiful lady and they have three very beautiful children.

And Aurelia Schwarzenegger, I ask? We have heard that the queen mother too stops by at Patrick's Roadhouse. 'She loves to come here to eat when she is on one of her two-month visits with Arnold.' Fischler mutters something about escaping Maria's cooking. Then he moves on to the subject of Sylvester Stallone.

'When he had a conference with Arnold one day at this table' – Fischler thumps it – 'he insisted that all the tables around be cleared.'

Fischler scowls at the memory, which seems to have been called up for comparison purposes. 'Arnold is always polite, though he doesn't like the public bothering him while he eats. Kids are different. He'll autograph anything for them. They stand there in front of him in complete awe, 'cos he's a great hero to young people.

'I'm not a prophet. I'm not a gypsy. But I would be surprised if he did not run for political office one day.'

I am ushered at last to the 'shrine'. This is Fischler's collection of mementoes, photos and magazine pieces about Arnold, housed in and around a battered-looking cupboard-cum-table. 'Most people I never ever show this to, but I will show it to you because you're quite an English gentleman.' Fischler fishes out a photo album. The first snap he shows me is of six elderly men sitting around a table. 'These are all German generals. World War Two. They've all been in here.'

Next, pictures of Arnold's wedding. 'Technically, you weren't supposed to photograph,' Fischler says, 'but I had a little camera about as big as the palm of my hand and I'd wave it as the people went by.

'That's Grace Jones and Andy Warhol. There, that's Mrs O (Onassis) and Caroline. And here, these are all Russian generals who were in here once.' The picture – six elderly men sitting round a table – seems to be the same as the Germans. But I let it pass.

'Here's Arnold and me at his bachelor party. That's Franco Columbu . . . Anyway, you'd better sit down and have breakfast as my guest.' The time is 8.45 and the diner is not yet officially open. A pair of timid prospective customers peer through the entrance door. 'Read the sign! 9 am! 9 am!' yells the proprietor before ushering me to a bar stool and introducing me to a passing top Hollywood agent. The agent looks through me and passes on.

'Here's the President,' Fischler says, showing me a photo of Bill Clinton jogging into Patrick's Roadhouse. 'He's been here twice. [Stage whisper] *Arnold doesn't like him 'cos he's a democrat!'*

Clinton would have to take a table below Arnie anyway at Patrick's Roadhouse, along with the rest of the world. For the restaurant acknowledges only one supreme being. Everyone else – especially the Hollywoodites – go up and down the diner's social order according to the yoyo-ing of their careers.

'Everything in this town is based on pecking order,' sums up Fischler. 'If you don't sit at the first four tables it means your business was not as good or your last picture was a big flop.'

As a plate piled high with eggs, sausages, bacon and hash browns is put before me, I realise I am in the restaurant's equivalent of outer oblivion. Right by the cooking area; down the steps from the stars' eating level; probably in a seat that indicates that my last twelve pictures have been flops and my next step is to move out in the smokers' patio with Emma Thompson.

(iii) Proposing and Disposing

A king is capable of good works on a national or local level; so we expect him to do them. Arnold was true to his crown throughout these early years of his movie fame. In October 1985 he recorded a rock video called *Stop The Madness*, together with La Toya Jackson and Herb Alpert, for Nancy Reagan's anti-drugs campaign. Around this time he started to donate money to the Simon Wiesenthal Center, giving a portion of his earnings from each new movie to this foundation for peace and racial tolerance. And he became ever more deeply committed to the annual Special Olympics.

This athletic event for the mentally impaired was founded in the late 1960s by Eunice Shriver, who ten years later secured Arnold's involvement as national weight-lifting coach. In addition to giving him a high charitable profile, the job helped to show Eunice how serious a son-in-law she was taking on. (At first she had tried to dissuade Maria from marrying an actor-athlete of dubious background, merit and intentions.) Arnold showed the Special Olympians how to hump weights and was able to act as an international liaison man for the event: writing letters to foreign leaders to set up host countries for the event. 'He's the embodiment of everything our athletes would like to be,' said Special Olympics executive director Harold Connolly. 'He's Charlemagne, Hulk Hogan and Alexander the Great all rolled into one.'

There are other stories of good works. Time and again grateful fathers – Reg Park, Paul Graham, Bill Fischler – have borne witness to this writer that Arnold has made a special effort to look after their sons in America: helping with jobs or education, or in the case of Graham's son with a learning disability requiring the attention of experts. 'Arnold helped us by recommending doctors through the Kennedy Foundation in New York,' says Graham, 'and he's assisted us with professors to help our son learn to speak correctly, He does things like that all the time.'

Arnold also took care to support his nephew Patrick after the death of Meinhard Schwarzenegger. He sent his brother's widow money; paid for her son's high school in Lisbon; and funded Patrick's education and living expenses when the boy later came to America.

Another beneficiary of Arnold's time and trouble has been California's penal system. In the mid-1970s, before he became a movie star, he started giving weightlifting classes in places like Terminal Island prison. (We see him conducting a seminar there in *Pumping Iron*.) He wanted to build up the inmates' self-respect as well as their bodies. 'That's much better than being dropped off at some bus station with twenty dollars in their pocket and back on the street committing crimes.' He was asked if it was not a bit risky, this honing up of the jail population. 'Not at all. Weight training has the opposite effect. Steam is let off, hostile feelings and stress are replaced by a more positive outlook on life.'

More recently, Arnold the philanthropist took on the East Los Angeles *barrio*. He has donated time, effort and over one million dollars to the Hollenbeck Youth Center, a non-profit rehabilitation programme for young people coming in off the drug- and crime-ridden streets. In the early 1990s he would become executive director of the same programme's 'Inner City Games', which for nine days each year gathers 100,000 children, aged eight to eighteen, from twenty-one Los Angeles housing projects. And in 1995 he would announce the extension of those games to five further cities.

For Simon Wiesenthal, whose Center in Los Angeles would honour him in the 1990s for his good deeds, this generous Arnold was the one he saw and knew ever since first meeting him. In the early 1980s, according to Wiesenthal, Arnold had approached the Center – before he raised those queries about his father – and asked if it was possible for non-Jews to contribute funds and to attend meetings and functions. Later Arnold and Maria threw a party for Wiesenthal on his eightieth birthday in December 1988 featuring, the honoree told me, a 'big cake which stretched from one wall to the other'.

'He has done so much for handicapped people without looking who they are, their race or their colour,' says Wiesenthal. 'Other people give only money, he gives both time and money. This should be honoured. The man is losing his free time to do something for these people, so they have a sense to live.'

Another feature of regal character, though, is that the king can get impatient – having grown used to a world pliant to his beneficent will – with minor examples of non-subservience in his home life.

(iv) A King at Home

First, the good news. Back at Pacific Palisades, Arnold is overcoming his one-time bachelor cynicism about the wedded state. 'I don't need to get married to get my shirts ironed,' he had once said. He is even contemplating the possible joys of multiplication. He and Maria 'have no heavy plans to start a family, but of course one of the big reasons you get married is to reproduce'. And how, one journalist asks him, will he handle fatherhood? 'I believe kids have to be treated with an iron fist,' says Arnold. 'They should know that they are not yet able to make their own decisions. They have to respect their parents completely. They have to learn – to polish their shoes, iron their shirt, arrange their things. Every day.' Gustav Schwarzenegger would have been proud.

And when small, pattering Schwarzenegger–Shrivers grace the happy home, will Arnold let them watch – presumably not? – his own violence-ridden films such as *The Terminator* and *Commando*? 'Let them?,' booms Arnold. 'I will *make* them. I will strap them in a chair, put the movie on and tell them, "This is Daddy."'

Every monarch should have a sense of humour. But sometimes too there are shows of temper. 'I'll get in the car screaming and Maria will say, "Oh yeah, look good, be brutal – look like the Terminator!"'

The couple's quarrels often stem from their different political outlooks and upbringings. 'I'm from a socialist country that has backfired on me and made me more conservative. She's from a democratic family, so that's the way she is. I don't mind.'

Or only sometimes. Maria's ability to be laid-back about wealth and clothes, for example, clearly rubs Arnold the wrong way. 'When we play football I will wear an old shirt,' he says. 'That's the difference between me and Maria – she will think nothing of putting on a cashmere sweater to roll around in the grass!' Arnold is amazed at this in more than one interview: at how his wife can wear that $400 garment 'so comfortably and sweat and throw a football or play tennis in it. I couldn't.' 'This, of course, is my upbringing,' he explains. 'In Austria, silk or cashmere wasn't heard of.'

If he stands by helpless as his wife's sweaters are dragged through the grass, on other clothing matters he takes firm action. 'I don't like to dictate to Maria, but I don't allow her to wear pants. I only like dresses and skirts. Maria understands that it looks more feminine.' And his mother? 'She also is not allowed to go out in pants with me.'

Maria, if not *Mutti*, could presumably have told him what to do with his sartorial sexism. If she did not, it may be because in 1986, the year of her marriage, Maria's own ego and career were poised like a nervous elevator between 'Up' and 'Down'. In June she had the honour to be chosen Regent of Georgetown University, the youngest ever in the history of America's oldest Roman Catholic university. Yet in the same month she learned that bad ratings for her CBS 'Morning News' show meant her contract would not be renewed. She was offered a position in Los Angeles, but according to the New York *Times* was 'said to be reluctant'. At summer's end she would leave CBS for NBC's '1986' news show, taking a large pay cut from $500,000 to $160,000.

Reluctance to take a job in L.A.? How odd, since it would mean her being able her to spend more time with Arnold. But perhaps the regime of being married without actually living together suited this as yet childless couple. Sometimes Arnold flew to the east coast for the weekend, getting a midnight plane in L.A. and meeting Maria for breakfast in New York. 'On the way home I read scripts, and now that there are phones on the plane I can make my calls. I don't lose one hour, and I can be with Maria. So far, so good.' Meanwhile Maria sat in New York during the week, where her alarm clock had been going off at 3 am during her stint with CBS 'Morning News' (her colleagues soon coined the nickname 'Maria Striver') and wondered what initiatives *she* should take over these weekends. 'I've got a relationship that's 3,000 miles away and that's tough. I'm here all alone, I'm thinking, should I go this weekend and see my parents or should I see Arnold?' Obviously, she felt she should not do anything so drastic as to re-locate in Lotusland.

Asked by Boston TV in June 1986 how he keeps his marriage intimate, Arnold says: 'We fly back and forth as much as possible and run up thousands of dollars in phone bills.' When all else fails, he adds, 'We have over-the-phone sex.'

This last statement caused a mild media earthquake at the time. 'Did we hear that correctly?' gasped a dozen commentators, speaking for a hundred Midwest matrons. Was it a blooper on Arnold's part – or was it the king turning joker again?

He cannot afford to do it too often. A royal personage must keep in dignified touch with his public duties. In 1986 the more serious Arnold could be found doling out his contributions to the Republican party – *USA Today* newspaper noted a $1,800 cheque in September alone – and answering questions about his ambitions for political office. Three years before, he had seemed to bat away hopes of preferment, aware that he was constitutionally barred from the Presidency. Now he seemed upbeat again. 'The joy in public office is a tremendous idea,' he fanfared. 'I think it could be the greatest challenge yet.' And he told *GQ*'s Jean Vallely that if he did run for office his sights would be set higher than those of actor-idol Clint Eastwood, famous as mayor of his home town Carmel. Said Arnold: 'I don't think I'm the type that could go for such a small city. Like Santa Monica. I mean, if I were going to run, I'd go after something major – like the governor of California.'

To keep in training, he contributed the occasional politically-tinged piece to magazines and newspapers. For its March 1986 issue, *American Film* sent the following whip-round question to various film personalities: 'Do the people involved in the recent spate of right-wing films hold deeply felt political convictions, or are they just making "entertainment"?'

Arnold managed to answer this exam question on one side of the paper but from both sides of the political divide:

> People who do heroic movies successfully and become big-ger-than-life stars get into the situation of being more than just an actor. You should try to keep the two apart as often as possible, because you don't want to alienate the other audience. You don't want to make just right-wing movies because you're conservative and alienate all the people who have liberal philosophies. Your films should be for everyone. It's a business and creative decision. But I would make an effort not to become a propagandist for communism in any way, or make a movie that Moscow invites to its Moscow Film Festival.

Two years later, Arnold would make a film *in* Moscow, playing a member of the city's police department who stomps over to the USA to demonstrate the Soviet way of enforcing law and order. But by 1988 Russia's political complexion had changed, changed utterly; and Arnold the politician would be there to show that his own complexion matched.

22

Running on the Spot

'I'm not into politics, I'm into survival.' Arnold Schwarzenegger in *The Running Man*

(i) Lycra Man

The Running Man is the most boneheaded movie of what we might call Arnold Schwarzenegger's 'mature' period. Made at a time when he had supposedly defined his film presence, it resembles a reject episode of British TV's 'The Avengers' dunked in the Tech Noir style of *The Terminator*.

Stephen King's original novella, written under the pseudonym Richard Bachman, is an unflamboyant but effective futuristic thriller about a man given thirty days to hide anywhere in the United States, in order to avoid a posse of 'stalkers' from a death-or-glory TV game show. The set-up is surreal, but we swallow it because the main character and the places he moves through are downbeat, vivid, recognizable. In the movie, directed by actor Paul Michael Glaser (late TV's Starsky) after Andrew Davis (later of *Under Siege* and *The Fugitive*) backed out owing to 'creative differences', we could be in a giant indoor sports park from start to finish. Slaloming around the prescribed narrative marker-posts – fights, chases, killings, flamethrowings – Arnold and his fellow fugitives move through settings that are alternately ill-lit and garish, wearing shiny jumpsuits as if they have been seconded from a ski-clothes commercial.

'There are elements in *The Running Man* that are definitely comic book,' Steven De Souza claims, 'but Arnold is certainly very human, with very real problems.'

Arnold's character is in fact pure pulp. He plays a cop framed for provoking a shoot-out during a food riot – year, 2017 – and then allowed a reprieve from his life sentence if he turns gladiatorial TV quarry. The show's compere, played by real US TV game-show host Richard Dawson, is a high-camp nastyboots, much like the one played by Michel Piccoli in the semi-identical French film *Le prix du danger*. Like Piccoli he steals the film. Whenever it 'cuts to the chase', leaving the gaudy television stage for fight and flight scenes in bizarre post-industrial settings (shooting was shared out between a steel mill and the Warner Hollywood soundstages), the film dies on its feet. Arnold and his hear identi-clothed co-runners, including Jim Brown, Jesse Ventura and token female Maria Conchita Alonso, spend ninety minutes seeking new ways to woo death, ambush and narrative non-sequitur.

The film is studded with Schwarzenegger self-referentialism. 'I'll be back, Killian,' booms our hero to Dawson's sleazy emcee. At another point – before the ski clothes set in – Arnold is seen wearing a 'World Gym' T-shirt. In real life he had recently bought the franchise to the famous gymnasium chain from Joe Gold. Later, for those with eyes still open, there is a split-second cameo by Franco Columbu as a security guard. The in-jokes, though, are as jaded as the film's violence. This runs the full, rich gamut from fisticuffs to chainsaws to a dynamite stick in the groin.

The badness of *The Running Man* is scarcely Arnold's fault, except as a career choice. With its directors 'coming in today, gone tomorrow' (his words), with its dubious baggage of market research (the film-makers, said Arnold, worked 'much more systematically for the female audience because we realised that the movie has a tremendous female appeal, through the studies they've done') and with its shooting schedule staggering upwards from fifty-four days to sixty, then sixty-seven, it became like an overweight aeroplane struggling for take-off.

'There's a formula for the successful film,' Arnold pontificated in the early publicity phases. 'If you combine action, adventure, some futuristic stuff and some comic relief, you're guaranteed success.' The film's belly-first landing at the box office in America, generating less than $40m, showed that no formula guarantees anything at all; and that no audience can reliably be browbeaten into passivity by Hollywood hype. *Last Action Hero* would teach the actor this, if *The Running Man* had not.

The runner, though, could afford to stumble. 1987 was the year when he proudly received his star in the Hollywood Walk of Fame. We see him leaning over the galactic paving-stone, with wife Maria, like a proud parent. In the same year he was honoured as 'Star of the Year' by NATO. This was not a case of bizarre cross-accolading, though the war industry would no doubt be next in line after the movie one to honour Arnold. It was the National Association of Theatre Owners' tapping of Arnold and Diane Keaton as their box-office superpersons of 1987. The awards spree was held at the Marriott Marquis hotel in Atlanta and saw Arnold in typically assertive, image-alert form. 'Could you stand up?', he tells a kneeling reporter. 'It would look better if I looked right at the camera.' To another journalist he sums up in two sentences his career trajectory so far. 'The executives saw I was making as much money with my clothes on as with them off. So I stopped getting scripts for Conan rip-offs or Vikings or gladiators and started getting parts for regular people.'

A life-or-death game-show contestant in 2017, a CIA mercenary fighting a creature from outer space, a commando who destroys an army to save his daughter: Arnold's notion of regularity at this time might be parting company from the world's.

That can happen to any superstar. While our hero believed that deep inside he was an ordinary fellow, he also knew that he was *extraordinary*. During a visit to Tokyo in June 1987 to promote *Predator* he was unable to sleep in his hotel and welcomed a 4 am call from *USA Today*'s Tom Green. Here in Japan Arnold must have felt like Gulliver in Lilliput. 'They're a little people. To them I'm a giant,' he tells Green. He means, presumably, giant in the physical sense. But was there an iconic dimension too? Did Arnold take some troubled moments to return to sleep after putting down that disconcertingly lightweight telephone receiver?

Consider the relentless culture-shock this man experiences. An Austro-American mega-person goes to Japan to trumpet the wonders of a film made in Mexico on either side of a honeymoon taken in Antigua with the daughter of German–Irish–Bostonian parents.

There are other disorientations, incongruities, anomalies: between the glittering socialising required of him and the post-nuptial call of domesticity; between the high-faluting hype he must lay over his films and the brute box-office results actually awaited; between being Arnold the role model for social climbers – the Kennedy husband who lines his office with Warhol silk-screens and Kennedy portraits – and Arnold the hard-working icon who cleans up, or tries to, at 42nd Street turnstiles. 'The reality is that my Jeep is standing outside, I go to work at seven in the morning like a plumber, and then I get dirty and I have to crawl around on the ground.'

There is one last source of tension in his life and soul. Arnold is very public with his jokes and badinage but not so sharing with his inner ruminations. He learned this habit in childhood. 'In my family we were very private with our thoughts,' he tells a reporter.

> No one discussed anything at the dinner table. The rule was, when you eat you eat. When I go home to Maria's house, everyone really shares all the things they've done during the day. If any problems come up, they discuss them with everyone at the dinner table. 'What should I do?' Everyone puts in their thoughts. I can make a decision within one second. I don't ever wait for anyone else's opinion.

Not even his mother's, who urges him to work less and relax more. She wonders how a man keeps his soul and identity anchored with such a crazy schedule. On her annual two-month visits to Casa Arnold, Aurelia will get up at a civilised time like 8 am and will stumble straight into Arnold returning from a workout. She: 'Why so early, why don't you eat first?' He: 'No, you have to train *before* you have breakfast.' She: 'This is healthy?'

When two of Maria's Kennedy nephews come to stay, Arnold

has them up early in the morning doing road-work, then push-ups and chin-ups. Maria protests, Arnold, they're here for a vacation, it's not boot camp.' Arnold says, 'Well, we gotta toughen them up, they might want to go into the family business, politics.' Arnold was keen that Maria keep fit too. 'How can a husband be turned on if his wife is sitting like a slug stuffing her face with pastries? Out of courtesy I would expect a woman to take care of herself.'

In the evening, according to friend and regular guest Jim Lorimer, Arnold's relaxation is to play tennis if he is not horseback riding or motorbiking. Only then, or after dinner, might he throw on a movie in his private viewing theatre, or play Strauss Waltzes on the music system while dancing with his daughter Katherine. He seldom watches television. Sometimes he reads; other times he sorts through scripts or projects till late into the night, with Maria's help and advice. 'She has very good instincts,' says Arnold. 'She reads fast, she analyses and – boom! – she has the notes. Like an agent.'

No wonder Aurelia shrugs and despairs. 'She thinks I'm a workaholic,' says her son. 'You have to remember that she's from Graz, a little town in Austria where people sit around and sip coffee – one cup can last two hours – and talk.'

No time for that; Arnold has another film to make. He will make do with a bowl of oatmeal mixed with raisins and bananas, followed by scrambled eggs, followed (or not) by a kiss hastily snatched from Aurelia and Maria. Then he will catch the plane to Moscow. *Red Heat* is the new movie; Arnold's role is that of a Soviet police officer modelled on Greta Garbo.

(ii) Amazing Changes

The director Walter Hill (*Southern Comfort, 48 Hours*) explains. 'I was trying to show Arnold the way to play it and I had him look at *Ninotchka*. "Look, you're Garbo in this thing. Don't *play* the joke, it'll be funny." And Arnold saw Garbo in the film and got it right away.'

In the screenplay co-written by Hill from his own story, Captain Ivan Danko (Arnold) comes to Chicago, USA, on a law-and-order mission: he must find and extradite a Russian drug dealer who killed Danko's partner. For most of the movie Arnold presents the same frozen Slavic solemnity with which Garbo got off the train in the Wilder-scripted, Lubitsch-directed spy comedy. Garbo ended up falling in love and, more famously, 'laughing'. Arnold ends up pulverising baddies, destroying cars and conducting business as usual.

At the same time, though, guided by Hill, he manages to be funny and endearing. Of Garbo in *Ninotchka* Arnold says, 'She plays the same kind of character I do in *Red heat*. She is a Russian who comes to Paris very cold . . . she falls in love with a French guy and whole new emotions are coming out that she was unaware of. I studied the film very carefully and saw it every day when we were filming *Red Heat*.'

If the new movie's representative of Soviet self-control does not exactly melt into transforming emotions in Chicago, he provides Hill's buddy thriller with its few moments of improving drollery. Partnered with a wisecracking James Belushi, few of whose cracks are funny, Arnold's echo-chamber one-liners, delivered in a Robert Easton-coached Russian accent, save the show. In response to Peter Boyle's harassed police chief asking his guest how the Soviets deal with tension and stress, Arnold resonantly deadpans 'Wodka'. And when Danko's partner warns him against threatening a suspect before reading the man his Miranda rights – 'You can't even *touch* his ass,' says Belushi – Arnold replies: 'I do not vant to touch his ass. I vant to make him talk.'

Add a straight-up haircut as alarming as Grace Jones's in *Conan 2*, a name that causes confusion at hotel reception desks ('Danko'. 'You're welcome') and a blithe ignorance of all manifestations of American culture ('Who is Doordy Herry?') and we could have had a winning culture-clash comedy. *Red Heat*, though, smoulders feebly. The clichés of its hunt-and-arrest crime plot smother the sparks of good humour, as even Hill realises with hindsight.

What we should have done was send an American cop to Russia and played it out there. The settings and locations were more interesting, the social dynamic would have been more interesting. Instead, when the film came out, to some it just played as another wrinkle on the American buddy-cop movie. It lacks the brio or freshness that a real super-hit has.

Hill also thinks audiences were not ready for Arnold playing a normal human being. 'They wanted him larger than life in the Terminator sense: being able to walk through walls and do the superheroic things.'

The movie is interesting mainly for the insights it provides – off camera and on – into Arnold at a career crossroads: an Arnold sharpening his political perceptions in the year that he began helping George Bush campaign for the US Presidency. During and after his mummer's mission to Moscow, the star takes every chance to de-brief himself loudly and publicly on the state of post-liberation Russia. Since an earlier visit to the country, he announces, 'Amazing changes have taken place. The people were much more relaxed about their freedom. There are now privately owned restaurants in Moscow. I have seen breakdancing, heavy metal rock bands . . .'

As a gesture of detente towards the new Russia, Arnold urges the US film industry to stop using the place as a villain recruitment centre. 'The Russians are fed up always seeing themselves portrayed as the bad guys in certain American action adventure movies.' So why did they welcome the *Red Heat* crew, the first Hollywood outfit ever allowed to film in Red Square? 'I think one reason they were pleased to have us there was because this is the first film where a Soviet has been portrayed in a very heroic and positive way.'

As if in gratitude for this image-enhancing initiative. President Gorbachev marked the first day of *Red Heat*'s Moscow shoot by announcing the Soviet pull-out from Afghanistan. Sylvester Stallone must surely have eaten his heart out. He had been sweating away in the Afghan desert, or nearest Hollywood simulacrum, making the now obsolete *Rambo 3*. Arnold Schwarzenegger, meanwhile, was in the Soviet capital tipping Chairman Mikhail's hand.

In stark contrast to the star's public declamations, Walter Hill once thought he espied a private Arnold. The film's stunt co-ordinator Bernie Dobbins died of a heart attack during shooting on the fight scene in the snow, a bizarre fisticuffs-in-the-nude sequence between Danko and a Soviet heavy that climaxes the story's Russian section. Dobbins, who had worked previously with both Hill (*Southern Comfort*) and Arnold (*Commando, Predator*), was obliquely responsible for bringing actor and director together on *Red Heat*. 'He used to say, "You gotta do a movie with Arnold"', recalls Hill. When Dobbins died, Hill shut down the set for the day, and the next day when they resumed the scene 'nobody's heart was there'.

Back in America, Arnold spoke a five-minute oration at Dobbins's funeral and Hill – not a man known for maudlin hyperbole – could not believe what he was hearing.

It was all about working in the movies, the mystery of life, and those that are called away too soon, and how none of us ever know what our fate is. I can't remember it word for word, but it was a *terribly* moving and insightful moment. I thought I knew Arnold better at that moment – and 'inside' Arnold – than I had while working with him during the whole movie.

23

Dreams and Nightmares

'I'm not a stern character who doesn't smile . . . I'm a peaceful guy who has a great time.'

Before he begins work on a new film Arnold has a recurring dream.

A week or so before I start, I always have a nightmare. I am sitting naked in the dark, with the cameras ready to roll. And I'm not prepared – I don't have my clothes on, the scene isn't ready, and I don't know what I am trying to shoot. Then I wake up, and it's the middle of the night, and I look around and I think, Wait, I'm not ready.

He brushes aside any hint of psychic revelation. 'I have no patience for my dreams – my life is quite interesting enough, and there's not much room for another dimension.'
But after *The Running Man* and *Red Heat* there was room – even urgency – for a new career strategy. If the hard man image was the faltering franchise that these films suggested (less than eighty million domestic dollars between them), it might be time to find a softer Schwarzenegger. 'I want people to know the real me,' he ruminates. 'Because the reality is that I don't take a gun in my hand to solve the situation . . . I'm not a stern character who doesn't smile . . . I'm a peaceful guy who has a great time.'

To bring this life-affirming Arnold into public view, he multiplies his acts of humorous self-deprecation. He has already begun mocking his early acting history. 'The critics used to call me a hunk. When I appeared in a movie with a horse, they said the horse had more facial expression.' Now he hints at a budding interest in playing comedy. 'I believe in systematically moving forward and not thinking that now I can do comedy because the studio will do it because I have power. I would put a little more into it because you have to make sure that the audience goes with you.'

During post-production on *Red Heat*, Walter Hill noticed the actor's increasing focus on comic devices.

When we cut the final movie, Arnold thought I'd been too severe in cutting some of the jokes. He had a couple of what I call 'wet' jokes rather than dry jokes. I didn't think they worked, they tried too hard. But Arnold likes those 'buttons', as we call them, at the end of scenes. That last word, you know – he throws a knife into a guy and then says 'Stick around'. Arnold loves those; I'm not such a big fan. We had a few and he thought up a couple and I practically cut them all out. There was a weird little meeting after the movie in which he questioned this.

Off-screen, the star got busy setting up other comic opportunities. The first stage in acclimatising the public to a newer, funnier Arnold was to have the 'hulk' persona laughed at by the right controllable people. Who better than his friend and neighbour, the comedian Milton Berle, who according to Walter Hill all but leans over the fence up there in Pacific Palisades and supplies Arnold with quips and epigrams? On April 5th 1988 Berle hosted a California Friars Club 'roast' in Arnold's honour, held at the Beverly Hilton Hotel. These evenings of ritual lampoonery are enacted yearly with a celebrity victim of choice. On Arnold's night Berle set the tone by introducing him as 'the illegitimate son of Kurt Waldheim. Waldheim said he was only following orders.'

If Arnold could chuckle at that, he could handle the rest. Berle: 'We are honouring a man whose breasts are bigger than his wife's.' Berle again: 'The number one box office draw in the world – he is to acting what Raymond Burr is to pole-vaulting.' Berle once more: 'Waiting for Schwarzenegger to win an Oscar is like leaving the porch light on for Jimmy Hoffa.'

Away from the social galas, Arnold's self-belittlement took a domestic turn. 'I do the washing up sometimes, you know,' he told *Time* magazine. 'Often, though, I do it for effect. I love washing up in front of my friends. "Look at the wimp. Hey, Maria, where's your whip?" they say. It's the kind of thing you can only do when you feel secure with your masculinity.'

Finally – impossible for the world to resist this – Arnold infected himself with eco-consciousness. 'You must be crazy if you're not interested in the environment,' he declaimed. 'We recycle newspapers and when we buy things like paper towels, we buy those that can be re-used or are biodegradable. I would never allow polystyrene dinnerware in the house, no matter what size party we have.'

This will seem sublimely dotty to people who have known Arnold hitherto as Conan the Republican, a man who would rather walk over hot coals than visit a bottle bank. But everything was now conspiring to whittle our hero down to his desired human shape, so he could fit into a caring, smiling world. Even his height seemed to be conforming. Six foot two had for years been the received wisdom, but in 1987, when Arnold visited the California Institute for Women in Frontera, a supervisor summed up the occasion to a reporter with a disappointed 'He's actually kind of short'. In March 1988 Britain's *Daily Mail* concluded, after meeting the giant: 'Sorry, Arnie, but I would have said six two on a *good* day.' And in August that year the verdict of Britain's *Time Out* magazine was, 'He appears to be a couple of inches shorter than the biogs state, unless he can pump bone.'

Amazing. Perhaps fate was reaching out to assist this Gulliver's attempt to adapt himself to the Lilliputian world of comedy. It was not the only force trying to cut him down to size. Other people and other voices, less goodhumoured, were seeking to sabotage the Schwarzenegger stature.

On or shortly after February 21st 1988 Arnold stumbled on a copy of the British *News Of The World*. Under the heading

'Hollywood Star's Nazi Secret', two British journalists, Wendy Leigh (from Hollywood) and Sharon Ring (in London), made a series of allegations – unrepeatable here for legal reasons – about the actor's political sympathies.

At first Arnold took no action. Only when the article began to be reprinted in other countries did he sue. The case took nearly two years to reach a settlement, but on December 21st 1989 the *News of the World* and Sharon Ring offered unreserved apologies. Thirty thousand pounds were paid in damages and a promise made never to repeat the allegations. Lawyer Robert Clinton, representing the *News of the World*, said, 'My clients accept that Mr Schwarzenegger has never espoused Nazi and anti-Semitic views and has never been an admirer of Adolf Hitler and what he and his evil regime represent.'

Only Wendy Leigh, planning her own biography of Arnold, held out against settling. She claimed she had supplied material for the article which she understood that the newspaper would research to its own satisfaction.

Arnold did meet Waldheim in August 1986, of course, as the newspaper reported, invite Waldheim to his wedding. He also seemed as the article touched on, disinclined, to discuss his father's history in public.

But were these the acts of a wicked man or merely a careless one? Or did they reflect an Arnold who by the late 1980s felt he had exorcised his family past and his father's guilt? Arnold claims he was unfamiliar with Gustav's Nazi membership until the early 1980s. It was around 1984, says Rabbi Marvin Hier of the Simon Wiesenthal Center in Los Angeles, that Arnold contacted him, seeking enlightenment about his father's political record.

When the press started bringing it to our attention about Arnold's father I told them they were second in their enquiries, because the first person to ask about Arnold's father was Arnold Schwarzenegger. He phoned me and asked if I could get records of his father's Nazi membership. He wanted to know everything the Center could find out about him, and I asked Simon Wiesenthal to help me.

Hier and Wiesenthal found that Gustav had not been a member of the SS or Gestapo, that he was on no official wartime lists, and that there had been no criminal charges against him after the war. 'I never heard anything negative of him,' says Wiesenthal. 'It was a matter of his father's existence, since he was serving in the Gendarmerie, to become a member of the party. There is a difference between that and being a "Nazi". A man may be in the party because he will lose his job otherwise. Another man may do something in the spirit of the party.'

Even if Gustav were considered blameworthy, says Rabbi Hier, why should that sin be visited on Arnold? 'My reply to the press was that for 35,000 years the Jews themselves have been victims of "collective guilt". We're not going to take it out on Arnold for what his father did.'

Arnold himself seemed reluctant publicly to disown his father's political affiliations, though he answered the *News of the World*'s charges about himself in a *Penthouse* interview in January 1989. 'I totally hate the Nazi period,' he said. 'When you come from a background like Germany or Austria, then you sometimes are joked about . . . I am so much against that time period. I despise it.'

Rabbi Hier thinks that Arnold found a way to repudiate his father's history too. 'He didn't attend his father's funeral,' Hier points out. Because of the Nazi factor? 'He was embarrassed. I assume he has a quandary.' Yet it is not quite clear, from either history or Hier, what the quandary is. Recalling that Arnold also failed to attend his brother's laying-to-rest, perhaps his quandary is about funerals in general.

Perhaps, also, Arnold's motive in contacting the Wiesenthal Center in or around 1984 was a political one: to pre-empt sensationalist media curiosity about his father's past and to limit potential damage to his newly stellar movie career. Hier admits that he cannot 'climb inside someone's consciousness', but claims that Arnold was in touch before the actor had reached 'his career peak.' The dates, though, suggest that contact was made after Arnold had completed his starmaking role in *Conan the Barbarian*.

Then there is the question of money: always a muddier of moral waters. Speaking on the Wiesenthal Center's behalf,

Rabbi Hier appreciates Arnold's generosity in giving 'more than a quarter of a million dollars' to the Center: much of it in the form of contributions made out of his movie fees. 'Every picture he makes,' says Hier, 'Arnold makes a donation to us. A week or two into each picture's release, always comes a cheque from him.'

Other sources, including a 1992 article in the San Francisco *Chronicle* by *Newsweek's* Charles Fleming, claim the star's total generosity to the Center is closer to $5m. Fleming, though, is vague today about where he got this figure from. He thinks it probably included donations by Arnold to the Los Angeles Museum of Tolerance, which was built by the Center.

These could be the acts of a man who wants to atone for his father's errors. They could also be the conscience sops and gesturings of a man who wants to shut down the controversy about his father, while he himself is not above flirting with an autocratic image. Rick Wayne recalls a contest in Germany in which Arnold, wanting to pep up a dullish climax, created a furore by turning sideways-on to the crowd and enacting a 'Sieg Heil' salute. When the spectators booed, Arnold stomped off to the dressing-room saying, 'These people are nothing without an Austrian to lead them!'

At other times, says Wayne, Arnold used to get together with the Jewish Joe Weider and do the famous comb-and-forelock Hitler impersonation beloved of schoolkids of all ages. (Yes, acknowledges Weider; 'but we did a lot of other impersonation too'.)

Even the best of us in provocateur mood enjoy bad-taste jokes. Hitler imitations would seem more a sign of satirical lèse-majesté than of idolatrous respect. As for the raised right arm, Wag Bennett claims that this wasn't a Nazi salute at all, but a posing 'classic' used by bodybuilders for years.

Arnold's own considerations on this subject may be problematic. However passionately he may hate the Nazi period, his charisma as a movie star is based on a comic-book machismo not wholly remote from our perception of totalitarian brutalism. Why should he jeopardise the frisson of ambiguity about his own personality? It feeds the box office. Arnold the *übermensch*; Arnold the grim reaper from alien realms or punitive regimes.

This Arnold must be maintained in the hangar – he will go back to it – even when he makes the occasional joy-flight in a different plane. Like his comedy of innocence and genetic engineering, *Twins*. A cross between The *Boys from Brazil* and *Rain Man*, this tale of two ill-matched test-tube siblings (Schwarzenegger, DeVito) reunited in Los Angeles, emerged from the brainpans of two Englishmen, William Davies and William Osborne. The unlikely pair of screenwriting aspirants – a lawyer and a barrister – travelled to California in the late 1980s carrying two scripts in a Waitrose supermarket bag. After days of doorstopping, they met *Ghostbusters* director Ivan Reitman. He wanted ideas – neither of the Waitrose scripts would do – for a comedy with an unusual theme. Davies and Osborne went off to the beach to think and came up with the idea of a genetic experiment in the Fifties, to create the perfect human being.

Arnold and Danny were inspirationally paired as the unlikely ex-womb-sharers; one a con man, round and squat as a cartoon bomb, the other a sweetly bewildered giant. In his new 'goofball' persona Arnold is a comic revelation. Dressed like an inflated schoolboy in thigh-length jacket and baggy shorts, he deploys a perpetual smile of gap-toothed serenity, plus an Austrian accent that must have fallen into the gene pool when the laboratory lifeguard was not looking. These components helped the film to $120m at the US box office after it opened in December 1988, handsomely lining the Schwarzenegger pockets since Arnold had waived his upfront fee for a percentage.

For all its brisk Christmas popularity, however, the finished film never matches the charm of its premise. Critics seized on *Twins* as an example of 'high-concept' cinema: one of those movies that promise the moon and deliver a few haphazard sparklers. Davies and Osborne's script, reworked by Timothy Harris and Herschel Weingrod (*Trading Places*), turns from a passably funny fraternal meeting-cute tale – the best scenes are the early ones of mutual disbelief as craggy, towering Arnold eyeballs, or tries to, human dumpling DeVito – into a mirthless road movie-cum-love story. The brothers, with token girlfriends in tow (Chloe Webb, Kelly Preston), hit the highway to find Momma and the meaning of their lives.

Arnold, though, liked the romantic dimension – 'In my last five or six movies, my love relationship was basically with guns, explosives, grenades and missiles.' And he enjoyed the fact that within this newer, amorous Arnold character there had to be a sense of awkward innocence. 'Julius' is a test-tube booby who comes straight from a monastic South Seas retreat into the revelatory world of pretty women. 'You can imagine me playing a virgin,' Arnold said, replaying his PR line from *The Villain*. 'It took tremendous acting, and I had to go way, way back into my childhood and pretend like I'm learning to kiss all over again and look clumsy.')

Director Ivan Reitman, though, perceived a natural innocence in Arnold. 'He has this lovely naive quality in real life. He's also very intelligent, very dedicated and very sweet. You don't often see that sweetness, and I thought it would be great to design a character that way.'

Oddly, Arnold *is* sweet in *Twins*. This is probably the Frankenstein syndrome: our tendency to feel protective towards the poignant or unfortunate, even when they are six-foot-plus monsters who pause from their mayhem only to throw us a disarming, retarded smile.

The funniest moment in *Twins* pinpoints Arnold's newly adapted charisma. On a busy street, a mugger on a motorbike tries to swipe Julius's suitcase from him. An insouciant flick of one of Arnold's 22-inch arms sends him tumbling to the ground. To the dazed onlookers Arnold says, 'I did nothing. De pavement was his enemy.' Unlike his terse action-movie one-liners, it is a defensive appeal from a man who genuinely does not know his own strength. 'I changed the rhythm of my voice,' he explained to one reporter. 'In action movies the heroes are much more appealing and believable if they say less. Only those people who are weak have to talk themselves out of trouble.'

The scene also suggests that a star's force of personality in one mode of behaviour may owe its power to the dormant presence of another or opposite mode. If Arnold is electrifying in *The Terminator* as an impassive avenging android, it is because we know or sense all the animated qualities he *can* invoke. (*Pumping Iron* showed them to us.) Those qualities 'repressed' inform and energize the performance. And if Arnold is charismatic in *Twins* as a bumbling, innocent giant, it is because the joke is made rich and generous by the hidden, menacing counter-energies we know from Arnold's action epics.

24

To Arnold and Maria:
A Schwarzenshriver

'I'd like to be a father. It's time.'

(i) Baby Shower

During the early summer of 1989 Maria visited Arnold in Mexico, where he was starting work on his new film *Total Recall*. She wanted to discuss the couple's autumn social calendar and nagged away at dates for this birthday party and that anniversary celebration . . . Ja ja, sighed Arnold, signing on every dotted line.

'Oh and it would be good if you have some time on December 1st', said Maria.

'What's that?' said Arnold.

'That's when you will become a father.'

Arnold reeled back against his exercise bike. A father? It seemed a miracle.

For yes, Arnold and Maria had laboured long and hard to produce an infant. The world's gossip columnists, suffering from sympathetic non-pregnancy, had been worried. There were rumours, admittedly in the baser press, that Mr and Mrs S had gone to consult the famous sex therapists Masters and Johnson, after fighting for the thousand days of their marriage over the question of infertility.

Then, claimed the *Star* newspaper, after one quarrel in which doors had banged and walk-outs been threatened or enacted, the couple enjoyed 'a glorious night of love' in a Washington Hotel.

The *Star* learned this from 'a confidential source' and went on to assure the world that *this very coupling* had resulted in conception. Maria did indeed become large with child. On December 13th 1989, after a fifteen-hour labour, she gave birth to a nine-pound baby girl, with Arnold cutting the cord.

'It's great to be part of the delivery,' he declaimed, after removing the white mask and surgical gloves. 'You really respect the woman more. The pain and the hours and hours of pure torture brought us even closer together.'

Cut to Casa Arnold. The baby has grown up three months and rejoices in the names Katherine Eunice. Arnold has rejected two film offers each worth $5m in order to stay in Los Angeles and tend the tot. (According to another source it is one $10m offer to make a long-mooted action adventure called *Sgt Rock* for Joel Silver on location.) Meanwhile Maria will return to work on the TV news show she hosts. 'Sunday Today'.

Arnold the new-age father went public to the press: 'I have my soft side and I help with Katherine in any way I can. I feed her and hold the bottle and have her lie on my chest in the morning and I burp her.' He even enjoys changing her nappies and 'getting up in the middle of the night to rock her to sleep'.

The world must have wondered how much the baby would appreciate this. What would her feelings be at the sight of Arnold Schwarzenegger coming in to rock her to sleep? Most of us would dash to the window and shin down the fire escape. The child, though, seemed to have few problems. Asked about parenthood on TV's 'Oprah Winfrey' show, Arnold was wondrous to behold. The eyes shone, the gapped teeth bared themselves in smile and the accent backpedalled to its most *gemutlich* Austrian. 'Dey come into de bed and lie on yer chest, and den dey smile and play with yer heer or scratch yer face. You jusd melt.'

Arnold, even with his millions, rejects the idea of round-the-clock help. 'I couldn't do what I hear your English aristocrats do,' he told a British reporter:

> Which is to leave their kids to nannies, see them for half an hour a day and send them away to school. Maria and I have a nanny, but Katherine's cot is in our bedroom. We want her to grow up knowing who her parents are. We want to be a close

family. A child changes your persona, too. In most movies I
have this iron face. When I'm waltzing around businessmen
making deals, I have a special face for that too. But when
I'm at home with my kid, I don't need those masks. I can
be as silly as I like.

Friends and movie colleagues join in this New Jerusalem
of parenthood for Arnold and Maria. At Katherine Eunice
Schwarzenegger's 'baby shower', director Ivan Reitman gave
Maria a camcorder. Her husband promptly commandeered it.
'We're like those wacko families you see on TV,' she said.
'Arnold never takes it out of his hands!' Or only long enough
to let someone else record him putting a nappy on his daughter.
'The first time, I got the waistband around the baby's neck,' he
laughed. It took three takes to get the sequence in the can.

Blithe with fatherhood, Arnold is not concerned about any
'Conan the Babysitter' backwash. 'Although it's wonderful to
have a child, it hasn't softened me. I can't afford to be like that.
When I walk out on the streets I have to be as tough as ever.
In Los Angeles they confuse softness with weakness.'

(ii) Blood Bath

To judge by his new feature release *Total Recall*, it was still
a mistake to regard Arnold as a softie. The violent futuristic
thriller about civil war on Mars was directed by Paul Verhoeven
from a much-travelled screenplay by *Alien* writing duo Dan
O'Bannon and Ron Shusett. The script had first been optioned
to Disney back in 1981. After that it was kicked around other
studios, producers and directors, including David Cronenberg,
who would have made it in Italy with Richard Dreyfuss, and
Bruce Beresford, who would have made it in Australia with
Patrick Swayze. Eventually, having racked up an estimated
seven million dollars in costs from false starts, the movie
gained inclusion in an American Film Institute course called
'The Ten Greatest Unproduced Films In Hollywood'.

'Arnold rescued it singlehandedly,' says Shusett. In the late
Eighties the actor told the production company Carolco to buy
the script for him from its then owner, none other than Dino De

Laurentiis. In a moment of sweet revenge for Dino's handling of his early career, Arnold told Carolco to bid substantially below the asking price: $3m rather than $7m. Since Dino's studio had gone bankrupt, the mogul had little choice but to accept.

Based on the story 'We Can Remember It For You Wholesale' by SF writer Philip K. Dick – another of whose tales had inspired *Blade Runner* – *Total Recall* is an insanely inspired space epic built around the plot gimmick of the memory implant. Has Arnold been to Mars before, or does he only believe he has because he volunteered for one of the memory-chip 'vacations' advertised by ReKall Inc? Explained the actor, gamely trying to clarify a complex plot: 'You believe you've actually been on a trip to these places (Mars), but when I go there (ReKall) and have the implant all hell breaks loose. I become very violent, and that's when I first find out I have this double life.'

Douglas Quaid (Arnold) is a restless construction worker with a knock-em-dead blonde wife (Sharon Stone, pre-stardom). Deep in his tormented memory he believes he waged a resistance struggle against the planet-polluting, worker-exploiting Mars bosses on a prior trip to the industrialised space colony. (We are in 2084 AD.) Events are now conspiring to send him back. He smuggles himself into Mars disguised as a large-built woman, removing his/her face only when trouble rears in intergalactic immigration.

This face removal is a *coup de cinema*. The 'layers' of the disguising giant head open up like a Dali-esque chest of drawers, revealing Arnold's own vengeful cranium atop the woman's yellow overcoat and Paisley-patterned scarf. Then he clutches the spontaneously re-formed head frozen in its hideous last grimace – this became a favourite image in the film's publicity – before making his escape.

Built on a quintessential Arnold plot formula, *Total Recall* is a vantage point from which to scan the whole movie canon, and to note how often the same morality drama is played out under cover of mayhem. A man with a troubled or beleaguered identity is recruited for a mission – or recruits himself – in which he must put aside vulnerable reflexes, from pity to pain, to mete out necessary justice. Performing this mission, he will rediscover his real self: a process incorporating, or symbolised by, a healing rapprochement with the key female in his life. It may be the daughter in *Commando*, or the exdrunken wife in *Raw Deal*, or the Mars-dwelling Melina (Rachel Ticotin) in *Total Recall*. It may even, more metaphysically, be Mother Nature in *Predator*.

Taking this view of the Arnold *gesamkunstwerk*, the discarding of the woman's head at immigration becomes more than a great sci-fi stunt: it is a pre-mission masculinisation gesture, a black comedy version of all those hieratic dress-to-kill scenes in films like *Commando* and *Raw Deal*, where the guns and leather are strapped on in an adoring kaleidoscope of camera angles, climaxed if possible by a shot of Arnie checking himself in a mirror. (In the postmodern age iconic self-awareness, even to the point of narcissism, is as important as iconic action. Pauline Kael described the mirror-checking shot in *Raw Deal* as 'the film's only love scene'.)

Later in *Total Recall* Arnold will clinch the sexual-existential symbolism by disposing of the false 'woman as anima' when he puts a bullet through Sharon Stone, revealed as a spy bent on nobbling our hero. 'Consider thadda divorce,' he barks to the perforated blonde, in another Arniegram that went straight into history.

'It is strange and bizarre,' piped the actor of the movie, 'and as much about the nature of reality and dreams as it is an action film.' Yes indeed. *Total Recall* is also about the reality and dream-power of the Schwarzenegger mystique. His character Quaid alliterates in more than name – there are assonances of iconography and idiom – with the film's elusive Mars resistance hero, Kuato. He, or 'it', appears near the film's close in the form of a living special effect: a quasi-foetal midget that pushes half-out from the stomach of his commander-in-chief.

This scene hints at what all Arnold's best films are about: the present pregnant with the future. (It is a rehearsal-by-proxy for the 'real' pregnancy he will have in *Junior*.) The sense of a hero who carries within him a momentously germinating Tomorrow is incarnate in Arnold's meta-human, hermaphrodite quality as a screen icon, and in the 'layers of being' of which his most memorable characters are composed. The robots who show unnerving flickers of humanity in the *Terminator* films; the hi-tech soldier secreting and releasing the warrior-primitive in *Predator*; the body-horror games his characters play with different skins and armatures; the hulk giving birth to reserves of gentleness in the comedies.

Only the outer public flesh of these characters remains, for the most part, constant: the muscled Colossus. It is the box-office gift-wrapping, the Schwarzenegger selling point. It says, 'Don't mess with me.' The best comical-dramatic treat in *Total Recall*, apart from the fly-apart head, is the robot cabbie who gives our hero a nightmare ride and then makes the mistake of requesting payment. Cabbie: 'The fare is 18 credits.' Arnold: 'Sue me, dickhead.' The robot ends up unscrewed and thrown into the back seat. Even on a Mars with as many time-conundrums as Marienbad, we need to know that Arnold can hot-wire justice by touching action to instant reaction, provocation to instant punishment. This is a man for whom taxi meters are a minor irrelevance en route to serving the whole universe with the fare for its wickedness.

25

Conan the Workaholic

'I sometimes do feel frustrated that I have more energy in me than I can get rid of, so much energy.'

According to *Forbes* magazine, which regularly counts the cash of the famous, Arnold's two-year income from investments and holdings up to late 1987 was $26m. His total 1987 income alone was close to $18m. In 1990, when *Forbes* again reviewed the figures, his yearly turnover was assessed at $35m. This would have included his remuneration for the 1990-released *Total Recall:* $10m plus 15 percent. Friends and associates of the actor, meanwhile, estimated his total assets at $40m.

Many men, on the strength of this lucre, might sit back in bubble baths quaffing champagne. That was not Arnold's style, except in publicity shots. His money-muscle would be used to aid the Republican cause; he himself would go out to claim a piece of the nation's political action. So we find him battling for George Bush in the pre-1988 Presidential campaign. He stood with Bush on the hustings, a Hollywood warm-up act beyond price for a White House contender. He delivered the designer soundbites: 'Michael Dukakis is the real Terminator!' He played twins with the Republican nominee in photo-opportunities: two men, oddly similar in their lean and lantern-shaped heads, smiling and laughing together as they gazed into America's future. Bush repaid Arnold by attending the *Twins* premiere in Washington.

The initial George-and-Arnold hook-up happened almost by

accident. In 1988, on the Friday before the Tuesday Presidential elections, Jim Lorimer invited Arnold to Columbus, Ohio, for a rally in Bush's honour. The star stood up to introduce the Republican contender, who was at that time Vice President.

'That same day, Arnold got on Bush's plane and went with him to three different cities,' Lorimer recalls. 'They fell into discussion on the plane, and a friendship struck up, and that was when Bush first put the idea of Arnold coming onto the President's Fitness Council if he won the election.'

He did win and quickly thanked Arnold publicly for his support. 'There are all kinds of courage. There is the courage of my friend Arnold Schwarzenegger, who more than once campaigned with me across the country – and then returned home to take the heat from his own in-laws!'

Neither Maria nor the Kennedys seem to have been unduly distraught. Arnold had his own ways of distancing himself from the dynasty anyway, and of keeping his agenda pure. He almost never, for instance, posed for magazine covers with Maria.

That's because I know then that an editor wants to do an Arnold-and-Maria story rather than something that will promote a movie. But it's not jealousy of Maria. If they want to put her on the cover instead of me, great; I'm very happy.

In the new White House regime Arnold was picked for the promised office. As chairman of the President's Council on Physical Fitness and Sports, he prepared to tour all fifty states, spreading the gospel according to Arnie. The public wisdoms tumbled forth.

Some 55 percent of girls ages six to seventeen and 25 percent of boys ages six to twelve cannot do even one pull-up.

When I was growing up in Austria, everyone who went to school had to do one hour a day of exercise.

A philosopher once said, 'Let the world be a better place, and let it start with me.' Think about that. It is the attitude each of us should take to help make our youngsters more physically fit.

If a kid grows up in a family where there's a fat mother, a fat father, and they sit in front of the TV set and just *chunk* hamburgers and French fries, this kid is gonna grow up and do the same thing.

So the incredible hunk went out to fight the incredible chunk. Even his daughter Katherine, five months old and fifteen pounds in weight, attended the 'Great American Workout' – Arnold's initiative for an annual promotion stunt – on the south lawn of the White House in May 1990. She nestled inside Maria's backpack while the great and famous threw horseshoes, shot baskets, rode exercise bikes and did arm-muscle stretches in tune to Arnold's orders from the podium. ('Okay, General Powell – *much* further!')

Watching Arnold hump weights on that perspiring summer day, the President turned to his visiting grandson Sam LeBlond and said, 'If Arnold can do that, why can't you pick up your socks?' Later the leader of the free world, after a short bout of aerobic dancing himself, quipped of his new fitness czar, 'He's stronger than I thought he was. He bench-pressed the federal budget!' The crowd loved it. Here, led by Arnold and Maria and George and Barbara, was a whole new decade of back-garden inspirationalism.

'I have been very impressed with the seriousness of our Council on Fitness and of its chairman, Arnold Schwarzenegger,' Bush said after the actor-sportsman had been at the job six months. 'People thought getting Arnold in there, we were going for some muscle-building big shot. He is the least biggest shot of any guy I have met. He is determined to set a good example. And he is.'

Unlike some slugabed superstars, Arnold wanted the public to know that he was putting physical fitness – his own and the nation's – above frivolous things like acting. 'I think it's great he shoots *Hamlet*,' he said of Mel Gibson. 'He maybe had time. That's a nice luxury to have, to hang out in Scotland and shoot *Hamlet*. I'd rather go to America and promote fitness.'

Consider the go-go energy of this man in five telling months of 1990. In March at the Arnold Classic bodybuilding contest in Columbus, Ohio, he had his picture taken one by one with almost a thousand people in just over an hour. ('That was tough. My face hurts.') Each person had paid $250 for a 'VIP package', which also included a banquet and an Arnold seminar. It was all part of the messianic self-promotion that had encouraged him to found this event the previous year in partnership with Jim Lorimer. The Arnold Classic included a women's contest, a 'fitness weekend', pose-offs, dinners, photo-opportunities ('A lot of the same people pay to have their pictures taken with Arnold every year', says Lorimer) and a quarter of a million dollars in prize money.

On April 4th Arnold took time off from preparing for his new Universal Pictures comedy, *Kindergarten Cop*, to co-operate in a long interview with BBC TV documentary-maker Nicolas Kent, then preparing a series on the American movie capital called *Naked Hollywood*. Arnold held forth on a ragbag of topics from his idol Clint Eastwood ('a man of real substance, not someone who screams all over the place'), via his own career rise, to personality politics in present-day Hollywood.

This included intriguing insights on charisma management.

> You as an actor never want to get involved in saying to a studio executive, I won't do this movie for you because you don't pay me enough money . . . That creates a problem because the person may be personally affected by that . . . and that can have an impact when he may have a negative attitude towards you at a later point when another decision has to be made. And so in general the whole system is set up so the actor, director, writer or whatever is usually the innocent and good person. [And the agent says] I demand for my client this money . . . and he plays the villain. And I would say more than in any other town that here in Hollywood there is this good and bad guy set-up that is understood.

Even when the camera was not rolling, Arnold sustained the charm offensive. In his warm-up chatter he aimed fond barbs at his current employer, Universal Pictures president Tom Pollock.

Arnold beams himself into the Avenue of the Stars, with matching smile from Maria.

Partying with daughter Katherine Eunice.

Quiet Austrian reunion. Arnold, Aurelia, Lights, Camera, Music.

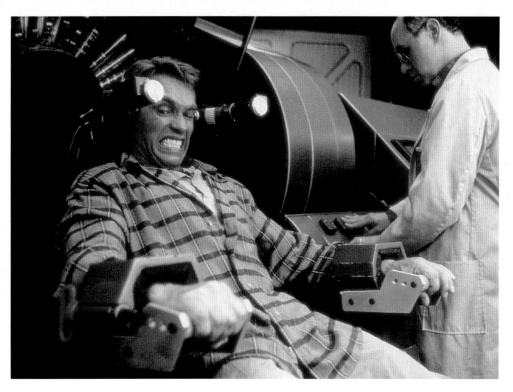

Arnold experiencing 'Total Recall'

Movie star turned fitness czar: *Kindergarten Cop*.

The White House celebrates the Great American Workout.

Arnie and Sly. Screen rivals hit the dance floor at the Cannes Film Festival.

Of Mice and Men

Eunice Shriver with her son-in-law.

Arnold experiences a moment of cyborgian transformation at the *Backdraft* premiere.

Arnold (right) introduces his first film director, *The Switch* for TV's *Tales From The Crypt*.

The largest lead balloon in history: *Last Action Hero*.

Three men and a franchise: Stallone, Schwarzenegger and Bruce Willis join hands for Planet Hollywood.

One man and a baby: Arnold delivers 'Junior'.

Arnold the suit - and future suitor for high political office?

'Tell him that Arnold suggested you follow him while his wife is beating him up! . . . It's not actually the men that rule this town, it's the women behind them that rule it, and she's smacking him around in the evening! That would be a good shot!'

At the Cannes Film Festival in May the star gave interviews, partied into the night, danced with Sylvester Stallone (*sic*) and visited a gymnasium in Monaco with a group of handicapped children who would later be competing in the July Special Olympics in Glasgow. He protected the children from the media riot outside the doors – 'I'm not gonna have these kids frightened by a mob' – but the story still exploded over local newspapers.

In June *Total Recall* opened and Arnold was the star of a lavish movie party held in L.A's famed Griffith Observatory (setting for the climactic scenes of *Rebel Without a Cause*). Here guests were treated to laser shows, tarot cards, psychics and palm-readers. In the same month his face adorned the covers of five American publications. And he promoted fitness to anyone who would listen, in any town that would empty an airport runway. His latest campaign slogan paid tribute to the soundbite that helped Bush win the 1988 election (and would help him lose in 1992): 'Read my hips: no more fat.'

In the following months Arnold found time to start intensive filming on *Kindergarten Cop*, to blueprint a plan to ship weight-lifting equipment to US soldiers serving in Saudi Arabia during the Gulf crisis, to receive notice that he would be Grand Marshal for the 59th Hollywood Christmas Parade (following such greats as Bob Hope and James Stewart), and to be sued for $1m by a Hungarian-American gunmaker. Lajos Goncz claimed that Arnold broke an agreement to put Lajos's name on the end credits of *Total Recall*, for which he provided weapons. He wanted the film withdrawn unless his name was up there. He had already told Carolco, *Recall*'s production company, what he thought of their idea of marketing real and toy versions of his hardware that would be manufactured overseas. 'All my creations are 100 percent US-made!' cried Lajos.

Arnold survived this dust-up. But superstars are bound to be a target for top-dollar lawsuits, legitimate or lunatic-fringe. The public perceives the star as a cash cow waiting to be milked.

In turn he will sometimes scatter his own writs around: either because he wants justice and can pay for it, or because he feels that a lot of snoopy people in the media deserve to have warning served.

26

Controlling the Image

'Because I come from Austria people put this Germanic trip on me . . . I am not a control freak. I just want things the right way.'

(i) Chicken on the Grill

In 1990 the publication of *Arnold*, a biography of Schwarzenegger by English journalist Wendy Leigh, raised some serious questions about Arnold's publicity-controlling techniques.

Leigh's book, first published by Chicago-based Congden and Weed, offers an arduously researched portrait of Arnold's early years, from pre-pubescence to *Pumping Iron*. (The movie career after 1977 is more sketchily covered.) Kiss-and-tell testimony is provided by Arnold's ex-girlfriends and Leigh unearths material about such controversial subjects as Arnold's money, his supposed familiarity with gay bodybuilding patrons and his father's politics.

The book's publisher and President of Contemporary Books, the imprint under which *Arnold* came out in America, was Harvey Plotnick. He claimed that when the manuscript was at the printers two bodybuilders who were 'mutual friends' of his and Arnold's phoned to give Plotnick some advice. 'In one case,' he says, 'the caller suggested that Arnold would do a joint book with me if I quietly dropped the biography, retained the rights, and paid the author off.' The other called, he claims, offered to reimburse Plotnick for Leigh's payment, and to contribute 'something extra'.

Shortly after, Plotnick says he received a phone call from a New York law firm in which Sargent Shriver, Arnold's father-in-law, was a partner. The caller said that the biography might well provoke a libel suit. Plotnick's attorney wrote back: 'We understand the implication in your letter that Mr Schwarzenegger has a sufficiently deep pocket that he can make life extremely difficult for Congden if it publishes his biography . . . We would hope he would not attempt improperly to use his muscle in an attempt to thwart the First Amendment.'

Later, mysterious phone calls were reportedly made to the Donnelly plant in Crawfordsville, Indiana, where *Arnold* was being printed. In an apparent effort to smoke out information about the book, one man rang up pretending to be Contemporary Books' production manager, another pretending to be Plotnick himself. Production was switched to another plant in Virginia and the publication date was moved up three weeks. Even in the new plant, security precautions were taken. Personnel had to refer to the biography by code under the title 'Chicken on the Grill,' a take-off on Contemporary Books' cooking series. If a caller successfully negotiated that password, he had to answer the question 'Who did the Cubs play?' The correct reply was 'The Houston Astros'.

Meanwhile rumours that Arnold himself wished to buy Contemporary Books were dealt with by his ever-alert publicist Charlotte Parker. 'The subject has never come up in conversation,' she told the Los Angeles *Herald-Examiner*.

The biography was cold-shouldered in much of the media after it was published, and the author's own promotion campaign soon ground to a halt. An interview with Leigh in the Washington *Times* by Elizabeth Hickey, scheduled to be printed in the week beginning 8th July, never appeared. The Los Angeles morning TV show 'A.M.L.A.' cancelled an item on Leigh, the writer claimed, the night before it was due on air. And the mass-audience interview show 'Larry King Live' played host to Arnold on May 11th after turning down Leigh herself as a guest. When King spoke to Arnold about how the biography seemed not to be selling well, the book's subject declared, 'Trash doesn't sell. People are smart enough.' King asked Arnold if he had read the book himself. 'No, I never read it, no.'

He did not want to hear about it either. Before a press buffet at the 1990 Cannes Film Festival, journalists were required to sign an agreement not to question Arnold about the book. On the few occasions he was persuaded to comment, he took a lofty, unfazed approach: 'Why should I be mad? I feel sorry for her. She's just a trash journalist and I'm a top box-office star.'

Leigh's biography survived the land of free speech unscathed by lawsuits, but before it was published in Britain her home country's stricter libel laws encouraged Leigh's lawyer Mark Stephens to make deletions. We cannot itemise those deletions here, since we would fall foul of the very same laws. (An article citing the affair in the London *Times* and its reflection on British justice was headlined 'Libel laws make us a laughing stock'.)

Asked why the world should give a damn about alleged attempts to suppress her underselling biography, Leigh replied: 'I think people should care because Arnold's extremely well-placed now for a career in politics. If he's allowed to muzzle me today, who's he going to muzzle tomorrow? He's only a movie star, but so was Ronald Reagan.'

In the *Sunday Times* on August 19th, marking the book's publication with an article on the trials of writing a celebrity biography, Leigh wryly lamented that Arnold had not yet sent her any flowers. She acknowledged that the unauthorised biographer is less popular as a breed than the 'the average showbiz journalist, who (after being whisked all over the world on a press junket during which he or she is anointed by an "intimate conversation" with the star) is willing to write an article declaring that the inner life of everyone on the planet will be vastly enriched if they buy a ticket for the star's latest film'.

Leigh relates the occasional threat and ominous incident that accompanied her research travails, including midnight callers insisting she take care since 'Arnold was a deity'. She records that she took advice from an international security consultant, but that no bombs were found under her car, nor did bullets fly through her windows. She spent some time, nonetheless, hiding in 'darkest Colorado' where she 'shredded documents daily and made sure that all tapes were sequestered in bank vaults.' 'After spending two years studying Arnold in depth,' she concluded, 'I feel that, over the next 25 years or so, he'll realise that unauthorised biographies come with the territory, then make that call to Interflora.'

Instead, Arnold's phone was busy with calls to his British lawyer. Having already held out for nearly two years against settling with Arnold over her part in the *News of the World* article, Leigh was to hold out for a further two before retracting her allegations in July 1993. Arnold's lawyer Martin Kramer summed up: 'Mr Schwarzenegger has at no time held Nazi views, been an admirer of Hitler's evil regime or been anti-Semitic. Instead the very opposite is the truth. He is an active supporter of Jewish charities in the United States and a friend and supporter of Nazi hunter Simon Wiesenthal.'

Wendy Leigh now lives in Florida, unable to comment on the case due to a silencing restriction that came with the settlement.

In 1990 another Briton experienced, to a milder degree, the Arnold empire's seeming obsession with controlling publicity. TV documentarist Nicolas Kent, in the episode devoted to Schwarzenegger in the *Naked Hollywood* BBC TV series, portrayed the actor as a triumph of self-marketing: a brand-name 'Arnoldproduct' created by Arnold, packaged by him and placed by his hands on the most conspicuous shelf in Supermarket Hollywood. For Kent this made him a paradigm of the new movie age. 'Schwarzenegger is in his metier in the free market,' he says today.

> He would have been Johnny Weissmuller, probably, if he'd been involved in the old studio system. It's unlikely he'd have been given the opportunity to re-invent himself or choose his own projects or put together packages of directors and writers and stars. His career is only possible in the new Hollywood.

For expressing this view on screen, and for intercutting Arnold the self-made showman with craftsman-actor James Caan, deliberately presented as a less flashy, more thoughtful movie artist, Kent incurred the wrath of Charlotte Parker. Four years later she was still using Kent's name to me as a demonic example in that long-running saga, Big Arnie versus Perfidious Albion. 'Lack of trust that one associates with Nicolas Kent' . . . 'British journalist community suspect for a long while' . . . 'Someone that high, I never dreamed that they would lie' . . . 'Everyone burned; nothing to do with you, Nigel, not personal.'

'I think she believed she'd been betrayed,' says Kent. He admits that the film, presenting Caan in a plainly-shot head-to-head interview while Arnold's own interview is intercut with power parties and press launches, showed 'quite nakedly the calculation and manipulation with which Schwarzenegger organises his career'. But he also thinks that the programme 'essentially reflected the agenda we had to begin with, to show Hollywood as a company town, to show Schwarzenegger as above all a businessman who was creating a brand-name superstar'.

(ii) Closet Commando

Is Arnold a control freak? Or does he just like everything to be his way? His controlling instincts, if so nameable, were not confined to public-access furores in the *press and media*. 'I am an organisation freak; sometimes I expect too much,' he admitted in that maelstrom summer of 1990. He illustrated this with a story about the sliding doors in his new Sun Valley vacation home.

Unable to find a box of training clothes he had forwarded to the house from Los Angeles, he became frustrated by the limited view of the closet interior. 'So I rip the doors out, throw them to the other side of the room. That way, the builder will get the point.' As Arnold ripped the doors off the second closet too, Maria walked in. 'This is so I can see the whole closet at one shot [*sic*] and find my shorts!' explained Arnold. His wife swiftly deflated his ego. 'She looks at me and says, "You look really rugged. Wow!" Then I have to laugh at myself.'

This tale of the closets is a domestic variant of 'going in to see the boss without using the door'. You *could* call it control-freak behaviour. But a truly vocational control freak, surely, would have methodically if monomaniacally extracted the said closet doors, laying them aside to acquire his wide-angle 'shot' of the missing-shorts area. Later, at his or his wife's requirement, he would have slotted them methodically back.

A control freak who does not want to *seem* one will want the world to envisage him as the Arnold of this story: a creature of equal-parts demented impulse and honest selflessness. Better still, he will lie in wait for an opportunity to be the victim of someone *else's* controlling behaviour. In 1989 Maria forbade Arnold to be a judge at the 1989 Miss America contest in Atlantic City. Days before the pose-off Arnold had to pull out. Charlotte Parker said that he was 'too busy' filming in Mexico. The media knew better, or liked to think they did. This was organisational Arnie being 'organised' back. 'Maria was unbudgeable,' said pageant director Leonard Horn. Her stated reason, he said, was that as a journalist at the event she could not allow herself to be biased by Arnold's presence.

No one could work out what direction this bias might take. Would Maria watch Arnold's judging pencil to see which girls he was most aroused by? Would she then report favourably on those girls or unfavourably?

We suspect it was a sweet conjugal ploy designed to let Arnold off the scheduling hook and to show the 'control freak' getting gently freaked back. That would help his new film *Kindergarten Cop*. For the Arnold comedy hero, while establishing his macho credentials in a few bold strokes at a story's outset, must be seen to crumble endearingly in the face of a seemingly ill-matched opponent. It may be a wife like Maria, or a pair of conspiratorial closet doors. Better still, it might be a classroom full of noisy children.

27

The Do-Gooder

*'I'm looking forward to the opportunity of working with forty or
fifty little children of the age of four to six in* Kindergarten Cop
and I always look forward to working with animals.'

America was knee-deep in family values in 1990. Arnold's ability
to recognize a zeitgeist was unsurpassed. While taking care not
to impugn modern faiths like feminism and environmentalism,
he embraced the George Bush emphasis on traditional morality.
Hymning the sanctity of the family, he cited his own enlightening
experiences as a father. 'Having a baby brings out a completely
new capacity for responding to emotion. I found holding this
baby, playing with her and seeing her smile, was something I
could use in *Kindergarten Cop*. It's very important to show the
emotional thing when you deal with children.'
   His move into comedy, coinciding with new parental status,
is an event for which he happily concedes credit to the director
of *Twins* and now *Kindergarten Cop*.

Ivan Reitman is singlehandedly responsible for my success in
that area. If you are one of his actors, he studies you like a
psychiatrist, spends enough time with you to analyse you, to
find what he can use in the films. He's been around me when
I was with Maria; with our daughter Katherine; in business
negotiation; when I am angry and mad.

Equipped by this exposure to the Arnold psyche, Reitman

could recognize the right project for the star. The director initially rejected *Kindergarten Cop*. The Murray Salem original screen treatment was owned by director Ron Howard, himself no slouch at the multi-generation comedy (*Parenthood*), but Howard's company Imagine Films was prevailed on by Arnold to send the screenplay to Reitman. The story of a cop who goes undercover as a children's teacher to track down a crook's stolen loot had 'high-concept' appeal; but the original script, says Reitman, 'played on the concept really hard, it didn't have any of the secondary themes . . . The strong family stories, the broken home, the child abuse and even the romance weren't there.'

Most of these secondary themes, when they got into the movie, capsized it beyond rescue. However, Reitman and Arnold no doubt thought that in the 'feelgood' Nineties a little sentimental moralising might help to sell the film to the public. Once the movie was greenlighted and Arnold secured a $12m acting fee, the star got right in there, approving the cast, learning the techniques of being an undercover cop (grow a beard, raincoat and hair extension) and helping to pick the hundred four-to-six-year-old child actors. 'Ivan Reitman took me into a real kindergarten,' he recounts, 'to see how I communicated with kids. The first time I went in there with a hundred of them, I was sweating. You say "Hi!" and they look at you strangely. You say "How are you today?" and they look at each other like you were talking Russian.'

The movie meanwhile was still in script stage. The old firm of Herschel Weingrod and Timothy Harris (*Twins*) had been shackled to their chairs at the Universal writers' table to provide more comedy, but this twosome soon turned into a Hollywood chain gang. As Arnold explained to Nicolas Kent, 'There'll be a writer on it just for relationships, there'll be a writer just for the action . . . and there would be a writer just to deal with the children and their relationships with the other children or with me. There would be specific writers who are hired that are experts at certain things.'

But too many experts can spoil the mix. *Kindergarten Cop* lurches from cop thriller to kids' comedy, then to love story (Penelope Ann Miller), then to sentimental fable about belonging, and finally back to cop thriller.

The only section that comes alive is the relationship between Arnold and the children. He offers up his multi-megaton gaucherie, a displaced Goliath among piping Davids. They take every unfair advantage they can. A biology chat turns into a sexual precocity demonstration. Tiny boy: 'Boys have a penis, girls have a vagina.' Arnold: 'Thanks for de tip.' When Arnold complains of a headache, a five-year-old helpfully volunteers, 'It might be a tumour.' A pet ferret offers brief and promising distraction. 'Yes . . . good . . . yeah . . .,' encourages Arnold, 'now we're having fun!' Soon, though, the noise and chaos are resuming, and the demands for bathroom trips force a Terminator-style brutalism: 'Dair *iss* no bathroom.' Arnold begins to crack. To his fellow undercover cop Pamela Reed, he complains that the children are walking all over him.' '*You* should be cleaning up the paint,' he says to her, 'you should be reading stories about bears that go shopping.'

Kindergarten Cop is another showcase for Arnold's skill at impersonating displaced aliens. This impostor-schoolteacher might as well be from another planet, for all he knows about relating to children, so his foreign accent seems deliriously *à propos*. Like the Terminator, flung from the future into a disorienting present where he must data-analyse each image through his heat-monitoring vision, our cop-turned-teacher must go back to the basics of human interaction to calculate how to relate to these dangerous, inadequately-researched homunculi.

In the comedies, the Arnold accent turns from a tool of menace to a badge of bewilderment. Although it is ten years since *Conan the Barbarian*, when Robert Easton strove to get Arnold to talk about Queen Victoria's velvet woollies, the actor still enunciates like a man with a mouthful of Austrian pastries. Something in our head says: 'Maybe they are now coaching Arnold in how to *keep* his accent.' Perhaps Easton is sitting at the side of Arnold's sets de-ironing the plainspoken Americanisms. 'No, no, Arnold, not "bears that go shopping"! *Beers dat go shah-ping*.'

But you cannot craft or manufacture this natural barbarian magnetism. In *Kindergarten Cop* Arnold is a monster of improbability whose gestures towards 'ordinary' humanity seem more touching for their very helplessness. He gives us a mighty hero undone by those tiny weapons of sabotage called children.

With its diselemented protagonist, *Kindergarten Cop* was a late arrival in the school of 'fish out of water' Hollywood comedies that appeared in the 1980s, as if showing an America twitching to recover its world-leader equilibrium after having its military might humbled everywhere from Vietnam to Iran to Beirut. A policeman who turns teacher to smuggle the law's might into a corner of rural America – and is then outwitted by seemingly 'inferior' forces – is no long stretch from a policing nation that sends its men in the guise of advisers (teachers) to remote corners of the globe, only to be likewise humbled by the natives. If America wanted to see its recent military adventures re-fabulated as Gulliver in Lilliput, here was the man to play Gulliver.

Yet *Kindergarten Cop* also hints at the healing age of peace-making with Russia and at President Bush's 'new world order'. The sentimental subplots about children reaching entente with divorced parents adumbrate both the messianic geo-political accords that had taken place under Reagan and the family-values mandates that had issued from his and Bush's White House.

Arnold himself was perfect casting as a national knight errant for the new president's 'kinder, gentler' America. Here was a warrior-lummox who had a charmingly unwieldy rapport with kids and plain people, plus an ability to spout folk wisdom about life-improving values in fractured English. In sum, he was a writ-large version of Bush himself. As a mixture of P.E. instructor to America and licensed jester mentor to pre-teeners, Arnold tirelessly babbled prescriptions for his fellow citizens' fitness. His statistics-crammed vocal memos were as ungraspably authoritative as those squiggly doctor's prescriptions that you cannot read.

'The nation's health costs rose from $230bn in 1980 to $606bn last year,' Arnold rumbled in early 1991. 'They may triple in another ten years if our physically deficient children become sedentary and sickly adults.' And the sound-bite simile came right on cue. 'The situation reminds me of a mechanic who suggests a new oil filter for a car. "You can pay me a little now or a lot later."'

Arnold told American kids to exercise while watching TV commercials, 'instead of stuffing your face'. If they do eat, they must take nutritional precautions. 'Anything that tastes good and delicious is usually bad for the body': except for veal and swordfish which are both 'good' and 'good for you'. Not surprisingly, when this man visited schools or gyms, children had difficulty reconciling the evangelistic Arnold with the movie star who killed people, shot up police stations and overturned cars with his bare hands. One child asked him: 'Can you lift up a whole school? I want to move it.'

For Arnold the entire year was marked by dotty generational interfacing. At Los Angeles' Four Seasons hotel a group of ill-programmed children – his co-stars on *Kindergarten Cop* – swirled around the TV cameras and tape-recorders, immortalising their diverse 'takes' on the megastar. A girl: 'Arnold was just a big mountain. He picked me up and told me I was a sexy devil.' A boy: 'We want to own big muscles and be like Arnold when we grow up.' Another girl: 'I like that he kills people. I like it when he takes two guys' heads and smashes them together and they go "boing".'

What George and Barbara Bush, having recruited Arnold for their family values bandwagon, thought of such endorsements is not recorded. Soon the Bushes would have their own problems *sub specie Arnoldi*. Two weeks after the *Kindergarten Cop* junket, the nation's fitness czar visited the first couple at Camp David and was there when Barbara crashed into a tree while tobogganing on the inner tubes of tyres with her children. 'There was no damage to the tree,' commented Bush. Mrs Bush sustained a small break in her left leg.

The First Lady's injury accorded with a year in which Arnold's health guru status seemed dodgier by the minute. As a fitness-celebrating twelvemonth, 1991 was a mixed success: culminating in some spectacular fall-out from Arnold's own former sport. By year's close the National Injury Information Clearinghouse in Washington D.C. had totted up nearly thirty thousand weight-equipment mishaps nationwide. They included 399 crushings, 459 dislocations, 681 amputations, 3, 701 fractures and 6, 191 lacerations. Perhaps it was safer to watch TV and chunk hamburgers.

Clearly some capricious force-field hovered around this man as he entered middle age. Turning forty-three in July, he wondered if he should now be a hellraiser or a do-gooder. On the surface he was sanguine about such watersheds. 'Since I just went through the first third of my life,' he says, winning low points for maths or high points for optimism, 'I don't have much to worry about.'

Arnie the do-gooder got a major workout – again with Bush at his side – in June 1991, when he was honoured with a National Leadership Award by the Simon Wiesenthal Center. Thirteen hundred guests paid $750 apiece – the most expensive table cost $50,000 – to pack the Grand Ballroom of the Century Plaza Hotel. The invitees list included Sylvester Stallone, Goldie Hawn, Lou Ferrigno, Eunice Shriver as well as seven studio chiefs and a cluster of super-agents. The famous producing duo Peter Guber and Jon Peters (*Batman*) were the evening's co-chairmen. Before the gala dinner, there was a march-through of concentration camp survivors carrying a US flag made in secret by the inmates of the Mathausen camp before liberation. Next up was a big-screen mini-documentary about Arnold's life narrated by TV anchorman Tom Brokaw. Then came dinner.

After the meal the US President made a speech in the star's honour. This included a joshing reference to Barbara's tree crash and how it seemed to have been precipitated by Arnold's visit. 'Come to think of it,' he said, 'you could be my special emissary to Congress.' The honoree graciously summed up his evening: 'To the President of the United States and everyone else who's here tonight – with a full and grateful heart this little boy from Austria thanks you.'

Although Bush himself picked up an award – the 'Cup of Elijah', for his work in airlifting Ethiopian Jews to Israel – it was Arnold's night. The guests were each given a blue-and-black duffel bag containing a *Terminator 2* T-shirt (the star's upcoming film) and a bottle of Fred Hayman perfume. 'It was one of the greatest evenings of my life,' Arnold told the press. 'We raised $1.5m. It's very important that the new generation shows leadership and speaks against prejudice and all that.'

Heads were mildly scratched in the media over what Arnold had done to deserve this orgy of good will and free publicity. Rabbi Marvin Hier says today, 'We honoured him for his concern, philanthropy and dedication to the Center. For eight or nine years he has been an active supporter. He is a friend of

Simon Wiesenthal. And he has contributed a serious amount of funds, as well as hosting private cocktail party fundraisers and opening his own home for these events.'

Nasty-minded people might murmur that Arnold was merely ingratiating himself with the philanthropic community. The trouble was, whatever community one turned to, there was Arnold acquiring a good name.

For disabled athletes, he lit the Olympic torch at the Athens Special Olympics on Pnyx mountain opposite the Parthenon, as well as attending a televised gathering of 6,000 mentally handicapped athletes in Minneapolis in August, along with Warren Beatty, Melanie Griffith and Whoopi Goldberg.

Satirical television comedians were wooed into his constituency. 'Saturday Night Live''s 'Hans and Franz' (Dana Carvey, Kevin Nealon), whose entire act is based on lampooning the Austro-American, were invited to the Arnold Classic one summer and spent the whole day, they reported, 'talking our lines to his secretary' with Arnold nearby. 'Now, how do you do de accent again?', Arnold would keep asking.

Even Hell's Angels got the olive branch. John Milius remembers the day he and Arnold were cornered in a hamburger restaurant in the Valley by a motorcycle gang who mocked the actor by chanting 'Conan! Conan! Conan!' and then invited him to arm-wrestle. Arnold held up a well-muscled limb and said, 'Have you ever seen such a beautiful arm? If I was to use this arm on you and hurt it, how would I feel?' Then one biker said, 'Hey, man, would you fuck my old lady?' Arnold inspected the girlfriend and said, 'If I fucked her, how would she feel with you afterwards?' Every provocation was defused. By the end of the afternoon Arnold was riding their motorcycles and being plied with the gang's colours and invited to join up.

In addition to turning the world into his family, Arnold became a father again. His new daughter, Christina Aurelia, was born on July 23d 1991 at St John's Hospital, Santa Monica, where Maria checked in under the assumed name 'Fitzgerald'. The baby had initial difficulty breathing and was put in an incubator with an oxygen tent. It was 'a mild respiratory, common condition', said a doctor, and soon she and her mother were travelling safely to Casa Arnold.

How can this man, who is now bonding with bikers, fathering children and working for charities, continue to play menacing movie figures? Perhaps he cannot. In *Terminator 2* Arnold reprises his starmaking role as a cyborg from the future. But this time he plays a 'good' Terminator.

28

Beyond Good and Evil

*'Don't think my character is a babysitter. I am as hard and as rough
as I was in the first movie'*

(i) Boys' Club

On the Fourth of July holiday weekend of 1991 *Terminator 2*
accounted for over half the cinema tickets sold in the United
States of America. In Hollywood jargon, a film with clear or
proven sequel potential is called a 'franchise': which means that
after picture number one everyone waits for number two to open,
and then number three, much like a new branch of Burger King
or McDonalds.

Like any sequel, this one had to be similar but different. 'It was
actually Arnold who got me thinking about it,' says film-maker
James Cameron; 'he loved the role and was interested in doing it
again.' It was no use, though, churning out the same plot about
a cyborg saving a mother and unborn son for the distant good
of the planet. Cameron and co-writer William Wisher initially
conceived of two Terminators: one handsome and heroic, the
other evil-looking and malevolent, both played by Arnold.
Cameron, though, saw the snag: 'It would have meant having
him in appliance make-up for the whole five months of the
shooting schedule, and I didn't want Arnold Schwarzenegger
cranky with me.'

It was decided to keep the two-cyborg concept; but Arnold
would play the robot we root for – thrown into the present from

the future to protect the now teenaged John Connor (Edward Furlong), destined messiah of the human race – while newcomer Robert Patrick was the villain, able to change shape, walk through solid objects and impale people with metallicised limbs.

For Cameron, though, hero-villain terminology was inappropriate. 'The Terminators exist outside of any moral framework – they're machines. It's like saying one gun is good and the other gun is bad.' Arnold concurs: 'I would not consider the Terminator to be a good guy. He has been programmed to protect the kid; but aside from that nothing much is changed. Ask any of the other people he destroys in the film.'

The choice is large. *Terminator 2* is a mayhem festival as before, the main difference being the lighter touch. Although the film cost $100m to make – at the time the most expensive in history – it plays like a cross between sci-fi shocker and picaresque comedy. Cameron builds the jokes around the Arnold character's alien manners: a creature of programmed responses and deadpan idiom, bringing his surreal affectlessness to an emotional planet Earth.

Most of the terrestrial wit the Arnold cyborg picks up, on the way to saving John Connor and his Mum (Linda Hamilton) as they sashay from mental asylums to desert hideouts to blown-up skyscrapers, is taught him by the boy: including the newest Arnold one-liner destined for history, 'Hasta la vista, baby!' The phrase's bi-lingual mish-mash of colloquialisms seems appropriate both for a disoriented cyborg and for an Austrian who became famous trying to be an American.

The boy-android double act is an inspired script invention. They teach each other not just different kinds of utterance but different kinds of anarchy and morality. 'You got a quarter?' asks the boy, wanting to phone his mother from a callbox: whereupon Arnold bashes in the coin-box and picks out one coin. Later, when the carnage starts, the boy shakes his head saying, 'You just can't go around killing people.' 'Why?', asks Arnold with unflickering robot commonsense.

At the same time Furlong's precocious, hang-loose manners highlight all Arnold's dotty formalism. The hip catch-phrases dispensed by the boy are picked up by the android, like a suspicious object dropped on a sidewalk, and tried out for size and style. The rapport is so wittily sustained that it lends credibility to the publicity stories about the two actors finding instant kinship. According to Furlong,

> I clowned around a lot with Arnold, and then Jim [Cameron] would walk by and get pissed off because he didn't like us clowning around when we were doing a scene. Arnold could just switch it on and off – from the Terminator to Arnold and then back to the Terminator again – but I couldn't do that. So sometimes Arnold would want to clown around and I wouldn't want to, but it was hard to say no.

Actress Linda Hamilton, left on the edge of this boys' club as the road-movie plot purred across California, remembers Arnold's 'filthy sense of humour'. 'You just had to go "Aachh!" He and Eddie Furlong would be together – both of them are about the same age emotionally – and we would be stuck in that car day in and day out. I would just sit there helpless while Arnold was giving Eddie tips on women. It was excruciating.'

It was of little help to Hamilton that she was living with the film's director. Cameron previously had been married to Gale Ann Hurd, his co-writer and producer on *The Terminator* (to whom he and his backers Carolco had to pay $5m for the release of the original film's rights) and film-maker Katharine Bigelow (*Near Dark, Point Break*). Now his new partner Hamilton looked on while her role, though studded with dramatic moments (gun battles, escape from criminal insane asylum) and entrusted with the film's voice-over narration, was effortlessly upstaged by her male co-leads.

There were also flashbacked love scenes shot for *Terminator 2*, featuring Hamilton and the earlier film's Michael Biehn, which the actress thought gave both her character and the movie an extra dimension. They hit the cutting-room floor. 'I was told they were an interruption of the pace of the movie. It got tender and quiet and they interrupted the build, Jim is an amazing editor and he cuts whole chunks of the movie that are brilliant – but if they don't survive the pace of the story, it's snip, snip, snip.'

Did she quarrel with the change? 'I was sleeping with the man and he didn't tell me, until we were looping, that there were no more love sequence and dream sequence. Ach! No courage at all! There was so much that had gone into that love scene with Michael Biehn. You were brought into the open heart of my character, which is just never opened in the rest of the movie.'

These scenes were restored in a 'Director's Version' released for video; but if anything they vindicate Cameron's original editorial decision. The filmgoer has no more interest in the inner workings of Sarah's heart in the second *Terminator* than in the first. The heart of both movies is Arnold, and the mystery of whether his character *has* a heart: this machine built for rough justice and rudimentary response, whose gift – and legacy to modern movie lore – is to find the shortest possible way to complete a desired action. In one defining scene in *Terminator 2* a top Cyberdene Systems scientist (Joe Morton) finds that his personal entry code into a high-security room does not work. 'Here, use mine,' volunteers Arnold, and blasts the door down with a shotgun.

Emotionlessness – or the cryptic rationing of emotional response – is a hard act to sustain, even for an actor who seems born to play androids. In one scene, Arnold explains, 'I had to walk calmly through this flaming doorway with all this shit going on around me, and reload my gun and fire away without once doing anything that would indicate a human reaction.' The dialogue delivery was as crucial as the physical actions. 'Because I was playing a machine, I had to sound like a tape-recorder and rattle off detailed technical responses without giving off human inflections. I could not pause. As soon as I did, they would cut and I would have to do the scene over again.'

The contrast between android Arnold and Robert Patrick's metamorphic T-1000 – changing shape, sprouting killing limbs, re-healing instantly after injury – echoes the oldest face-off of all in our hero's career: Conan the Barbarian versus the slippery transformation-cultists of Thulsa Doom. Arnold's reason-for-being as a movie hero is still to embody the universe's Mr Stand-fast. While others deal in changeability, he favours the monolithic, the monosyllabic. Even when he does change or mutate, it is merely a hiccup in that hieratic wholeness. In the process Arnold has come to seem not just macho but macho-monstrous.

(ii) The Art of Hulking

As with all great screen ogres, there is something endearing about Arnold's monstrosity. Strongmen have been part of movie lore ever since Maciste, the power-muscled slave from Ancient Rome who made his first appearance in the 1913 Italian silent epic *Cabiria*. Later this popular hero-hunk was re-named Samson for foreign audiences, presumed to be struggling Laocoon-like with the Italian vowels and consonants. 'Ma-chee-stay', though, offers a perfect and prophetic Schwarzenegger conflation: 'macho' plus 'machine' plus a hint of 'masochistic'.

To those bigger-than-life qualities Arnold has added a bizarre humanity that makes his ancestry seem wider and his appeal more poignant. 'Movies have always had their sympathetic hulks,' says Pauline Kael. 'Think of Victor McLaglen. Arnold Schwarzenegger could probably have played the Informer if he could have put his tongue around an Irish accent.'

McLaglen was the massive Irishman with the squashed-truck face who 'graced' films like Ford's *The Informer* and *The Quiet Man*. Like him, Arnold combines a monumental *joli laid* presence with a built-in comic pathos. But he also has an undercurrent of wry commentary on his own 'otherness.' 'He was lucky in playing the Terminator so early,' says Kael, 'and he was smart to play it again. He's ideal for playing not quite human figures. He makes them droll – they end up seeming more human than the humans he plays.'

That rogue humanity raises Arnold above the tradition he 'ought' to belong to by virtue of his athletic background and minimalist acting style. Try to pin the sportsman adventure-hero label on him – to align him with the Buster Crabbes and Johnny Weissmullers, the Reg Parks and Steve Reeveses – and we realise how much more than a mere body-in-motion he is. You would have to interbreed Reeves with Lon Chaney (junior or senior), or Crabbe with Boris Karloff, to get anywhere near Arnold's blend of the photogenic with the primitive, the eugenic with the high-Gothic.

This sense of Arnold as an Impossible Synthesis, played up to in movies like *T2*, inspires the constant jokes that he is some kind of assemblage – born of mad science rather than of man and woman – and also gives him an avant-garde edge in our own dawning movie age of the 'Synthespian'.

In the near future any actor's appearance will be alterable, *ad infinitum*, by computer. This writer stumbled last year on a special effects lab – high in the Hollywood hills – where hush-hush tweakings were being visited, on computer screen, to Sylvester Stallone's appearance for *Judge Dredd*. There was the Stallone face looking out at me like a mask on the back of a cornflakes packet: flayed into two dimensions, number-coded, ready for desktop surgery.

I was told to say nothing, but pixel-manipulation is now an open secret and Arnold must be reckoned its John the Baptist. *His* face has gone through more advanced-science contortions than any other actor's; from *The Terminator* to *Total Recall*. His face has a joyous mechanistic otherworldliness to it even when not being pixel-ated. And when the Book of Synthespians is published, he will surely be marked down as first, finest and most formative.

Arnold the New Age assemblage, though, can be as baffling and ambivalent to critics as Arnold the more evolutionary hero-ogre. Where *Kindergarten Cop* posed questions about whether Arnold's size and strength were assets or handicaps, *Terminator 2* sowed confusion over whether he was playing *übermensch* or *untermensch*.

Terrence Rafferty in the *New Yorker* complained that 'the whole movie is based on the insane conceit that Arnold Schwarzenegger is the underdog'. J. Hoberman, by contrast, writing in *The Village Voice*, hewed to the older and in leftish circles still ascendant belief that Arnold the movie star is a sinister power totem sent to us from Greater Germany's Aryan culture. Hoberman's ripely provocative essay, later reprinted in Britain's *Sight And Sound*, dwelt at length – indeed was entirely built around – the relationship between the actor and the philosopher who has been most often invoked in the same breath, Friedrich Nietzsche.

(iii) Also Sprach Schwarzenegger

Called 'Nietzsche's Boy', the essay takes off from the Nietzsche quotation that John Milius had pinned to the opening of *Conan*

The Barbarian: 'That which does not destroy us makes us strong.'
Fantasising the image of a giant survival machine, a Golem
powered by box-office success, Hoberman refers throughout
to 'The Arnold' or 'Der Arnold'. He sees him as a composite
of past movements and past and present disasters. 'To become
the Arnold, Schwarzenegger required the 80s fitness craze, the
fifteen-year regime of "body horror" movies, the proliferation
of environmental cancers, the plague of Aids, the Reagan *jawohl*.'
(The exact part played by Aids and eco-cancers is unclear.)

Arnold required all this to become the post-Nietzschean figure
Hoberman identifies and shudders at. 'Unlike any other previous
star,' he writes, 'he embraces and embodies the covertly admired
Teutonic virtues.'

There *are*, of course, correspondences between the German
thinker and the Austrian thespian. It has been a popular invoca-
tional pairing. Film-maker John Milius was still going around in
the 1990s proclaiming the kinship: 'Arnold is very Nietzschean.
He believes in will.' And George Butler in his photo-monograph
Arnold Schwarzenegger: A Portrait, published in 1990, mentions the
actor's allusions to a career 'master-plan' that Butler describes –
without providing much further detail – as a 'campy mixture of
Nietzschean philosophy and Soviet Five-Year Plan'.

Yet Nietzsche, placed in the Arnold landscape, tends to
turn the signposts away from rather than towards the clichéd
iconography of totalitarianism. Read attentively rather than
Reader's-Digested, Nietzsche's writing shows that his priority
shibboleths were team morality and the evil of received ethical
systems; and that the Arnold he would have seen as a brother,
far from being Hoberman's Aryan hit-man, was the budding
sportsman who turned his back on team activities as a boy and
the new-world achiever who mocked, self-delightedly, each of
his successive career incarnations.

Laughter is the great fanfare of exultant defiance for Nietzsche's
allegorical protagonists. Every new wisdom derides and destroys
the last one. His war on absolutism is at a virtually opposite
pole to the millenarian dogmas of Teutonic dictatorships in this
century. ('There are *no eternal facts*, just as there are no absolute
truths.' *Human All Too Human*.) And his war on communal ideals
blueprints a hero who never joins or champions other people's

causes: 'One has to get rid of the bad taste of wanting to be in agreement with many. "Good" is no longer good when your neighbour takes it into his mouth.' (*Beyond Good and Evil*).

Nietzsche's writing does seem at times like an annunciation of Arnold's life and career, but in surprising, even particular ways. He gives us what might be an encoded paean to the bodybuilding ideal: 'What is the heaviest thing, you heroes? so asks the weight-bearing spirit, that I may take it upon me and rejoice in my strength . . . There are many heavy things for the spirit, for the strong, weight-bearing spirit in which dwell respect and awe: its strength longs for the heavy, for the heaviest.' (*Thus Spake Zarathustra*).

Nietzsche's delight in transfiguration fables also lays out a groundplan for Arnold's bizarre progress through serial vocations. In *Thus Spake Zarathustra* the human spirit goes through three changes on the way to wisdom and beatitude. First, it becomes a camel: a beast of burden, a bearer of weights. Arnold the bodybuilder. Then a lion: 'it wants to capture freedom and be lord in its desert.' Arnold the action star, real-estate millionaire, power broker. Finally a child: 'innocence and forgetfulness, a new beginning, a sport, a self-propelling wheel, a first motion, a sacred Yes.' The Arnold of *Twins, Kindergarten Cop, Junior*.

Sometimes, too, Nietzsche's writing can seem a vivid sketch for the Arnold manner. 'The will to economy in the grand style; to keeping one's force, one's *enthusiasm* in bounds' (*The Anti-Christ*) is a prescription for the laconic, emotion-proofed heroes of *Red Heat* or *Predator*; while *Commando* is prefigured in another passage from *The Anti-Christ*: 'One must be accustomed to living on mountains – to seeing the wretched ephemeral chatter of politics and national egoism *beneath* one.'

Sadly, Nietzsche did not live long enough to get a job as a Hollywood copywriter. Otherwise the town would ring to his matchless one-liners for the Arnold posters. 'I am not a man, I am dynamite.' (*Ecce Homo*). 'Courageous, untroubled, mocking, violent – that is what wisdom wants us to be' (*Thus Spake Zarathustra*).

Theories of rapprochement between a modern film star and a past philosopher are ambitious, probably delirious, at the best of times. But the Nietzsche invocation suggests that a culture giant subpoena'd by the sceptical prosecution, in the People versus Arnold Schwarzenegger the movie image, can be used just as easily by the defence, with a little homework and sympathetic imagination.

29

Lost Action Hero

'We never stay on top all the time. No one ever has and no one ever will.'

Anyone bold enough to interpret Arnold's life as the fulfilment of a long-term plan would have to deal with the year 1992. It is a bewildering, at times dismaying twelves month. Our hero runs about like a one-man jobs noticeboard. He is opening eateries, directing TV shows, taking on career-changing movie projects. His success in these areas is mixed, though his enthusiasm is unflagging.

(i) Arnold the Foodie

In February 1992 Arnold opened his own restaurant in Venice, California. He had bought the name 'Schatzi' from a German deli in Santa Monica for a sum reported by one newspaper to be $21,000. 'Not even close,' says Lilo Finston, the deli's sexagenarian owner, without specifying if it was larger or smaller. 'Arnold used to come here all the time because he liked our sausages,' says Finston. Soon, though, the aggrieved proprietor was being besieged with misdirected calls for the other Schatzi.

That restaurant's first two years were marked by high-visibility hirings and firings. Chef Lisa Stalvy from the famed Spago's restaurant, that epicentre of Hollywood schmoozing perched in an eyrie above Sunset Boulevard, got her walking orders after a week. Maria didn't think the burgers fatty enough. Three more chefs would be tried before the Schwarzenburgers were satisfactory.

Amid the whirr of revolving cooks, manager August Spier set out to establish a simple style of eating, with the stamp of Arnold and Maria's personalities on the Styria-meets-Southern-California decor. Maria picked or approved the designs of carpeting and crockery. Arnold's signature is to be found in the bathroom, where a mysterious voice, issuing from behind the walls, gives the visitor German lessons while he attends to nature's needs. This invisible Mr Berlitz favours words and phrases like 'to control', 'to discipline', 'to correct'. (Has the ghost of Gustav been wandering, from Weiz cemetery, Austria, to Venice beach?)

What is one restaurant, however, to a man with the power to open a hundred? Soon Arnold stood shoulder to shoulder with Sylvester Stallone and Bruce Willis at a series of frabjous photo-opportunities, as the three men launched their Planet Hollywood franchise across the world. The chain's actual founders and co-financiers were New York businessman and film producer Keith Barish (of Arnold's *The Running Man*) and British restaurant and entertainment tycoon Robert Earl (also, with Barish, involved with the financing and administration of Schatzi on Main). For front-men, though, this duo had picked three of the world's mightiest promoters. Once these megastars stepped on a bandwagon, the vehicle would be unstoppable.

At publicity events Arnold was the face most often in the forefront. When Planet Hollywood opened in Santa Ana, California, one wet night in autumn 1992, he broke through security ranks to thank hundreds of screaming fans for their attendance, while Sly and Bruce stood back nervously waving. 'It's a matter of intelligence,' Arnold told a reporter later. 'These people standing in the rain made you a *star!*'

The most fanfared Planet Hollywood, though, was in New York. Clustered inside the interior created by *Batman* set designer Anton Furst – pillars in the shape of Marilyn Monroe's legs, omnipresent TV screens flickering with old films – were such memorabilia as James Dean's motorbike from *Rebel Without a Cause* and the full-metal cyborg from *Terminator 2*.

Food seems incidental here, though it too has a demotic dementia. Dishes named after popular movies or stars; sizzling hamburgers chased down by polychromatic ice creams. Whenever the menu gets too predictably American, enter Aurelia Schwarzenegger. Arriving from Graz on one of her yearly visits, she walks through the door and homes in on the nearest skillet. 'Every time she comes into the restaurant in New York,' enthuses Arnold, 'she has a new idea about what ought to be served. Then she goes into the kitchen and makes something. All of my success is down to her upbringing. You know how I became a world champion bodybuilder? It had nothing to do with weight-training and everything to do with my mother's cooking.'

Explaining his own role in the restaurant chain, Arnold vouchsafes: 'I'm involved in everything from finding sites, picking the next town for openings, choosing what memorabilia will be inside and how much money we'll spend. We are involved together in every business decision right down to the architect's blueprints.'

'A lot of crap,' comments Jackie Stallone, Sylvester's mother. 'They're getting paid for the use of their names, they're frontmen. Maybe they put a dollar in.'

Nonetheless, the trio troops off to major openings across the world. The first European outpost for Planet Hollywood was in Piccadilly, London, where the target for customers was two million a year. A ground-breaking ceremony in August 1992 was followed by a party for Arnold hosted by British film-maker Michael Winner. Among the glittering were John Cleese, Michael Caine, Lord (Lew) Grade, Ridley Scott, Billy Connolly; but Winner recalls the spectacle of the glitteratissimus himself, a giant among pygmies, charming even as he spilled a glass of his favourite pear schnapps over Winner's furniture.

'He was very embarrassed. He stained my dining-room table. He said to his wife, "If anyone did this to me in Beverly Hills they'd be banned from society."'

Arnold atoned by chatting to each guest, queuing for food with everyone else, making a droll speech – 'Michael is more than just a best friend to me; he's a complete stranger' – and staying until one in the morning advising Winner on the director's new private gymnasium. The next night Arnold returned the hospitality by dining Winner at Tramps.

For a man determined to wrestle to himself the reins of career control, it is a short step from restaurateur to movie auteur. Arnold had announced his film-making ambitions before: 'I think it's a big challenge. I don't know how Clint Eastwood does it. I ask him so many times.' Now he was offered the chance to direct a 25-minute episode for the TV horror series *Tales from the Crypt*. In this small but serviceable spinechiller, a lovelorn old man pays $6 million to swap faces and bodies with a handsome youth, wishing to win over the girl of his dreams. The twist ending is that she goes off with the other man, now older-looking but much richer.

The show is stolen by Arnold's Hitchcock-style introduction. He comes on in a purple-coloured *Tales from the Crypt* T-shirt and wraps a friendly arm round the series' mummified-corpse compere (who is wearing a sweatband and humping a barbell formed of two skulls and a cross-bone). 'Tonight's story is about an old man who finds a new wrinkle in de fountain of youth – a tvisted tale dat we call "De Svitch".'

The Switch, a literal tale of 'body-building', probably appealed to Arnold for the *grand guignol* spin it puts on physical self-improvement. Stylistically the episode is unremarkable, apart from one grace-note which coincides with what seems to be Arnold's theme for the year: eating. The mad scientist masterminding the occult surgery is seen slicing a salami while discussing a transplant of the old man's most intimate body part. (German humour?)

'After I directed that little *Tales from the Crypt* I felt ecstatic,' raved Arnold. 'It was something I never expected. To work with actors and mould a scene. It's wild.'

He moved on to a larger project, a TV feature called *Christmas in Connecticut*, recycling a 1945 Barbara Stanwyck comedy about a celebrity cook-housewife who knows almost nothing about either activity, and whose gourmet dishes are put together by someone else. Arnold found himself working with an actress whom better directors than he had moulded. Otto Preminger,

Paul Mazursky, Sidney Lumet . . . Hollywood's finest had had
a go at shaping Dyan Cannon.

'At first I thought, Arnold, fine,' remembers the actress.

But can he direct comedy? I had director control and I was
doubtful. But he was very open and had very good ideas. He
listened to everyone. We'd be standing around and there'd be
a set-up we'd have to do in five minutes and I'd say, 'You
know, Arnold, wouldn't it be funnier if da-da-da-dah.' And
if he liked the idea he'd switch the whole thing round to
do it. Your ego has to be pretty settled to do that. We
had little preparation time, being TV. We shot five days a
week, rehearsing Saturday. Most of us had 'flu during the
shooting.

The film's producer Stanley Brooks was startled at how
efficiently Arnold coped. 'He storyboarded every single shot.
Before filming, he spent six to ten hours with Ivan Reitman
going through every shot. And on the set he had it all down in
a notebook on a music stand. On a TV movie with a twenty-day
schedule that's enormously helpful.'

Not helpful enough. *Christmas in Connecticut* ends up as ninety
minutes of ill-judged whimsy. Faced with a witless script, studio-
bound snowscapes and a Who's Who's of Yesterday cast – Tony
Curtis, Kris Kristofferson, Richard Roundtree – Arnold makes
the mistake of getting everyone to 'act up'. The camera leaps
from face to face, capturing each semaphored line-reading, while
the audience prays for a moment of repose. When all else fails,
Arnold resorts to self-promotional in-jokes: Kristofferson doing
bodybuilding workouts in his home gym (he plays a forest ranger
who used to teach comparative literature); a clip from *Twins* on TV;
the Cannon character's leather-and-shades-sporting son booming,
in a voice dubbed for the line by Arnold himself, 'I'll be back'.

What took place off camera – as often in this star's career
– was droller than what happened on. When a reporter from
TV Guide visited him during a postproduction looping session,
Arnold told her, 'You cannot just observe, you will have
to participate.' The scribe was required to post-synchronise
the cry of a woman struck to the floor by Tony Curtis.

'You inhaled!,' cried Arnold. 'You don't inhale while you are falling!'

Later he put his weight behind promoting the film. Seven hundred and fifty guests attended a party in the Directors Guild of America building; and at the American Film Market Arnold buttonholed nearly everyone to ask 'Did you buy my movie?' When Charlton Heston made the mistake of drifting away from a poster of the film, Arnold cried, 'Hey, Charlton, let's promote *Christmas in Connecticut!*' The ex-Moses and Michelangelo was dragged back for a smiling two-shot in front of the hoarding.

In the run-up to the film's spring broadcast on the Ted Turner channel, Arnold appeared in promotional spots, answering the imaginary question why a Christmas film was airing in April. 'Because I said so,' he boomed. It seemed to pay off: *Christmas in Connecticut* became the fourth highest-rated programme in Turner Television history.

(ii) The Titanic

Couch potatoes tuning in listlessly to the latest TV movie are one audience. The great filmgoing public, however, make an effort for their entertainment. They order babysitters, put on galoshes, back the car out of the garage, drive through streets booby-trapped with ice or garbage, pay twelve pounds or twenty dollars for a pair of tickets plus coke and popcorn, sit through the trailers and commercials, and then watch – *Last Action Hero*.

Like the Titanic the film began as an 'unsinkable' project. Approved for launching by Columbia Sony Pictures, it would be an action comedy featuring every watertight gimmick the movie fan could require. Special effects; car chases and crashes; young boy hero to bring in the kids; in-jokes and ludic movie references to bring in the more sophisticated moviegoer; Arnie to bring in everyone else.

Although the budget was large and would spiral to $93 million, it was still less than *Terminator 2*. Defining his policy on choosing projects for the studio, Columbia President Mark Canton said: 'We've stopped overpaying . . . We used to say, "We want it, no matter how much it costs." Now we've adopted the mantra of all well-run businesses: "We want it, but only if the price is right – or if Arnold is in it.'"

As *Last Action Hero*'s biggest champion, the star announced that the hour had come to take American action cinema in a more pacific direction. Building on the hints of generational bonding in *T2*, *Last Action Hero* has a missionary innocence about it: the tale of a boy (Austin O'Brien) who finds a magic movie ticket that transports him into the screen, where he teams up with the movie-within-a-movie's gangbusting action star Jack Carter (Arnold). They romp about in a fantasy dimension where guns blaze, vehicles collide and no one gets hurt.

'The country is going in an anti-violence direction,' stated Arnold. 'I think America has seen now enough of what violence has done in the cities, and while it was okay for the Arnold of the Eighties to kill two hundred and seventy-five people on screen, it is not for the Arnold of the Nineties.'

He had pushed aside several high-profile properties in favour of this one. He could have played the title role in *The Count of Monte Cristo* but said. 'How can this work with the accent and everything?' He was briefly piqued by the fantasy possibilities of *Curious George*, based on a children's book about a monkey's misadventure in Africa, accompanied by a man in a yellow hat. (He would play the man in the yellow hat.) Finally he narrowed the field to a comedy called *Sweet Tooth* – producer Norman Lear, director Ron 'City Slickers' Underwood – and *Last Action Hero*.

The first of these was about a US marine who is asked by his dying tooth-fairy father to carry on the family tradition. Nice for children. But we wonder if Arnold felt nervous about the possible media response to the project. Reporters who like comparing life and art might ask: 'Arnold, what sort of family traditions did *your* father try to hand down to his son?'

Last Action Hero seemed free of personal booby traps and had a potentially gymnastic appeal. It lunged towards the avant-garde by mixing reality and illusion, it went back to basics with its cleanly demarcated heroes and villains.

Meanwhile the pre-teen market was to be wooed, but wooed wholesomely. When the sales people, early in the shoot, came up with a gun-toting Jack Slater doll, the first ever toy licensed to bear the star's exact likeness, Arnold sent it back to the drawingboard to be disarmed. Children would have instead a nice fifteen-inch Arnie doll, price $22, that dispensed punches not bullets and uttered the new film's catch-phrase, 'Beeg mistake'. The message on the packaging would read: 'Play it smart. Never play with real guns.'

Based on an original screenplay by two ex-university unknowns, Zak Penn and Adam Leff, *Last Action Hero* received a major script polish from Shane Black (*Lethal Weapon*) and David Arnott (*The Adventures of Ford Fairlane*). It then had a four-week, one-million-dollar re-polish by William Goldman (*Butch Cassidy and the Sundance Kid*, *Misery*). It would be directed by Arnold's old comrade John 'Predator' McTiernan.

So the Titanic set sail. One of the passengers, who caught the ship late, was actor Charles Dance. Cast as the dimension-hopping villain, he got the role as second choice to another Englishman, Alan Rickman, who had turned it down. Says Dance: 'When I got to Culver City in Los Angeles, where they were shooting, I had the props people make me up a sweatshirt which read "I'm cheaper than Alan Rickman". John McTiernan was horrified that I knew, but Arnold chomped on his cigar and thought it was a big joke.'

Dance was swept up in the convivial nimbus created by the stogie-chomping star.

He creates an extraordinary atmosphere on the set, because everyone in the film industry is rampant with insecurity and paranoia. Everybody's being nice to each other for fear of the next job. But the more I worked, the more I realised the good atmosphere actually came down from Arnold. He's very friendly with everyone. He's a 'people's champion'. And that goes for his view of movies too. He was sitting around in the make-up trailer one night, talking with some people about the nature of the film industry, and as I walked in he said, 'You see, Charles, you make your "art films", but I make films for the polyester people.'

Several of these polyester people, or cotton-polyester, seemed to be among Arnold's own retinue. Loyal to the last, the star still had his stuntmen pals from the old days around him. 'Enormous guys,' recalls Dance, 'strolling around in singlets that were too small so that they revealed more of their muscles. There was an exercise bike outside Arnold's trailer, in regular use. And at every lunch there were these vats of vitamin pills sitting around the tent for them all to dip their hands into.'

So much for the gym and health club on the Titanic. What of the captain's bridge? Was the vessel being steered correctly from point A to point B? It began to seem not. Wild and interesting risks were being taken. With Arnold's approval, McTierman inserted in-jokes and frame-breaking fun into the film, which became more postmodern by the minute. In the sequence where Arnold plays himself, the star persuaded Maria to play herself at a glittering movie premiere within the movie. 'It took some heavy, heavy midnight discussions,' he recalls.

> I told her, 'All you have to do is be yourself and give me hell about the way I always plug my Planet Hollywood restaurant – just like you do when we go to any event.'

The giant new Columbia-Sony lobby was used as the film-within-film police headquarters. Here audiences could play spot-the-star with passing 'real' celebrities: Sharon Stone, Robert (*T2*) Patrick. In a video-store scene the filmgoer could giggle as Danny the boy hero looks at a poster advertising 'Sylvester Stallone in *Terminator 2: Judgment Day*'. And in an early vignette in a school classroom Joan Plowright, aka Lady Olivier, introduces a clip from Laurence Olivier's film of *Hamlet*, which a daydreaming Danny re-fantasises as an action movie trailer with Arnold playing Prince of Denmark. 'Something is rotten in the state of Denmark and Hamlet is taking out the trash!'

Last Action Hero was reaching that point common to many multi-screenwriter productions: secretly, everyone began to realise there *was* no script. An army of authors was labouring long and hard to produce a something-for-everyone film that contained little of substance for anyone. Even Charles Dance joined the contributors, writing his own dialogue and devising new scenes with McTiernan's encouragement.

I played two whole scenes to the camera, and I did a soft-shoe shuffle in one of them on 42nd Street with a bag lady at three o'clock in the morning. It was after shooting the guy I kill and saying 'Doesn't anyone care?' I turned to the camera and sang, 'What a day this has been, what a rare mood I'm in, it's almost like being in love . . .'

The scene hit the cutting-room floor. So, come post-production, did vast lengths of celluloid from all over the rambling movie. For alongside the pressure of trying to edit several hours of volitional chaos, there was the horror of the summer deadline. Columbia had decided that *Last Action Hero* would open in early summer, giving McTiernan just two and a half months for post-production. Soon triple crews worked around the clock, and tensions were such that a masseuse was summoned to relieve aching muscles. 'There was no panicked, oh-the-movie's-a-turkey feeling,' insists writer Shane Black. However, another gang of ill-omened birds was gathering: the media vultures.

The first public test screenings took place as quietly as Columbia could manage. The studio even denied that one ill-received sneak preview, held according to the *Los Angeles Times* in Pasadena, ever occurred. 'It absolutely never happened,' said Mort Gill, Columbia's Vice-President in charge of Publicity. 'I was never told about a screening in Pasadena.'

When the film opened, it was a night to remember. Out in Westwood, L.A.: the gala premiere, complete with searchlights, a hundred feet of red carpet and a giant inflatable effigy of Arnold straddling the village. Back in the scribes' and journalists' offices: the sound of a thousand men and women forming themselves into a human iceberg. The Titanic was approaching. Said 'Today''s Gene Shalit, making the sharpest incision in the hull: 'It was supposed to be a movie within a movie. Turns out it's a movie without a movie.' For another critic, it was '*Cinema Paradiso* from Hell.'

Charles Dance believes *Last Action Hero* was punished for not being an assembly-line Arnold film – and, top-secret previews apart, for being so relentlessly hyped.

People were afraid, according to one L.A. journalist, that they were being 'Schwarzeneggered'. It's like a gorgeous product in the supermarket imploring you to buy it; then you take it home and it's empty. It was not essentially Arnold's fault. It was the fault of the 'committee', because these kinds of films are always made by committees ultimately.

Columbia tried to make light of the debacle. In May Arnold was there in Cannes, along with his inflatable effigy moored at sea (the Mayor had forbidden it within the town), doing the kind of promo wonders that only he could do. However much he did, though, it was too little, too late.

On February 28th 1994 the *New Yorker* devoted a nine-page article to the effect of the film, and of other management decisions, on the balance sheets of Sony's first three years as a player in movieland. Despite assurances to the *New Yorker* from a Sony spokesman that *Last Action Hero* would eventually break even, an internal Columbia profit-and-loss statement revealed that after three months of release there was an 'unrecouped balance' of $124,053,994. This gave *Last Action Hero* precedence over *Heaven's Gate* as the largest flop in Hollywood history.

(iii) Postmodern Arnold

What would be the reaction of a man reared almost exclusively on success to his first major movie humiliation? Perhaps he would offer an Arnold paraphrase of Norma Desmond in *Sunset Boulevard*. 'I *am* big. It's the audiences that have got smaller.' Or he might summon his advisers to an Oak Plaza summit to remodel the Arnie image and career plan.

Or he might shrug it all off. Stanley Brooks remembers lunching with the star at Schatzi on the day the 'numbers' on *Last Action Hero* started coming in. '*Jurassic Park* had opened just before and it was obviously doing bigger business. *Variety* had some headline like "Lizards eat Arnold for lunch". But you could never tell from his manner. He was as upbeat and gregarious and confident as he was at the first studio screening, when everyone thought it would be a smash.'

Last Action Hero was a daring film: even an avant-garde one. It tried to go further than the norm but went too far.

The reality/fantasy agenda is no more outrageous than in *Bill and Ted's Excellent Adventure*. But while audiences throng to see a Zen screwball like Keanu Reeves break the bounds of the comical-dramatic universe, they associate Arnold with everything that is insanely steadfast. When he mocks himself in a movie, it must be deadpan, not semaphored. Any suspicion that Arnold on screen is 'in' on the joke as much as we – even though off-screen we know he is – destroys the fun.

Last Action Hero does not so much break the frame, it annihilates it. When everything can be postmodernly destabilised, why should the audience reach for any handhold or foothold? The gags are arch and self-advertising. Prattling to reporters at a gala premiere in one scene, Arnold-as-Arnold says, 'Dis movie, we only kill 48 people, compared to the last one, where we killed 119.' What was funny, though, about Arnold's previous real-life body counts was that we thought they might be serious.

Another self-defeating scene is Arnold's encounter with a cabbie. Charging through the streets with the boy hero at his side, he accosts a taxi and hauls its surly driver half out of his window. 'You've seen dose movies where they say, "Make muh day" or "Uh'm your worst nightmare,"' he breathes. 'Well, listen to dis one: "Rubber baby buggy bumpus."' Then he turns to the boy. 'Ha! You didn't know I was going to say that, did you?'

This joke on the talismanic one-liner is disastrous in two ways. First it announces, with a self-congratulating smirk, its awareness that these lines are little more than cynical marketing ploys to help a movie seduce its audience. Then it misunderstands, or seems to, their very magic. They are not nonsense mantras, but everyday sayings lent a scary-hilarious resonance by their new context. 'Make my day' was a lifeless cliché transformed by Clint Eastwood. Arnold's own 'I'll be back' took the dullest phrase in the language and used context to give it an uproariously brutal spin.

In a satirical essay on Arnold's postmodern tendencies, Ed Porter of *The Modern Review* fantasises a visit to the latest Schwarzenegger production only to find our hero impaled on the horns of this dilemma. States the superstar, after invoking Shakespeare, Stoppard and Pirandello: 'A civilised moviegoer should have the capacity to acknowledge a film as a fiction while simultaneously involving themselves whole-heartedly in that film.'

Arnold goes on to invoke Brecht's *verfremdungseffekt* – alienation effect – and other high-faluting reference points to champion the postmodernist impulse: all the while battling the man-hungry crocodile that has been thrown into a sewer with him.

It is hard to think of any other popular star today who could produce this delirium of mock-critical address in a thinking media journal. Porter's conclusion that Arnold cannot have his action cake and postmodernly eat it is proved right, it could be argued, by *Last Action Hero*.

At the same time self-invention and self-commentary, including self-mockery, are the leitmotifs of his whole career. As Adam Mars-Jones noted in his review of *Last Action Hero*, even the man's sporting background fits the pattern. 'In one way, Arnold Schwarzenegger should be ideal as the Aryanised icon, since bodybuilding is inherently a post-modernist sport . . . The prize-winning body is a piece of muscular development that is already in quotation marks; it wins prizes not for what it is capable of, but for what it looks like it is capable of.'

No wonder the world presses its nose to the PR bubble surrounding Arnold, trying to work out where amid the multiple inverted commas of his image, actions and words the truth lies; and if indeed the 'truth' does 'lie'. Shortly before *Last Action Hero* began shooting, a *Spy* magazine article by Charles Fleming flitted through the rumours and controversies that have accompanied Arnold's rise to fame. But the real subject of the piece is media manipulation.

Fleming quotes an unnamed Paramount executive as saying, 'Arnold exercises power the way the oldfashioned moguls did – they could make any problem go away.' When *Time* did a feature on him, reports Fleming, his publicist Charlotte Parker 'explained that the interview would be ended instantly if the reporters introduced the subject of Wendy Leigh's book, the Nazi affiliations of Arnold's father, or steroids.' Parker also once offered a magazine only thirty minutes of Arnold's time, claims *Spy*, in exchange for a cover story: she said, 'We don't want one of those long pieces that try to figure Arnold out.'

But how *do* you figure out a postmodern hero? Arnold the

public figure, if not Arnold the private individual, re-arranges himself constantly while we look. The man whose majoring subject is 'True Myths' keeps putting fresh quotation marks around himself, and the public accepts them. How else explain his ability to emerge unscathed from the brief flurry of media questions that followed the *Spy* article. After disarming newspaper reporters with the comment, 'It was wonderful fantasy writing, I can't wait until the movie', he was no less adroit on TV's 'Oprah Winfrey' show. Of the most scandalous item in the *Spy* pages – a full-frontal nude photograph dating from the 1970s, which Fleming had received from another unnamed source – Arnold chuckled, 'Why should I be upset about a nude photo I posed for for an artist, a sculptor? I've nothing to hide.' (Supportive laughter from audience.)

We search our minds in vain to remember hearing of any nude paintings or carvings of Arnold. Francesco Scavullo has since told this author that the *Spy* photo was one of those he shot for the never-published *Cosmopolitan* centrefold. 'It was such a bad print that I wasn't sure at first it was mine. But later we realised it was. I didn't feel like suing, though – you know, what for?'

On 'Oprah' the mystery/inconsistency of the photograph is no more followed up, in this media love-in masquerading as a talk show, than are other points of interest or controversy. When Winfrey asks about the Kennedy and Shriver family's reaction to the William Kennedy Smith rape trial Arnold shows his only moment of unease. He mutters something about not wanting to get into that and firmly but courteously clams up.

The reason he gets away with re-mythologising himself is that he does it with such a blithe, broken-accent charm and such hard-earned box-office credibility. Almost no one in America tries to stop him. Why should they? An Arnold kept happy is a meal ticket to journalists and TV reporters. In a 1993 poll he is voted the man most Americans would want to spend time talking to on a long-distance flight. The only person to outscore him is a woman – Oprah Winfrey – and lagging far behind are President Clinton, Madonna and Boris Yeltsin.

Arnold must go on as long as he amuses the great US public viewers. 'Never say die' is the motto both of his movie characters and of his own success; and it is the imperative that his American public has thrust upon him.

However, he *has* just made *Last Action Hero*. He *has* directed his first, underwhelming feature. And he *is* approaching middle age. 'Never grow old' may be a different proposition.

30

Man and Menopause

'You get to be a certain age, it's a plus.'

(i) Accessorise

In July 1992 Arnold reached that menopausal watershed, the age of 45. At the same time he put down a new marker as an action star by invoking the 'Age equals character' ruling. He told the *New York Times* in March 1993:

> Bob Rafelson said to me years ago: "Don't do any war movies or Westerns till you're forty, forty-five, because that's when you start looking interesting. You have good bone structure: it'll get better. I was insulted. I thought, wait a minute, I look great. What's he knocking my face for? But he was so right . . . You get to be a certain age, it's a plus.

Above the neck it might be. Below, matters would not improve with age – especially for a running, jumping, fighting action star – so other virility accoutrements became important. More than ever, in the early 1990s, the Pavlovian press panted in the wake of an accessorising Arnold. They reported on his cars, his offices and his speed-, status- and celebrity- symbols. Instead of the bulging pin-up for whom sloughing clothes was the significant action – the heroes of *Conan* and *Commando* and *Predator* the new Arnold donned new layers of machismo insignia.

Money was one. Knowing every dollar he owned, Arnold kept the public *au courant* with his Midas status even while seeming to mock it. Asked on TV whether wealth creates happiness, he said: 'No. Now with having fifty million dollars, it doesn't make me any happier than when I had forty-eight million.'

When his daughter Katherine visited the set of *Last Action Hero* he handed her a copy of *Daily Variety*: 'Here, Katherine, read the grosses, they're really interesting.' Katherine was three. Minutes later Arnold invoked the money question again to discourage her from standing next to him while a scene was being shot. 'Katherine, this company can afford only one Schwarzenegger, not two.'

Good knockabout stuff. However, it kept the idea of limitless wealth and eminence in front of the public's eyes. And as a good Republican, Arnold had a duty to champion power and prosperity in the dangerous, liberal-egalitarian age of Clintonism. In June 1993 a visiting GQ interviewer glimpsed the ominous mismatch between Arnold and the political times as they watched TV together.

> I am looking straight into Arnold's face at the very instant he learns that Clinton's income-tax surcharge is going to cost him close to $4m a year. If Arnold is sweating I cannot tell, since he is already wet (from a workout), but the tax package seems to have little visible impact. He continues chewing that cigar and sipping Swiss pear brandy and munching macadamia nuts and watching CNN without flinching, which is how movie heroes are supposed to act when they get bad news.

After 1992, Arnold's Democratic wife was able to crow over a national polls victory for her party: that cannot have been pleasant for him either.

In June '93 Arnold ventilated his discontent with the zeitgeist by writing to Clinton resigning as national physical fitness supremo. In the same year he accepted the chairmanship of the California Governor's Council of Physical Fitness and Sports. A thumbs-up for the favoured state from the man whose nation was now out of favour with him ideologically plus perhaps a hint of gubernatorial ambitions to come.

Besides, Arnold was building his own sovereign empire: who needed handouts from the White House? His greatest accessory as he fortified and embellished his middle years was his own office. Occupying half the third floor of his building complex in Main Street, Venice, it was a 2,500-square-foot monument to male self-assertion. 'For any guy,' says Arnold, 'an office is the only place where you can say, "This is exactly how I want it."'

It was designed by Japanese minimalist architect Ted Tanaka, who suited form to theme: 'Because of his bodybuilding background, I used some curved lines on the walls to express muscle and body tone.' Into this bio-visual space, aided by interior designer Waldo Fernandez, Arnold cast his trophies and treasures: the Conan sword; the bronze elephant sculpture, symbol of Republicanism, by Lorenzo E. Ghiglieri; the Robert Berks sculpture of JFK (a Democrat, but still an icon and in-law).

Under the seventeen-foot-high ceiling sits the two-thousand-pound solid aluminium conference table, with heavy screw-shaped legs designed by Arnold himself in the style of Austrian wine-presses. And the 'Austrian room' itself is nearby, where the star has set off a small, enclosed space for a bed and a dining area. Here amid the pine panelling Maria and the children will spend their visiting hours as if time-warped to old Thal. (A print of the village hangs on the wall.) Also conspicuous is the cradle where Arnold used to rock baby Katherine. 'I put it next to my desk and attached a rope that I would pull on. She fell asleep every time.'

This place is Arnold's grandest accessory: a home-from-home where the husband is master, housekeeper, cradle-rocker, chatelaine. But a fortress, even built by a Japanese minimalist, is too large to move. So more accessorising is needed. Wealth on wheels: virility as internal combustion.

What an idiosyncratic collection of wheels Schwarzenegger's are at this time. They indicate a man joyously aware that he encompasses the extremes of rugged pioneer and suave plutocrat. In April 1992 an English reporter poked his nose into the Casa Arnie vehicle compound. 'In the garage of his Spanish-style mansion in Pacific Palisades there are a Porsche, a Mercedes, an antique El Dorado Biarritz convertible, a Jeep and a Harley-Davidson motorcycle; but since Operation Desert Storm Arnold has been driving an ex-military Humvee (High Mobility Multi-Purpose Wheeled Vehicle).'

The Humvee was a seriously out-front acquisition, since no private citizen in America had one before Arnold, or was allowed to have one. Without the optional gun turret it cost the star $45,000. (The price paid by the US government for the basic Humvee was $26,000 when it bought twenty thousand of them for the war in the Persian gulf.) Arnold fell in love with the vehicle and drove it to and from World Gym. The children loved the Humvee. Only Maria resisted. 'She hated it at the beginning,' explains Arnold. 'She said to me, "I can't hear you at all, I can't concentrate." I said, "That's why I got it."'

Maria preferred the Gulfstream III private jet. This was reportedly given to Arnold as part of his *Terminator 2* deal. Arnold denies the report and says he bought it himself. Nineteen seats; grey carpet, blue-grey upholstery; VCR and stereo, plus a video screen system showing the plane's location on a map. It is said to have cost Carolco, the production company, (or Arnold) $12.75m.

However, the most spectacular vehicle of all to pass through his 'collection' must have been the NASA space rocket: not owned by him or driven by him but emblazoned with the title of his movie *Last Action Hero*. It crouched in its silo waiting for take-off in the summer of 1993. The name Schwarzenegger was spelled out in bold black letters along each of the six boosters while the film's title was daubed on the main fuselage. Arnold was wild about this publicity stunt initially; though his and Columbia's enthusiasm waned as the film's receipts came in. One studio executive ended up wringing his hands over the $500,000 folly: 'It's so embarrassing. It's like a joke. It's like putting Howard the Duck on the side of your rocket.'

Perhaps, *Citizen Kane*-style, we should search for a 'Rosebud' in Arnold's childhood to explain this *amour fou* with costly and overweening machines for motion. What formative joy made a steering wheel or joystick seem the definition of romantic, manly omnipotence?

Maybe it was the tank or tanks that meant so much to him in

boyhood. The one that took him to school, trundling majestically from Thal to Graz; or the one he might hitch a lift from, while traipsing home from the Graz gym in the early morning. These tanks contained, in legend at least, those people from a magical land – Americans! And finally there was the Austrian *panzer* he got to command during his own military service. Where is that vehicle now?

In America. It stands in front of one of the Planet Hollywoods, in Santa Ana, California. Arnold, through the Planet Hollywood company, bought it for twenty thousand dollars. As with the Humvee, no one was allowed to buy a military tank. But in August 1994 the Austrian cabinet sat in special session to agree that, at Arnold's request, an exception could be made for their most famous living expatriate.

(ii) Wheels With in Reels

For a movie star enamoured with vehicles, *True Lies* is the ultimate dream or nightmare. There are a horse, a helicopter, a Harrier jump jet: all subjected to violence or adventure. There are cars galore, screaming round streets or jumping off blown-up bridges. But the biggest vehicle of all is the movie – and that in turn was the biggest movie of all.

The estimated final cost was $120m, beating the previous record-holder *Terminator 2*: at least by the time this ultimate male accessorisation orgy – incorporating political incorrectness and lashings of sexism – had gone months over schedule and called on more expensive hardware than any film in history.

Arnold himself had approached director James Cameron with the idea after seeing the French comedy *La Totale*. He had been introduced to the movie by his brother-in-law Bobby Shriver, whose reward for bringing it round to Casa Arnie would be an executive producer credit on *True Lies*.

Arnold and Cameron used to go tooling around the canyons on their motorbikes – or 'hogs' as they called them – and when they stopped off at Patrick's Roadhouse the business talk would begin. 'I have the picture you want to do next,' the actor announced to the director, outlining the plot about an international spy whose double life ran to a mutually suspicious relationship with his wife. The high concept that appealed to Arnold was: here was a superhero influencing world events who could not handle, indeed was totally lost in, the smaller arena of his marriage.

We can only speculate about a connection between Arnold's interest in the theme of connubial tension and the fact that Maria was now spending more time – much more – with her family. In 1990 she had signed a new contract with NBC allowing her to be based in Los Angeles. The bi-coastal commuting was over: not least the two and a half years in which she had triangulated between L.A., New York (to anchor the Saturday edition of 'NBC Nightly News') and Washington (for 'Sunday Today').

Arnold and Maria therefore stumbled over each other much more often in Pacific Palisades. Neither could simply come home, slough off shoes and sit in mute solitude before TV, book or newspaper. The infrequent and manageable 'How was your week?' was replaced by the remorseless 'How was your day?'

Even if Arnold's interest in *La Totale* as launch-point for *True Lies* had no autobiographical subtext, the movie offered a new dramatic dimension. A middle-aged star tiring of *ubermenschkeit* could put some weathered humanity into the hokum. Half the film might be taken up with zapping the heavies with overkill toys (including a nuclear bomb). The other half – or middle third – would give us Arnold the actor, pixilated by marital crisis.

Also, the film would allow Arnold as suave CIA agent Harry Tasker – a quip, a tuxedo, a mission to save the free world – to pay tribute to his beloved James Bond. 'The past ten or fifteen years have not seen any of those great Bond movies,' the star expatiated. 'We wanted to bring that idea – the gadgets, the ballsy way Bond would do things – into the 90s.' Cameron put it more tersely. 'Bond's an ageing, alcoholic Brit. C'mon!! Let's pump some new blood into him!'

Filming began in August 1993 in a heat-wave. It ended one hundred and eighty shooting days later – Cameron claims a hundred and thirty – after a production history that made *Gone with the Wind* seem a quota quickie. Cameron's behaviour was true to his martinet reputation. During preparation on important stunts – almost wall-to-wall in the finished film – he would not allow people to wander off even at nature's call. Anyone who went to the bathroom could keep walking. That included Harry

Tasker, strapped into his Harrier jet hired from the US Defense
Department (cost of fuel $15,000 an hour).

> I am suspended twenty stories, thirty stories up, [recalls
> Arnold] and I have to go to the bathroom and he screams.
> 'No, you can't, you're now a military man on a mission.
> What if you're really a pilot and you have to fly an attack?
> Are you going to land and go the bathroom?' . . . *He* would
> rather pee in his pants than leave the scene when things are
> clicking.

Visual Effects Supervisor John Bruno, in constant attendance
at this time, has no memory at all of bathroom requests or
complaints. He recalls total compliance from Arnold, and even
that the star cried out at one point during the Harrier stunt
filming, 'Dis is where de money is!'

Still, filming was no paid vacation. 'In a scene on the rooftop
of the hotel,' says Arnold, 'the horse freaked out and almost
stepped literally over the rooftop. If he had taken one more
step, we would've fallen thirty feet to the ground.'

Meanwhile extras were hurled across the landscape in explosions; cars were thrown like confetti; and co-star Jamie Lee
Curtis, playing Arnold's wife, screamed and gesticulated at an
overhead rescue helicopter while trapped in a runaway limousine
fast approaching the end of a broken Florida bridge. 'The trick
to that is she was never in the car,' explains Cameron. 'She
was attached to the helicopter and the helicopter flew up and
matched the speed of the car and dropped her in there. So there
was never a way that she could go off with the car.'

Danger was in the eye of the deceived beholder. Another form
of trickery – computer opticals – ensured that there was no real
risk to actors or stuntmen in the Harrier jet sequence, which
provides *True Lies* with its deeply satisfying, deeply deranged
climax. Most normal action pictures would have ended with the
preceding scene: Harry Tasker and wife clinching, somewhere
on the Florida keys, against the backdrop of a nuclear explosion.
Instead we have a bonus ten minutes of the hero bouncing around
the Miami skyline in a metal monster, firing on high-rises and
bashing out skyscraper windows with the plane's tail while trying

to rescue his daughter from an Arab terrorist who has chased her to the edge of a building crane's arm.

After *True Lies'* stunts, special effects and overtime demands some crew members swore never to work with Cameron again. They took to walking past him wearing T-shirts blazoned with the message, 'TERMINATOR 3 – NOT FOR ME.' And the chief electrician would go up to the director while they prepared the latest set-piece to say, 'There's probably a way to make this harder, but you just haven't found it yet.'

Soon parties would rise up, however, who would make life hell for Cameron. The film's excuse for a global conflict was a group of gone-nuclear Muslim extremists called the 'Crimson Jihad'. Before *True Lies* opened, Arab-American organisations caught wind of its plot and began protesting to 20th Century Fox, even calling for the film's boycott. M.T. Mehdi, head of the National Council on Islamic Affairs, said: 'The movie will increase prejudice against the Arabs and Islam, pouring dirt on the image of 1.5 billion people who are opposed to terrorism.' Although Fox stuck a disclaimer on the end of the credits – 'This film is a work of fiction and does not represent the actions or beliefs of a particular culture or religion' – Mehdi claimed he had received 10,000 letters and thousands of phone calls from outraged viewers after the film's July opening. In Washington protesters gathered outside the film's opening, carrying placards parodying favourite Arnold mantras: 'Open Your Eyes and Terminate the Lies,' 'Hasta La Vista, Fairness.'

In the age of political correctness there is no such a thing as an innocent action film: especially if it steps into global politics. But the controversy over *True Lies* did not stop at outraged Muslims. Feminists resented the treatment of Jamie Lee Curtis's character: a mousy housewife who is first hauled through a CIA interrogation process after husband Arnie finds her *in flagrante* (as he thinks) with a car salesman and then tricked into performing a humiliating striptease. 'This is really to be taken lightly . . .' said a beleaguered Arnold on ABC TV's 'Good Morning America'. Asked at the film's London opening if the strip scene did not demean women, he sallied: 'No. I let my wife strip for me too. I don't know what household you have, how kinky you get in your house, but I think those kinds of things keep a marriage alive.'

As for the film's violence, deemed excessive by some, Arnold insisted on its cartoonish innocence. 'It's like *Raiders of the Lost Ark*, where the violence itself means nothing. That's one of the things we've done like the Bond films, where you really pay very little attention to showing bones crack or skulls being blown in.'

At the box-office *True Lies* went into immediate overdrive – $28m on the opening weekend – and then throttled disappointingly back. It would soon be overtaken by an unheard-of movie called *Forrest Gump*. The bad political reaction may have done it less harm than a general – and accurate – audience perception that Arnold was trying, for the second time in a row, to do a something-for-everyone epic; a comedy-action-romance that was firing on too many cylinders. *Daily Variety*'s critic summed up the film as '141 minutes of extravagant fodder for an enticing 3-minute trailer'. *Time* magazine pronounced the film 'a loud misfire', but predicted that audiences would like it. 'They will enjoy the lavish squandering of talent by Hollywood's shrewdest showman.'

The most effective Arnold moments, though, are the least lavish. He has a window of comic opportunity, gleefully opened, in the early scenes of the jealousy subplot. He does not so much 'act' jealousy here as signpost it. The Schwarzenegger voice, not known for its tendency to ricochet around the octaves, levels into a grimly comical monotone. The accent produces a new and menacing Arnold coinage: his wife is having an 'affee-ar'. And the glower is in the finest shape of his career: a mask of high-camp menace hewn from granite, with two searchlights for eyes. One moment this gaze is levelled from the passenger seat of a car at his suspected cuckolder (Bill Paxton); another it burns across the dining table at Curtis. Later still, magnified by the cockpit glass of the Harrier as the jet rises up behind a skyscraper window, it will spread panic among the baddies.

This is the film's grandest moment. Deus ex machina *in* machina. Arnold the avenger behind two walls of glass, his blurred and frowning face as mysterious, as majestic as the Turin Shroud.

After *Last Action Hero*, *True Lies* restores his credibility as a menace to humanity, or its most dangerously businesslike messiah. Though the hints of misogyny in the jealousy plot may not enhance the film's appeal to liberals, they help repudiate the larky, self-deprecating Mr Nice Guy of the earlier movie. It is refreshing to eavesdrop on one interview – with Michael Cartel of the *Vally Vantage* – and find that the public Arnold's chauvinist sexual politics are still in place.

> There was this whole thing with Tia [Carrere] and Jamie Lee [Curtis] [recounts Arnold]. Who would get to kiss me *more*? She [Carrere] sat on my lap for a long time and she kept kissing me and kissing and looked over at Jamie Lee Curtis and she says, 'I don't know how long *you* kissed Arnold' and all that, 'but this is what I do.' And she [Curtis] says, 'Bitch, get off his leg,' and all this. So in reality there was this jealousy, and who was doing the tango the longest with me and all those kinds of things which I enjoyed because I didn't egg that on.

'Oh, he wished!' was Jamie Lee Curtis's only comment.

True Lies the movie and *True Lies* the promo campaign are full of the sound of Arnold backpedalling from PC postmodern pieties. Was our hero returning to his gung-ho roots? Certainly in November 1993, after two previous fatherhood bouts that had produced daughters, Arnold made amends to the god of machismo with a newborn son, Patrick. The boy entered the world at 6.30.am – bodybuilder's wake-up time – and weighed nine pounds.

To celebrate, Arnold expanded his domestic empire. With three children and a wife it was clearly impractical to live in a mere seven-bedroom, 6,500-square-foot house in Pacific Palisades. So Arnold bought the house next door from actor John 'Dynasty' Forsythe. The price was around $3m. The purchaser would maintain both homes, using Casa Forsythe initially as a guest house. In addition he installed a $100,000 basketball court for his baby son

The new, improved, territorial Arnold is also reported to have paid $3,150 to a local lobbyist, Kei Uyeda, to help speed through City Hall an application to regain a 300-by-40-foot plot of land adjoining Casa Arnie. The city had taken over the land to extend a road, but under Arnold pressure they agreed to shelve the plan. 'You can't fight city hall,' goes the American proverb. Arnold told the proverb to drop dead.

It is bracing, in these early years of the pre-millenial decade, to find Arnold counterattacking whenever he has a setback. After *Last Action Hero* he stormed back, more or less, in *True Lies*. Piqued by the Clinton accession, he turned from Washington and acquired a nameplate in the California corridors of power. After two daughters he begat a male heir, destiny assisting patriarchal desire. And after the minor humiliation of seeing his Hollywood Boulevard 'star' dug up in April 1994, when his and other performers' paving stones were removed during extension work on the Los Angeles underground system, he had the consolation in July of plunging his hands and feet into wet cement in another ritual sacred to the Avenue of the Stars. Arnold wore size-12 cowboy boots, signed his trademark line 'I'll be back' and told the 3,500 watching fans, 'This is absolutely a great honour and a great pleasure.'

Arnold was so comfortable now with his own achievements and his own masculinity that he could take the ultimate leap of courage. He could play the role we have unspokenly dared him to. A woman; or rather a man who gets pregnant.

31

Germination

'I think that you could play anything you want. But the audience wouldn't believe it. I couldn't play Tootsie. I'm too big to put on a dress and put on high heels.'

(i) Pregnant

There were a lot of movie ideas floating around in late 1993. Almost any producer with $15m to spare would want to hire Arnold, even after the shock to the star system that was *Last Action Hero*. *True Lies* had not been completed, but it was expected to restore the actor to his rightful place in the pecking order: number one.

Producer Bernie Brillstein tried and failed to get Arnold for a self-spoofing comedy turn – 'We'll only need him for two or three or weeks' – in his Columbia project *Hans and Franz Go to Hollywood in Search of Arnold* (still unmade). Perhaps the star drew the line at too broad a mocking of his image. One Schwarzenegger taking the mickey (himself) was permissible. Three people doing so – himself plus 'Saturday Night Live's Dana Carvey and Kevin Nealon – might be overkill.

As if to make the point, Arnold accepted a solo spot as 'himself' in another film. Ivan Reitman cast him in a tiny cameo in *Dave*. Arnold is the fitness supremo barking dietary orders at President Kevin Kline as the two men host a White House children's party: 'Let me tell you a little bit about di*ssoo-erts* [desserts],' rasps Arnold. 'What you don't want to do is eat doughnuts.

248

No doughnuts!' Arnold hurls an offending pastry away, then joshingly turns his handshake with Kline into an arm-wrestle forcing the world leader to the floor.

Meanwhile a third project was in play that proposed Arnold for the role of Arnold. His wife Maria was labouring at a script based on their own life. The idea for this 'sentimental comedy' had been lodged with super-agent Mike Ovitz, then head of the powerful Creative Artists Agency, much to the fury of Arnold's agency, the equally powerful International Creative Management. Maria's plot concerned a Republican who marries into a Democratic family. Ovitz placed it with Universal and Ivan Reitman was lined up to direct. Since 1993, however, the project has vanished into limbo or into development hell.

So what *would* be the next star vehicle? Two projects beckoned. One was another Reitman comedy: the story of two scientists, to be played by Arnold and Danny DeVito, who stumble on a miracle pregnancy drug and seek a male to male to test it. For this low-budgeter, as with *Twins*, the two stars would waive upfront fees in return for a percentage of the gross. By contrast *Crusade*, a Paul Verhoeven project, was an awesome mega-bucker set in the 11th century which promised to deliver Arnold to the world on a horse. He would play the knight Hagen, caught up in the First Crusade, and would claim his $15m before the first clapperboard struck.

Written by Walon Green of *The Wild Bunch*, *Crusade* became a logistical and financial headache. The production company Carolco wanted to make sure they would get value for money. The budget would almost certainly climb to $120m, with battle scenes and location sequences. So Arnold would have to be surrounded by fine actors who did not cost much. John Turturro would play the evil brother. Newcomers would play significant other roles. Robert Duvall might play a guest cameo.

A well-known British actor who prefers to be nameless was also sounded out. The script did not impress him.

It was like Monty Python's *Holy Grail* without the laughs. Well, the laughs were there, but I don't think they were intentional. The part they wanted me to play gets chopped in half with a broadsword and his lower trunk falls to the ground. It's just like the scene with John Cleese getting quartered and saying 'Come on, fight me!'

You can imagine it on the big screen, though. One scene in the script describes the camera pulling back and you see *thousands* of people going off to the crusades. It would look absolutely sensational.

Paul Verhoeven, not surprisingly, agrees. Hence the sticking point of a nine-figure budget.

The more I know of the logistical difficulties, the high price of shooting in Europe, I don't see how I can do it for less. I'm talking about scenes where you take 10,000 people, move them through the mountains, then have battle scenes with that many people and 1,500 horses. My vision in developing the script was to make it an epic, and I've said to Walon Green that if you make it smaller, it's not the *Crusade*, it's *The Wild Bunch* in the 11th century.

The film was abandoned by Carolco in May 1994 as too expensive, even with Arnold offering to trim his fee by $5m in return for a share in merchandising rights. By year's end, though, the actor had secured the rights himself and was encouraging a bidding war, with Warner and Buena Vista making the loudest noises. In October Mikhail Gorbachev sat across a table from the actor at the Environmental Media Association's awards ceremony in Los Angeles. The Russian offered to negotiate the deal. 'I used to be a lawyer,' explained Gorbachev. Arnold made a note.

Junior was the chosen film for an early summer shoot, with a view to Christmas release. As a Schwarzenegger project it has a high-concept surrealism – Arnold gets pregnant – and would surely be ideal for a reunion with DeVito. After they had played twins, little else could 'up the ante' in saleable preposterousness than to cast them as male mother and surrogate midwife.

Arnold brushed aside doubts about the effect on his image.

'When you're a stud like myself, and you're so gutsy and ballsy, you can communicate with your feminine side. I don't have any hang–ups about that . . . I've always sympathised with my wife when she was pregnant and understood something of what she was going through.'

'I remember her throwing up in the car' he recalls.

'on the way to a major party or something. We stopped the car on Sunset Boulevard so that she could stick her head out over the gutter. She – [he makes gagging sound], and then sat back in the car. We went on to the party and never talked about it again.'

Actress Emma Thompson, swirling in from Britain to play the scatterbrained doctor who 'fathers' Arnold's child by donating one of her eggs, applauded the actor's nerve. 'I've always been fascinated by him. He is a self–made myth, someone who has invented himself and stayed in control of himself. Then he makes this film in which he loses control of his body. Arnold of all people.'

If there was a squeak of appehension here, there was a seizure of anxiety in the mind of longtime Arnold collaborator Adam Greenberg. The cinematographer who had perfected the infernal palette for the Terminator films now sat behind the camera, thinking up nursery pastels for what he considered a wholly misguided Arnold project.

It's not a sympathetic story. It's not pleasant to see a big, well–known star like Arnold pregnant. I didn't express myself, but we'd be doing the movie and I'd be looking at Arnold asking myself, 'Why does he do the film? With his image, why does he go so far?' But I told myself I was wrong. Everyone else – the producer, director – thought it would be well received, and Arnold was so excited.

Even Arnold *might* have been aware that he was entering dangerous territory. There was the risk of trauma, for instance, on his children. They visited the set on the day their father was in disguise for his visit to the maternity clinic. 'I was wearing a dress, wig, glasses and for the role I was eight months pregnant. The girls were saying, "Mummy, where's Daddy?" Maria pointed to me. They said, "No way – this is not Daddy!" I had to take the wig off to convince them . . . I think they were a bit worried.' (He adds to another reporter, 'I picked the dress myself by a way. Did you like the minty colour?')

Director Ivan Reitman too became worried. 'When I was dressed as a woman, people treated me differently,' says Arnold. 'They treated me much sweeter and nicer . . . Ivan caught himself touching me more and sitting with me. He said, "I don't know what's the matter with me: Every time you sit down, I feel like hugging you."'

Arnold on screen seems to take the role to heart. He does not clatter about in a chaos of parodic denial, like a pantomime dame. Instead, catching a myopic gentleness of manner from the round-rimmed specs he wears as fertility doctor Alex Hesse, he plays recessive male to Emma Thompson's batty colleague. Finally, he becomes bizarrely touching as his new pregnancy turns TV-watching into an orgy of sentimentality – he weeps at a commercial depicting nuptial bliss – and reacts to his bodily changes with a series of sweetly muttered asides: 'Muh nipples are very senzitive.'

Has Arnold been taking illicit doses of Stanislavsky – or sneaking off to Eric Morris again? When he talked during production interviews about 'acting' pregnancy, he sounded disturbingly earnest. 'It was not the obstacle I thought it would be. It's great when it's really big, it's more hard physically. All of a sudden I can't tie my shoes anymore, and you do feel the weight. When I take Katherine to school, I watch the pregnant mothers wobbling around, just to get a feeling of how much there is.'

Arnold's performance won a Golden Globe nomination for Best Actor in a Comedy or Musical: his first whiff of an award since *Stay Hungry*, though he was beaten to it by Hugh 'Four Weddings and a Funeral' Grant. The figures coming in from the box office, however, were less flattering. After enthusiastic early notices and word-of-mouth – *Variety*'s review predicted that *Junior* would take the 'seasonal box-office crown' – the film slid down the charts. It performed especially poorly in the American South, where conservative audiences shunned the biologically surreal premise. Co-screenwriter Chris Conrad admitted that the concept was 'really a test for men' and 'a shock. 'The ones who are secure go easily, the ones who are not secure don't,' she said. 'It is a new concept and people are afraid of the new.'

The final American tally was a mere $30m: poorer even than *Last Action Hero*, though from a more modest budgetary starting-point. *Junior* had disappointing reviews outside America, especially in Britain. But it scraped together $100m worldwide.

'I think the movie was done in too serious a way,' opines Adam Greenberg. 'It it had gone more into slapstick comedy, it would have worked better. It's too serious and it scares the audience, they pull away.'

Longtime Arnold fans, most of all, may have pulled away: those who never wanted to see a dent – let alone an incongruous swelling – in that macho physique. An Arnold sometimes accused of taking too few risks with his box-office image might have taken one too many.

But what should a star do? Sit back and let the public dictate his output – let movie audiences get him serially pregnant with the roles *they* want him to play? Or should he indulge his own whims and instincts, however high-risk?

Designing Arnold – the self-made icon who tirelessly patterns his own career – co-exists with 'Designer Arnold', the label formed in his name and from his raw material by other people. These may be film-makers, or the public influencing the film-makers. Or they may be the Arnold chroniclers and mythographers who wage constant war over their rival perceptions of Arnold's life and image.

(ii) *The Song of Arnold*

This is a true myth zone all its own, with its own contrasting minstrelsies. Take two examples: one Arnie fan, one foe. The fan is Robert Kennedy (no relation to Arnold's in-laws). He is the editor of *MuscleMag*, a Canadian-based magazine whose regular 'Arnold Hotline' is the world's – or the Schwarzenegger world's – most fulsome outpouring of obsequious gossip and journalistic kiss-blowing.

Arnold and Maria's new baby! Arnold and Maria's new restaurant!! Arnold's latest box-office record!!! Kennedy is there feeding it to his readers in a cataract of ragged-right prose on shiny coloured paper, with pin-up insets of Arnold looking ever young, ever smiling.

Kennedy is also well to the fore in defending Arnold when scandals threaten or when *Spy* magazine full-frontal nude photos hit the stands. 'Personally,' he writes, 'I think that Arnold's *Spy* pic further emphasises his state of comfort with his whole body . . . it seems to us that everyone's making a big deal out of a very insignificant matter [sic].'

The Arnie foe is the man who supplied *Spy* magazine with the nude picture in the first place. Los Angeles-based Lacey H. Rich Jr devotes his life, or much of it, to circulating all the bad news he can find about the actor. He has a computer and fax machine, crouched in an apartment berserk with files, dossiers, overflowing ashtrays and unprocessed coffee cups. He runs whatever is the opposite of a fan club – a fiend club? He regularly bombards leading newspapers and magazines, as well as private subscribers and Arnold ill-wishers, with updated news on the megastar from Middle Europe.

Much of the malevolence is aimed at current or former Arnold friends or associates with allegedly shady pasts, in the hope that it will bounce off them and hit the man himself.

When I ask Rich why he is doing all this, he says it is for his close friend the bodybuilder Mike Mentzer. Mentzer fell apart emotionally (claims Rich) after Arnold snatched that controversial Sydney 'comeback' trophy in 1980. Rich helped to look after him, since he managed the apartment building where Mentzer used to stay. Mentzer has no comment on this, beyond acceding that I can take Rich's word for most things and wryly commenting on the breadth of Rich's expertise on everything relating to the years after that controversial Mr Olympia contest. 'When I hear Lacey discourse on the subject,' says Mentzer, 'I'm literally amazed at how extensive his knowledge is, much greater than mine.'

It may *be* that dubious deeds have been committed in the past by people close to Arnold: deeds that Rich is eager to circulate but that no magazine or newspaper in America seems to want to print. Maybe the media think the 'mud' is too vague and unverifiable – let alone non-specific to Arnold – to stick. Maybe too, as *Newsweek*'s Charles Fleming theorises, journalists are waiting for Arnold to attempt the leap from screen to political platform before activating any smear campaign.

'The Hollywood reporters are one thing,' says Fleming. 'But it's nothing to what "real" reporters could do if they really got him. They'd eat him alive. If there are scandalous facts in his past, they would be exposed to the harshest sort of light if he was a candidate for the governorship of California.'

Arnold's friend and business partner Jim Lorimer surprisingly agrees.

> He's got tremendous pressure to run for office. There's strong money and inclination for him to run, from top Republicans [Lorimer declines to name them] and he'd be a very viable candidate for California. He's an attractive personality, he's extremely bright and he 'lives' the American Dream. But my counsel to him is to continue the career he's in. Going into politics creates burdens and pressures for you and your family. There are people out there ready to tear you apart if you put yourself up for public office.

If he did, though, how good or bad a politician would Arnold be? Wendy Leigh, we know, sees him as another, worser Reagan. Lacey Rich, when I press him further on why he conducts his vilification campaign, says:

> *Pumping Iron* was an exercise in brainwashing and we've never recovered from it. It's the whole male mystique of the superior man . . . We are talking today about a bodybuilder turned 'actor' who potentially could become senator or governor, then President of the United States. If he could get the Constitution changed. And with Arnold's track record I'm not sure he couldn't manage that. And I'm damned if I'm going to see this hypocrisy elected to public office in this country.

But a skill at using the mythmaking machinery of PR and image salesmanship hardly seems a disqualification for high office. Every leader, popular or unpopular, uses it. More likely to disqualify Arnold is his lack of – well, qualifications. Few of California's top political pundits seem to credit the idea of 'Senator (or Governor)' Schwarzenegger.

'It was talked about a couple of years ago, but the story hasn't had much play recently,' says Bernard Weinraub, Los Angeles bureau chief of the *New York Times*. 'Arnold comes out when he has a fitness thing to promote; he may have done a little campaigning in the last election; but as a political personality or campaigner he's not very visible.'

Sam Popkin, Professor of Political Science at the University of California in San Diego, begins by citing one major Austrian-born precedent for high office in the USA: ex-Secretary of State Henry Kissinger. But then he casts doubt on whether Arnold has found the political footholds from which to climb to state or congressional power, let alone to the presidency.

If you compare him to Ronald Reagan, Reagan was the President of the most powerful union in the state, the Screen Actors Guild. He'd had a lot of hands-on experience. He had campaigned for Goldwater, he had been a radio commentator and a spokesman for capitalism. Running for Governor was the third or fourth step, not the first. Also, Reagan came up when two or three strong positions were what were needed. What's Arnold as a gung-ho Republican going to offer? We already have the death penalty in California; we already have three-strikes-and-you're-out imprisonment.

I can't imagine the Republicans feeling they need him. People of high visibility and glamour are grasped when it's felt that nobody else can do it. But the Democratic party looks so messy right now that all the Republicans think they can win and they don't need a big hunk to run for them.

Even some Arnold admirers who think he *could* make a go of politics are not sure he should. 'I don't know if this is good for him,' says Simon Wiesenthal. 'He is working in one field, successfully, and should remain, and do charity. When I talk to him, I think he feels that fame and money give him an obligation: to carry on doing something for people who are in need.'

Arnold himself has long realised that politics may be a loser's game. Interviewed by the *New York Times* back on the set of *Last*

Action Hero, he said, 'Why should I run for governor? Look at the life I have now. I can sit here casually, smoking a cigar. I couldn't do that in the Governor's office. They'd attack me immediately and say I looked like a gangster.' Instead he can sit on movie stages 'having schmoozing sessions with film journalists who are quite different from political journalists who are always on the attack'.

Today, says Jim Lorimer, he is still resistant. 'He hasn't warmed to the idea. But he's forty-seven and you have to ask, what new goals and challenges does a person look for who's succeeded in so many areas? That's the factor that might count: that he's looking for some new hill to climb.'

Especially now that two out of three recent films – *Last Action Hero* and *Junior* – have tottered at the box office, prompting us to ask if Arnold is a victim of the zeitgeist. Is he an Eighties movie hero (Reaganism, patriotism, self-help) fallen on soft times – a macho-man trapped in the feelgood, irresolute Clintonite Nineties?

'That's too facile,' believes film critic Pauline Kael. 'If he's an Eighties phenomenon, why isn't he accepted now along with the Republican revival and Newt Gingrich? He should be having a recrudescence. Maybe his celebrity days are numbered unless he can find another alien to play.'

If Arnold's political future is under siege from the sceptics, we should remember that 'Can't be done' or 'Shouldn't even try' is what everyone said about his previous careers. Skinny Austrian boy could not be Mr Universe. Man with unwieldy name, accent and body could not be major movie star.

Since late 1994 his political manoeuvres have kept us guessing. In October '94 he crossed party lines to support his uncle-by-marriage Ted Kennedy's campaign to be re-elected senator for Massachusetts. Then he made amends to his own party in April 95 by turning up on Washington's Capitol Hill to support the Republican man of the hour, Newt Gingrich. 'Our leader!', proclaimed Arnold, in a phrase whose Nurembergian ring put the press on thrilled red alert. 'Sieg Newt' ran one headline.

In July, pushing his political horizons still further, Arnold visited Israel. During a 24-hour stopover in Tel-Aviv he spent half an hour with Prime Minister Yitzhak Rabin talking about 'some of the important things in peace negotiations that are going on now which I'm fascinated with'. Having received the keys of the city, he then released a white dove from a restaurant rooftop and cried, 'Shalom! And I'll be back!'

Even Sylvester Stallone in these momentous Ninties, has contributed his genuflection to statesman Schwarzenegger: albeit on screen, albeit ironically. In the sci-fi thriller *Demolition Man*, a time-transported Sly finds himself in a 21st-century cab with futuristic heroine Sandra Bullock. She is updating him on world crises. 'I have in fact perused the newsreels from the Schwarzenegger Library', she says. 'Hold it,' interjects a shocked Stallone; 'the *Schwarzenegger* Library?' 'Yes, the Schwarzenegger Presidential Library. Wasn't he an actor when you –?' 'Stop. He was *President*?' 'Yes. Even though he was not born in this country, his popularity at the time caused the 61st amendment, which states that –'. Stallone cuts her off with an emphatic groan: 'I don't want to know. (looking away) *President!*'

It makes good comedy. Yet for all the historical and logistical obstacles strewn in his path, Arnold's political preferment also makes disconcerting sense. Since this man has already turned every fence to matchwood as he smashes through the Great American Dream Steeplechase, a United States faithful to its historical self-image as a giant immigrants' jump-off almost *owes* the Presidency to its greatest modern hurdle-crasher.

We should add to the actuarial calculations Arnold's own competitive streak, exacerbated by twenty years of love-hate intimacy with the country's 'first family' in politics. How long before the fuse runs out on this man's patience with the Kennedy legend, igniting his urge to outperform it?

32

Endgame

'There's something very outrageously funny about sitting around a table and listening to me, all the crap that I have to say and all this stuff. It's all funny. Life is funny.'

(i) Ownership and Disposal

The year 1995 was a typical one for a superstar and public figure. Arnold once more increased his domestic domain in Pacific Palisades. Two years after taking receipt of John Forsythe's front-door key, he bought the two-million-dollar, 5,000-square-foot mansion of his other next-door neighbor, actor Daniel J. Travanti. He now owns three houses in a row, with a combined bedroom count of fifteen and a total value of just under $10m.

Not to be housebound, Arnold spent the rest of the year kissing babies, glad-handing statesmen and cutting ribbons: not least on his own expanding empire of cities hosting the Inner City Games, those sports jamborees for underprivileged urban children. He was in Miami in spring 1995 at a Hollywood binge where the price for two guests – dinner and pre-reception – was $5,000 and where for another $84 you could join the 'adopt-a-kid' scheme. In Atlanta he took five sledghammer whacks at a wall in a 'wallbreaking ceremony', to mark the enrolment in Arnold's Games of the city soon to spread its attention to the Olympics.

Together, Arnold and Maria blessed another opening in November 1995. As benefactors of Santa Monica's St John's Hospital they had funded the rebuilding and decorating of its nursery. In the very maternity wing where Maria had delivered past Schwarzenshrivers she accepted a commemorative plaque, declaring, 'This is a place near and dear to our hearts. It makes me want to have another baby.' Standing at her side, Arnold gave a gentle smile.

The couple had weathered a difficult year. In April there was the embarrassment of a paternity lawsuit. 'Arnold Love Child Scandal' cried the tabloids when Debra Wrenn, a Texas mother, claimed that the bodybuilder had impregnated her in Indianapolis on January 14th or 15th 1982, after the couple had met at the Naughty Lady nightclub.

The evidence, said the mother, was thirteen-year-old Christina: a child bearing no discernible resemblance to the Austrian Oak, though the plaintiff insisted the bairn was his. 'Maybe he felt he had to prove himself as a man,' she theorised, 'during that long gap between the time they were going together [Arnold and Maria] and when they got married.' Arnold's lawyer in turn theorised that his client had never been in the said city on the said date. In August the case was thrown out by a Texas court when Arnold agreed to take a DNA and blood test.

The actor also emerged unscathed from the revelations of Heidi Fleiss, a Hollywood 'madam' keeping the gossip presses whirring during 1995 with tales of errant stars and executives. In July Arnold won a lawsuit against the French magazine *Voici* for reporting that he had bought one of the lady's prostitutes, according to the testimony of an ex-Fleiss employee who claimed he had been her client. 'When publications and tabloids print those statements about me,' the star averred, 'I intend to take swift action to protect my good reputation that I have established.' Though the magazine refused to print a retraction, it paid undisclosed damages, which Arnold gave to the Special Olympics in France.

As well as repudiating sex rumours, the Schwarzeneggers survived the latest round of tattle about their political differences. As America readied itself for a new White House contest, the Clinton-supporting Maria reaffirmed her tolerant views of a husband still attached to the other party. 'When you marry someone, you marry them in sickness and in health. Republican politics is Arnold's sickness.'

Arnold, though, seemed healthier than his supposed political betters. In May 1995 Presidential contender Bob Dole visited Hollywood to expatiate on the film industry and lost no time in placing his foot in his mouth. Addressing a dinner for six hundred business leaders and party stalwarts, Dole excoriated libertine film-makers such as Oliver Stone *(Natural Born Killers)* and Quentin Tarantino *(True Romance)* for their violent movies – 'a line has been crossed, not just of taste, but of human dignity and decency' – while mysteriously describing Arnold's mayhem-intensive *True Lies* as 'friendly to the family'.

The newspapers purred in delight, sensing a super-gaffe. Dole's aides made matters worse by pointing out that the Senator had not seen all – or possibly any – of these films. And one Hollywood VIP, director Rob Reiner, spoke up for the rest when he said, 'The only reason he doesn't lambast a film like *True Lies* is because Schwarzenegger is a Republican.'

Arnold showed a pro's skill in standing away from this furore, but soon backed into another one scarcely less noisy. A script of the unmade *Crusade* found its way to England and sprang leaks all over the Sunday newspapers. To the media's righteous glee, this long-nursed Schwarzenegger project boasted material so violent and provocative that even Republicans might struggle to class it as family entertainment. Attention was brought to two scenes in particular, in one of which Christians eat their Muslim victims, while in the other freshly-lopped Muslim heads are used as catapult missiles. In America the Atlanta-based Christian Film and Television Commission vowed to place advertisements in Hollywood trade journals publicising 'the grossly false depiction of Christians', although non-Western historians countered that episodes of Christian cannibalism, if not of human heads used for ammunition, are well documented.

It is a far cry from Planet Hollywood, where both the menu and the milieu enjoy trans-denominational approval across the world. Although the Arnold-Sly-Bruce restaurants have now extended into twenty-nine international sites, from New York to Honolulu and Helsinki, business experts were still surprised in February 1996 when plans were announced to float its shares for an anticipated $1.2bn. Rival restaurant tycoons claimed this was twice the chain's value. Though the company turned a profit in

1995, it had spent the previous four years losing money, with reported debts of $120m.

But perhaps Wall Street saw the 'futures' potential in hype and Hollywood input. Provided the stars stayed in close conjunction with the Planets – that is, Arnold and company continued to eat and be ogled at the brand-name burgeries – here was a bankable universe: one whose actor-stakeholders would be worth the $40m each that the flotation was expected to bring. Meanwhile, the company identity must be ruthlessly protected. In late 1995 Arnold stood elbow to elbow with Sylvester Stallone as the two men brought an action against a whippersnapper Indian eatery in London that had dared to call itself 'Planet Bollywood'.

It was tactical for other reasons to keep in with Sly. The veteran superstar's career was showing startling if erratic signs of revival. In 1995 Stallone began piling up movie contracts like gold bars, crowned by a $20m deal for an untitled Warner project that was deemed the highest offer ever made to an actor by a major studio. On June 3rd Stallone received the Icon Award as history's top-grossing action adventure star at the Blockbuster Entertainment Awards.

But any professional envy Arnold may have felt was dispelled by the performances of Sly's movies. One by one *The Specialist, Judge Dredd* and *Assassins,* all projects that had once been whispered as Schwarzenegger vehicles, tottered or collapsed at the box office, demoting the Stallone career to normal stardom. In 1996 the actor expressed his disappointment with destiny by changing agencies. He deserted ICM for William Morris, piqued in part (claimed the trades) by his failure to secure the coveted role of Mr. Freeze in Warner's promised major production for 1996, *Batman and Robin.* The refrigerating villain, once played with memorable Teutonic menace in the *Batman* TV series by Otto Preminger, would now be played by an even more famous Teuton: Arnold Schwarzenegger.

(ii) Eraser

This assignment, however, was not yet a gleam in Arnold's agenda during the long summer of 1995 when, after *Junior's* disappointing birth, he pondered the best way to return to screen in a commanding role. In July he briefly re-activated the *Terminator* franchise to film a $50m 3D spectacular, under James Cameron's direction, for the Universal Studios theme park in Florida. Despite one miscarried stunt – 'I'll be back', Arnold boomed to onlookers as he was stretchered off to hospital for a few hours – the *Terminator* attraction was wrapped and is due to open in April 1996.

Then again, directing a movie himself might be an option: especially since most people had forgotten *Christmas in Connecticut*. That film's producer Stanley Brooks asked Arnold if he had any ideas. Something 'a little more dramatic that stayed in the family area', Brooks was told. 'Something like *Heidi*.'

Heidi? Directed by Arnold Schwarzenegger? 'It takes place in his homeland,' Brooks points out. But even he thought it was stretching things. Also, there was the risk that people might confuse one Heidi with another, expecting a tale of loose-lipped Hollywood madams. So the two men agreed to consider another girl-comes-of-age-in-beautiful-surroundings story, the 1950s children's novel *The Good Master*. A script went into development by Jenny Wingfield, who had written a favourite sentimental movie of both Brooks and Arnold, *The Man in the Moon*.

As an actor, though, it had to be back to manly heroism, perhaps with a fresh vision behind the camera. Arnold's last five films had all been directed by Schwarzenegger veterans: James Cameron (*T2* and *True Lies*); Ivan Reitman (*Kindergarten Cop* and *Junior*); and John 'Predator' McTiernan (*Last Action Hero*). Scored up, that was one success, two narrow victories and two humiliations. Time for a new face shouting 'Action'.

On the ski slopes of Aspen and Sun Valley, Arnold had befriended Charles 'Chuck' Russell. In 1994 Russell had put himself in the A-list of Hollywood directors with *The Mask,* a crazed special-effects comedy, whose greatest special effect was newcomer and overnight star Jim Carrey.

If Russell could make stars, he could remake them. Arnold and he pored over scripts through summer, fall and winter of '94. *Captain Blood* was the early favourite, with Arnold pencilled to re-enact the Errol Flynn role. But was the world ready for an Austrian pirate? *Attila the Hun* was a more serious, form-fitting proposition: the tale of a musclebound tyrant who was stopped by history at the very gates of Arnold's near-native Vienna. It was full of blood, violence and primitive politics. It would need careful nurturing, though, if it was not to seem a back-flip to the *Conan* days.

Finally they found a crime thriller they liked called *Eraser.* Its debut writer Tony Puryear was a serial careerist after Arnold's heart: he had been a painter, chef and advertising executive before writing. His screenplay was inspired by news stories suggesting that America's famous 'witness protection programme' – whereby endangered informants plus families are whisked off to new homes and identities by the FBI – was a disaster waiting to happen, or a scandal waiting to break.

'For the price of a cup of coffee you can bribe an FBI agent,' says Puryear; 'these formerly spotless guys who're now riddled with corruption. I thought, suppose there were some last incorruptible men – for whom it's a mark of honour to protect anyone, no matter how scummy'. So his plot revolves around one of these last just men, who has a damsel to protect, a perfidious colleague to outwit and miles to go before sleeps.

The first 'Arnold' with whom the script landed was Kopelson, not Schwarzenegger. The producer of *Platoon* and *The Fugitive* saw *Eraser* as a star vehicle. Steven Seagal was sounded out, but Kopelson thought they could do better. Harrison Ford and Mel Gibson were mooted. Then, enter a large Austro-American.

Puryear, who had crafted his FBI hero in the tough-underdog mould of late Clint Eastwood, was aghast – 'Who you gonna get to beat up Arnold Schwarzenegger?' But he set about the required revisions, which included trying to explain the Arnold accent. 'We handled it by saying the hero had been an orphan kid from the war in Europe. And he'd had this really fuckcd-up childhood before joining the US army. We wanted to establish that our FBI "erasers" came from the military'.

Soon Puryear became privy to the strange world of an Arnold pre-production. The star would ring him up in the middle of the night to ask what clothes he would be wearing. 'You mean, symbolically?' Puryear would say, 'like, are you wearing a veil of black in pain?' 'No, no,' said Arnold, 'what do I way-er?' (Puryear gives the accent full value.) 'Because you know, Tony, in *Toorminater* I'm wearing de leather chacket, in *Commando* I'm wearing de vest and nice haircut. So what do I way-er?' Puryear soothed him with sartorial suggestions and returned to sleep.

Earlier, the writer had spent a long day at Arnold's office and at Schatzi's going through the star's copious script notes. Bodyguards stood about with walkie-talkies, flunkies danced attendance with plates of fresh-picked strawberries as Arnold riffled through the queries he had jotted on four pages of a legal pad. 'On page 34, you know, I'm wondering, is this de woman or is dis not de woman, because she's in disguise heah...'

According to Puryear, Arnold never once behaved like a star on probation.

> There was no hint of 'Oh I need this because I need to re-establish myself as an actor'. He behaved like the pretty girl at the prom, whom everyone wants to dance with. He passed out cigars at table and Arnold Kopelson went like, 'Oh Arnold, these are the best cigars I ever had!' It was like everyone was sitting there, before the Prince, blowing smoke up his ass.

Finally, in September 1995, with Arnold joined in the cast by James Caan, James Coburn and the singer and former 'Miss America' Vanessa Williams, *Eraser* went before the cameras.

And stayed there, month after month, with remission for Christmas. Rumours of a ballooning budget and schedule issued from the set of what had started as a $72m 90-day shoot. Stunts went awry, including an explosion that set fire to Arnold's hair and a suspended cage that crashed, injuring and hospitalising the stars' stand-ins. In addition, an entire $600,000 set at Warner studios was scrapped unused when scenes were re-located. And Arnold was said to be having difficulties with the director, who was fond of eight-take sessions. 'Look, Chuck,' the star declaimed one day, 'you're making the same mistake Jim Cameron made. I'm a bodybuilder, not an actor. Do it in two takes.'

Producer Arnold Kopelson did his best to spin-doctor matters into tranquillity. 'These are usual things on an action movie of the scope of *Eraser*,' he told the press. 'You build in a 10 percent contingency on every schedule and budget.' Finally, a happy, action-packed, if a little bloated, *Eraser* headed for release in the summer of 1996.

TRUE MYTHS

(iii) The Real Arnold

Guns, identity confusions, blowings of cover, killings: it could only happen in a movie. Or could it? Somewhere in the vicinity of that witness protection programme known as SAS ('Sheltering Arnold Schwarzenegger') an even odder thing happened in February 1995. A British fan who cashed a social security cheque to buy an air ticket to fly to America and see his idol was shot dead while trying to burgle a house in Los Angeles.

The victim, who had Arnold's fan club address in his diary, had been receiving treatment for schizophrenia. The house-holder, seeing only a stranger wielding a handgun outside his house and being well-trained (possibly by Schwarzenegger movies) in the virtues of safety-in-overkill, shot him six times with a Smith and Wesson .44 automatic. Then he chased him into the street to deliver one more bullet to the head.

A few months earlier, another British fan had gone to America, with less violent consequences. It was this author. As narrated at the outset, I pursued the trail of clues to Schatzi's restaurant where I arrived at breakfast-time one Saturday morning. Eating a bowl of cereal on the public patio, I noticed at a nearby table a powerfully built man with carrot-coloured hair and an Austrian accent.

It was, of course, Arnold. He was sitting at a power breakfast with director Paul Verhoeven, producer Alan Marshall and agent Lou Pitt. They were holding, I deduced from higher-volume conversation snatches, what must have been the last full-dress summit on *Crusade* before Carolco pulled the plug.

Briefly deserting my bowl of muesli, I went up to Arnold's table. I think (but cannot be sure) that we shook hands. The great one turned on me a pair of alert but impassive eyes. I thought I heard the sound of whirring machinery deep inside the Schwarzenegger frame. Was I being recorded on his bio-mechanical video camera? I muttered some semi-prepared words about my book, assuring him that it was written from the standpoint of an enthusiast and admirer, and saying I did not want to end my visit to Los Angeles without doing him the courtesy of letting him know I was here, while at the same time not wishing to put him under pressure.

ENDGAME

As sycophantic speeches go, it just about went. Arnold graciously and sonorously intoned 'O thank you' and returned to his breakfast. I returned to mine. He did not look round again.

But I looked up a few times. The large hand was waving a stogie with alert, robotic command. The enormous-seeming head, with its all-over tan, poured forth Arnyisms of enthusiasm or business elan: I caught 'I like it, I like it!' and something about 'negotiate de price'. The Arnold presence seemed powerful enough to obliterate everyone else at the table; yet at the same time it seemed to have no graspably idiomatic human configuration at all.

This was avant-garde Arnie before my eyes: Digital Man, surrounded by Analogue Man. Digital Man extracts the clearest, most vivid sounds and colours of the human personality to create something beyond hi-fi – sci-fi. Analogue Man has all the sonic fluff and in-betweening: all the warmth of the accidental. You could see it in every other person sitting on that Schatzi's patio. All the people I did not know, I felt I knew. The one person I and everyone else 'knew', I felt none of us knew.

It is a part of the Incredible Vanishing Celebrity syndrome. A superstar, building his image-carapace, retreats with his real personality (full of normal quirks and weaknesses) into the recesses of his official personality. That way, there will be no *faux pas,* no ill-calculated spontaneities that will return to haunt him, amplified by media response. At the same time part of the unknowability is affirmative. It is that teasing, magical 'Find me if you can' charisma special to every superstar, from Garbo to Brando.

'There's something essentially mysterious about Arnold,' says director Walter Hill today.

Whatever you think he is, he's something else. If you think he's a movie star, he's also a real estate tycoon. If you think he's a real estate tycoon, he's also a modern Theseus. There's something elusive about the exact nature of this guy. I used to call him a 'force of nature'. He's not an actor in the normal sense and he doesn't pretend to be. But he is one of the great stars. They project something that's far beyond dramatic talent, and that 'mystery' is part of it. The greater the magnitude of the star, the greater the source of the mystery.

Paradoxically, too, the more 'Arnoldish' the star becomes on screen, the more elusive the real Arnold becomes. His in-tray for movie projects in the early-to-middle nineties showed him increasingly playing himself on screen or being invited to. Yet the Arnold-as-Arnold of *Last Action Hero* or *Dave* was even more cartoonishly one-dimensional than the grizzled, fictive action men of *Commando, Predator* or *Total Recall.*

Meanwhile, the two 1996 vehicles being wheeled into position on either side of *Batman and Robin* – a spring-filmed sentimental comedy aimed at Christmas release called *Jingles All the Way*, about a father seeking a perfect gift for the son he has neglected, and *With Wings as Eagles,* a World War II character-driven action epic about a Hitler-resisting German officer – leave the Arnologist dizzy with contrary indicators. They seem to promise both an extension of his range and a hardening-up of that impenetrable Nazi/nice guy dichotomy that has kept his persona going both on and off screen.

George Butler realised some years after *Pumping Iron* that a synthesising process had begun, in which the real Arnold Schwarzenegger was being set aside for the super-artefact. 'There was a natural, catchable, ingenuous Arnold that I thought we showed in the film, and I think it's a great record for him to have. Since those early days he has become a lot more calculating.'

More elusive too: even for past or present friends. When Butler prepared a photographic book about Arnold in the 1980s, he visited Los Angeles to show his subject the choice of pictures. Arnold told him to ring up when he arrived and not bother with an appointment: he would see him right away. Butler waited in his hotel from Sunday to Friday. Finally Arnold riffled through the photos with Butler in the short time the star had before leaving for Palm Springs. The answer was no: he would not co-operate. Arnold planned to write his own autobiography and he rehearsed for Butler, right there in the office, his imaginary bargaining session with agent 'Swifty' Lazar.

'I'll get you a million dollars in advance,' Swifty says.
    I say, 'No, I want five million!'
    Swifty says, 'That's the biggest book deal in history!' He says, 'Arnold, you are crazy.'

I say, 'What do you expect, Swifty? You are the hustler!'

Then Arnold [he was now speaking about himself] does another movie in three months. Ten weeks on the set. Bang! Twelve million plus 6 percent of the gross. Arnold establishes more value for Arnold! This allows Arnold to tell Swifty he has to pay ten million, making it twice as big as the biggest book deal in history. But already it is too late again, because now Arnold wants twenty million for his autobiography.

Butler retreats, outmanoeuvred by this spectacular show of third-person ego-flexing. A legend who sees himself as a legend is a hard act to connect with: you have to interpose yourself between him and the mirror. Even then – and even for fellow legends – it may be difficult to attract his attention.

'Sometime when I met Arnold,' remembers a wistful Simon Wiesenthal, 'I said, "When you come to Austria, to visit your mother, please call me so we can spend time together, a few hours". He promised. But then I have heard he is in Austria and he never called me. I'm sure he is occupied by so many people'.

Others look more fondly on the vanished Arnold: and with more amazement on the man who has left earthly gravity for his own time, space and astral priorities. Wag Bennett, sitting in his East London gym, gazes at the bench once occupied by a nineteen-year-old Austrian who could speak barely a word of English.

'I wake up in the morning and it's like a dream,' says Bennett.

I think: it hasn't really happened. He said he was going to be the greatest bodybuilder in the world and I sort of looked at him. Then he said he was going to be a film star, and I'm thinking in terms of Gary Cooper or Cary Grant, and I see him sitting there like some 260-pound monster, with a big fat face. And I think, what's *wrong* with this boy? I think, 'Some hopes.'

But it happened. Even George Butler, having to hustle for the star's time after being the man who introduced him to stardom, acknowledges Arnold's place in the annals of the American dream.

He feels that when he arrived on earth he was king of the world. What I find so charming and interesting about his story – the most important aspect – is how difficult his struggle was. I'm awestruck by what Arnold went through to achieve what he achieved. It's one of the great Horatio Alger stories. There's nothing like it.

Arnold Schwarzenegger lives in the promised land, on the mountain-top of success, protecting himself against the jealous, malicious, usurping. Sometimes private Arnold sends public Arnold forth – the truth despatching the myth – to act in a movie, speak to the press, campaign for a politician.

Made in response to the world's needs and shaping perceptions, this public Arnold is one of the great show-business creations of our time. Long after history has forgotten the 'real' Arnold's stumbles or mini-scandals – steroids and Hitler allusions, sexual peccadilloes and petulant lawsuits – iconic Arnold will survive; as the Aku-Aku statues outlived the Easter Island natives who built them.

We will celebrate, awed and uncomprehending, the colossal frame, the high-boned classic head, the lunatic accent, the unpronounceable name, the ten-ton charisma, the defiant, alien presence. We will wonder how they ever got established on the terra firma of Tinseltown. And we will rejoice that we live in a world where the unimaginable, bordering on the downright impossible, can still happen.

As for politics, Arnold has had two recent imprimaturs. Audiences polled last November by a leading American cable TV network voted him their second-favourite celebrity to become President, behind the inevitable Oprah Winfrey. The other endorsement, or perhaps warning, came from a man intimate with the worlds of both cinema and statecraft, as well as with the extended ambitions of that extended family, the Kennedy-Shrivers. Gore Vidal prophesied that the 2004 Presidential election would be between Norman Schwarzkopf and Arnold Schwarzenegger.

Arnold's own most recent thoughts on that supreme office?

'I'm more than happy to help this country, to help this world, in the future. . . . '

ACKNOWLEDGEMENTS

This section of a biography is usually the 'without whom it would not have been possible' part. Dozens of people indeed made *True Myths* possible, generously lending their time and powers of recall. Before thanking them, though, I should like to mention some of the people without whom the book had to stumble along as best it could. They are the close Arnold associates who withheld their assistance.

Ivan Reitman was approached by me at a Venice Film Festival move-makers' symposium in 1993. It was, I now realise, an ill-matched encounter. He was there equipped with an haute couture black suit, possibly by Armani, and a top Ameriican publicist (PMK's Leslee Dart). I was there in a 'Save the manatee' T-shirt and a seen-better-days Italian-made baseball jacket.

He said he could not help me as he was leaving Venice shortly. This was literally true; though he neglected to add that he was scheduled to return almost immediately to promote *Dave* at the festival: a film featuring Herr Schwarzenegger.

Later I faxed Reitman's PR people in America. Their only reply, when apprised of my imminent trip to Hollywood, was a return fax couched in urgent B-movie language: 'Hold your jets'.

James Cameron's office received one fax and told me they had mislaid it; requested another and failed to respond to it.

Literally dozens of other directors, actors, producers and Arnold associates declined to talk to me. Many of them pled 'friendship' with the superstar. Others told me they would check with Charlotte Parker and were never heard from again.

Parker's role as a human Bermuda Triangle also accounted for writer Charles Gaines. I had approached him as the man intimately connected with Arnold's first two serious movie ventures: *Stay Hungry* and *Pumping Iron*. Gaines said he was willing to talk and only needed Charlotte to fax him an 'OK'. She declined to fax.

Even some of those who did talk to me offered strange insights into Hollywood protocol. Walter Hill, walking me to the door after our interview, said he would not have agreed to see me if he had had 'anything bad to say about Arnold'.

Other people parenthesised their more judgmental remarks with 'This is off the record'/'between you and me'/'not for attribution'. Vince Gironda, talking freely and frankly down a long-distance telephone, twice interjected, 'Don't make me sue you, Nigel.' Gironda also started off with a remark that may reveal more about Arnold than anything else in this book. 'There are a lot of things I would like to say about Arnold, but I daren't because he is so powerful.'

On two occasions I received telephone calls from intermediaries hinting that Arnold himself might be willing to talk. The first call, I later realised, was a fact-finding mission disguised as an Arnold overture: it was never followed up by any willingness from the star. Months later Arnold's lawyer Martin Kramer said to me 'You'd obviously like to talk to Arnold.' I said it was a little late – the book was virtually written – and that I had become wary about telephone probes masquerading as friendly approaches.

In Europe, by contrast, my days seemed blessed from the moment I crossed the Austrian border. I speak no German beyond phrasebook monosyllables. But basing myself in Graz, I had barely picked up the phone to begin my campaign – using sentences taught me by the hotel receptionist – before Kurt Marnul, Arnold's boyhood trainer, was in the lobby wearing a large moustache and Styrian braces.

Then Fraulein Laurinzer, headmistress of the Hans Gross School in Thal, agreed by telephone to supply me with a list of Arnold's former classmates. I drove to the village, first stopping by the house that had been Arnold's childhood home. David Anderwald, teenage son of the current residents, spoke to me in English and showed me Arnold's room, with its view of the nearby castle ruins.

At the school Fraulein Laurinzer, whom I had envisioned as a school mistressy woman in tween and comfortable shoes, was a svelte blonde resembling the late Lee Remick. Helpful and English-speaking, she armed me with a list of Arnold classmates still living in Thal. I asked if she could recommend an interpretar, hoping she would recommend herself. She and her colleagues were too busy, she said: teachers' meeting. So out of the blue I called David Anderwald. He agreed to tear himself away from homework and accompany me on my interviews.

Later that day, passers-by would have witnessed an English film critic and Austrian schoolboy accosting the bewildered members of a bus queue, to ask for small change to use the public telephone. Finding the interviewees was one thing; giving them polite notice of arrival was another.

David Anderwald deserves one of the biggest votes of thanks in this book. For most of that day, I was in semi-shock. As well as recovering from a bad cold, I was stunned by the kismet which has sent me the son and heir of Arnold's boyhood home to be my guide through Arnold's boyhood. His energies were unflagging and his social graces put people at ease before they had a chance to put up their guards.

Even his warnings when we parted were well-meant, albeit in line with Schwarzenegger protocol. 'You must not write bad things about Arnold,' he instructed me, 'or your book will not sell.'

Of the many people who spoke to me for *True Myths* or whose reflections on Arnold have featured in the book, I must thank the following:

Gordon Allen, Wag Bennett, Stanley Brooks, John Bruno, John Bubb, George Butler, Dyan Cannon, John Citrone, Boyer Coc, Jeff Corey, Charles Dance, Ivan Dunbar, Wayne DeMilia, Robert Easton, Bill Fischler, Richard Fleischer, Charles Fleming, Vince Gironda, Paul Graham, Adam Greenberg, Linda Hamilton, Josef Heinzel, Lance Henriksen, Franz Hermann, Rabbi Marvin Hier, Walter Hill, John Irvin, Pauline Kael, James Karen, Nicolas Kent, Franz Kicker, Martin Kramer, Mark L. Lester, Jim Lorimer, Karl Malden, Kurt Marnul, Mike Mentzer, Eric Morris, Hal Needham, Reg Park, Edward R. Pressman, Professor Sam Popkin, Tony Puryear, Lacey H. Rich, Sir Jimmy Savile, Francesco Scavullo, Arthur A. Seidelman, Barbara and David Stone, Brigitte Verschink, Rich Wayne, Ben Weider, Joe Weider, Bernard Weinraub, Vernon Wells, Simon Wiesenthal, Michael Winner.

Three books about Arnold Schwarzenegger were invaluable. Wendy Leigh's *Arnold*, though prone to novelettish style and dubious psychologising, is awesomely well-researched. She left future biographers, including this one,

ACKNOWLEDGEMENTS

a ready-blazed trail of witnesses' names and identities. I am also aware that my account of the Schwarzenegger libel case is incomplete without her present-day contribution, unobtainable due to the silencing restriction imposed on her by the legal settlement.

George Butler, as well as providing first-hand testimony, gave me contact numbers for Arnold friends and associates and pointed me to his own book, *Arnold Schwarzenegger: A Portrait.* Rich in insights and revealing moments, this is the best sketch of Arnold by an Arnold friend.

Our protagonist's own *Arnold: Education of a Bodybuilder* provides an important perspective on his early years and an articulate attempt to 'explain' bodybuilding. I thank Martin Kramer, of Theodore Goddard in London, for his courteous response to my request for permission to quote from it.

Out in the Hollywood jungle, my friend and researcher Barbra Paskin hacked through initial obstacles to make the whole *True Myths* enterprise possible. And Sandra Archer of the Motion Pictures Academy library sent consignments of 'cuttings', from which I grew my own information forest back in Britain.

My thanks also to Ned Comstock, curator of the film library of the University of Southern California; and to Elan Steinberg of the World Jewish Congress in New York, who furnished documentation relating to Arnold's father.

Back home the British Film Institute library in London and the British Library's newspaper collection in Colindale were vital information sources. At my newspaper the Financial Times, Peter Cheek, Malcolm Rutherford and Jurek Martin, pestered by me at different times for different things, all responded with helpful alacrity.

Malcolm Whyatt, treasurer and archivist of the National Amateur Body Builders Assocation, supplied material on Arnold's years in Britain. And Nicolas Kent lent me illuminating transcripts and videos relating to his research for the *Naked Hollywood* series.

Alexander Walker, himself a distinguished biographer, gave this writer the benefit of wit, wisdom; and my agent Michael Shaw offered much-needed advice and suggestions for re-polishing, pressing them further when they were needlessly resisted.

My editor Matthew Hamilton kept sending the entire book back to me with red scrawls through it. After initial shock, I realised that almost every scrawl was sensible; a year hence I shall probably realise they all were. In addition he kept suggesting fresh avenues of approach to that sometimes impregnable fortress called the life of Arnold Schwarzenegger.

Finally, I should like to thank the subject of this book himself, For being courteous to me at Schatzi when he could have socked me on the jaw. And for never once making a midnight call to me or my publisher suggesting that the best biography would be no biography.

Nigel Andrews

Sources

Chapter 2

p. 11. 'an excellent bone structure. . .' ARNOLD:
EDUCATION OF A BODYBUILDER by
Arnold Schwarzenegger and Douglas Kent Hall
'Nobody had a phone . . .' *Rolling Stone*, 17/1/85,
'Pumping Arnold,' by Nancy Collins
Information on Gustav's Nazi membership from
Berlin Document Archive
Austrian Nazi membership before 1938 from Herr
Stein at Austrian Interior Ministry
p. 12. 'These look a little dirty to me . . .' *New
York Times*, 17/5/82, by Chris Chase
'Sit in front of this book . . .' *Rolling Stone*,
17/1/85, N. Collins
'We would have to write an essay . . .' *Washington
Post*, 9/1/83, by Marguerite Michaels
'He would correct them . . .' *Playboy*, Jan. 1988,
interview by Joan Goodman
p. 13. 'That's not too bad' *Chicago Tribune*,
17/6//87, by Cheryl Lavin
'He had no patience . . .' *Atlanta Journal*, 31/5/87,
by Dotson Rader
'There was a real wall . . .' *Rolling Stone*, 17/1/85,
N. Collins
Religious upbringing and sports from
EDUCATION OF A BODYBUILDER
p. 14. 'You really screwed up . . .' from the
documentary CHAMPIONS (1990)
Gustav's drinking, from Wendy Leigh's ARNOLD
Gustav's music-making, from ARNOLD and
N.A. interview with fellow band member
Franz Kicker
'My father played soccer . . .' *USA Today*,
24/3/93, by Nanci Hellmich
'I remember having nightmares . . .' *GQ*, July
1986, 'The Promoter' by Jean Vallely
p. 14. One of the best mothers, from *Rolling Stone*,
17/1/85, N. Collins
p. 17. Aurelia's tolerance from N.A. interview
with Arnold's boyhood trainer Kurt Marnul
'(She) had to go around . . .' *Playboy*, Jan. 1988, J.
Goodman
'I remember, we were all standing . . .' *Sports
Illustrated*, 7/12/87
'If I got sick . . .' *Rolling Stone*, 17/1/85,
N. Collins
p. 16. Aurelia with trophy, from EDUCATION
OF A BODYBUILDER
Gustav carrying the trophy, from CHAMPIONS
Calling out doctor, from N.A. interview with
Josef Heinzel
p. 17. 'I remember as a boy . . .' *Atlanta Journal*,
31/5/87, D. Rader
'to be in the military . . .' *Playboy*, Jan. 1988, J.
Goodman
p. 18. 'I always ran around with it on' ibid.

Chapter 3

p. 19. 'I felt like Leonardo . . .' *Guardian*, 27/9/77,
by Angela Neustatter
Bobdybuilding at lake, from ARNOLD'S
FITNESS FOR KIDS AGES
BIRTH TO FIVE by A. S., quoted

USA Today, 24/3/93, Nanci
Hellmich
Weight-lifting for soccer, from EDUCATION OF
A BODYBUILDER
'It fascinated me . . .' *Guardian*, 29/9/77, A.
Neustatter
p. 20. First gym visit, from EDUCATION OF A
BODYBUILDER
'I disliked it when we won . . .' ibid.
'The worst thing I can be . . .' *Rolling Stone*,
17/1/85, N. Collins
'Why, Arnold, why do you want . . .' N.A.
interview Kurt Marnul
'I was so weak . . .' ibid.
p. 21. 'She said she'd rather . . .' N.A. interview
Kurt Marnul
'After he had finished . . .' ARNOLD
SCHWARZENEGGER: A PORTAIT by
George Butler
Arnold training, from N.A. interview Kurt Marnul
p. 22. 'Reg Park looked so magnificent . . .'
EDUCATION OF A BODYBUILDER
p. 23. 'When I was ten and twelve . . .' *New York
Times*, 17/5/82, C. Chase
'I'd have to walk in backwards . . .' *Time Out*,
10/8/88, by Brian Case
'released a kind of desire . . .' 'You' Magazine
(*Mail on Sunday*), 22/11/87, by Douglas
Thompson
'Everything I wanted as a kid . . .' *Time Out*,
10/8/88, B. Case
'I loved the huge cars . . .' *Atlanta Journal*, 31/5/87,
D. Rader
'While my friends were talking . . .' *Playboy*, Jan.
1988, J. Goodman
p. 24. 'They would say I was totally insane . . .'
GQ, July 1986, J. Vallely
'Showing him the bird' and following, from N.A.
interview Josef Heinzel
Seeing Johnny Weissmuller, from Wendy Leigh's
ARNOLD
'Caesar, Charlemagne, Napoleon . . .' from
EDUCATION OF A BODYBUILDER
p. 25. Arnold bring his work home, from ibid.
'All the other boys . . .' CHAMPIONS
documentary
'There were a certain number . . .' and following,
ibid.
p. 26. Old-worthy chivalry, from N.A. interview
Brigitte Verschink
'I didn't allow myself . . .' EDUCATION OF A
BODYBUILDER
'I set a goal . . .' 20th Century Press Biography,
August 1982
'A lot of people do it . . .' N.A. interview
Robert Easton
p. 27. 'I'd grown up in a disciplined . . .'
EDUCATION OF A BODYBUILDER
Arnold getting up at five etc., from *Guardian*,
22/8/85, by Jasmine Birtles
Junior Mr Europe contest, from ARNOLD and
EDUCATION OF A BODYBUILDER
Other people at contest, from ARNOLD
p. 28. Sitting in jail, from EDUCATION OF A
BODYBUILDER

SOURCES

'I was like a black . . .' *Atlanta Journal*, 31.5.87,
D. Rader

Chapter 4

p. 29. 'I knew I was a winner' EDUCATION OF
A BODYBUILDER
'Wag had told me . . .' N.A. interview Gordon
Allen
Arnold staring at Reg Park, from EDUCATION
OF A BODYBUILDER
p. 30. 'He said that he was inspired . . .' N.A.
interview Reg Park
Reinhard Swolana story from ARNOLD,
documentary by Jeff Forrester (1994)
'Hello, you old pig . . .' from ARNOLD
'He wore a German-style corduroy suit' and
following stories and quotations, from N.A.
interview Wag Bennett
p. 32. 'His legs were his faulty part . . .' N.A.
interview John Citrone
'After he came second . . .' N.A. interview Wag
Bennett
'Not since Reg Park . . .' *Health and Strength*,
10/11/86, Ivan Dunbar
p. 33. 'One of the other bodybuilders . . .' N.A.
interview Wag Bennett
'He had the biggest dose . . .' N.A. interview Sir
Jimmy Savile
'Posing is pure theatre . . .' EDUCATION OF A
BODYBUILDER
p. 34. 'In Paris you get more response . . .'
AFTER DARK, February 1977, by Norma
McLain Stoop
'We didn't get finished . . .' N.A. interview Ivan
Dunbar
'There is one very important thing . . .'' *San
Francisco Chronicle*, 21/3/77, by David
Scheiderer
'In the old days . . .' *Playboy*, Jan. 1988, J.
Goodman
p. 35. 'He'd literally insinuate . . .' N.A. interview
John Citrone
'He was very ambitious' and following, N.A.
interview Reg Park
p. 36. No money and 'I was kind of like . . .' from
EDUCATION OF A BODYBUILDER
Arnold at Mr Olympia, from ibid.

Chapter 5

p. 37. 'I feel that I must have lived . . .' *Options*,
January 1989
'seemed to have been tooled down' and
crying all night, from EDUCATION OF A
BODYBUILDER
'America is still the only country . . .' *Time Out*,
7/10/77, by Scott Meek
p. 38. 'I asked my agent' N.A. interview Joe
Weider
First magazine exposure for Arnold, from *Muscle
Mag*, August 1991, Robert Kennedy
$200 a week and 'We helped him edit them', N.A.
interview Joe Weider
Yellow Volkswagen from *Muscle Mag*, Aug. 1991,
R. Kennedy
Arnold's inability to driive and 'We'd train at
Vince's . . .', from N.A. interview Paul
Graham
p. 39. 'Joe Weider paid me . . .' and following,
from N.A. interview Vince Gironda
p. 40. Steroids and 'He was a fanatical trainer . . .'
N.A. interview Rick Wayne

'Arnold was learning to drive . . .' N.A. interview
Paul Graham
'I do not mention the movie . . .' N.A. interview
James Karen
p. 41. 'They asked me if he could act . . .' N.A.
interview Joe Weider
'Weider was such a hype artist . . .' *Sports
Illustrated*, 7/12/87, 'Hot Stuff'
'I frankly was against dubbing him . . .' and
following, from N.A. interview Arthur A.
Seidelman
p. 42. 'I'd never see anyone like him . . .' N.A.
interview James Karen
'He had a couple of practice sessions . . .' N.A.
interview Arthurr A. Seidelman
p. 43. 'He said to me very early on . . .' ibid.
p. 44. 'Arnold hates to go to sleep . . .' *Sunday
Times Magazine*, 24/4/92, by Russell Miller
'You may have seen walking . . .' *Santa College
Magazine*, (undated issue), by Valerie Hirschl
p. 45. 'When we came out with . . .' N.A.
interview Joe Weider
Picture of Arnold, by George Butler, featured in
his ARNOLD SCHWARZENEGGER: A
PORTRAIT
'Being at the beginning . . .' *Hollywood Reporter*,
57th anniv. issue
Bennett Irving Park story 'favoured version' in
Wendy Leigh's ARNOLD
'I've read that story . . .' N.A. interview Reg Park
'It's absolute nonsense . . .' N.A. interview Wag
Bennett
p. 46. 'Arnold had gone from . . .' N.A. interview
Gordon Allen
'In bodybuilding you don't . . .' *Chicago Tribune*,
19/7/81, by Peter Koper
'He didn't just have physical . . .' N.A. interview
Wag Bennett
Arnold/Oliva psych-outs from N.A. interview
Rick Wayne
p. 47. 'The judges thought Sergio . . .' N.A.
interview Wag Bennett
'This is great . . .' *Washington Post*, 9/1/83, by
Marguerite Michaels
'At one point we went . . .' N.A. interview Wag
Bennett
p. 48. Essays on Weider from N.A. interview Rick
Wayne
'If he didn't understand . . .' N.A. interview Joe
Weider
'It was initially . . .' N.A. interview John Bubb
'Weider had the IFBB . . .' N.A. interview Wag
Bennett

Chapter 6

p. 50. 'When you have parents . . .' *Playboy*, Jan.
1988, J. Goodman
'wonderful paintings' and following from *Rolling
Stone*, 17/1/85, N. Collins
p. 51. Details of Meinhard's life from Wendy
Leigh's ARNOLD
p. 52. Rolling Stone version of funeral story, from
Rolling Stone, 17/1/85
'When we were shooting . . .' N.A. interview
George Butler
p. 53. 'What actually happened . . .' ARNOLD
SCHWARZENEGGER: A PORTRAIT by
George Butler
'I couldn't go to the funeral . . .' *Playboy*, Jan.
1988, J. Goodman
p. 54. 'All of these magazines . . .' *Sports
Illustrated*, 14/10/74, by Richard W.
Johnstone

'We all make mistakes . . .' N.A. interview Joe
Weider

Chapter 7

p. 56. 'I set out to be the best . . .' *Sun*, 13/12/86
'We've always loved . . .' *USA Today*, 30/7/85, by
Jack Curry
'started with people . . .' N.A. interview Vince
Gironda
p. 57. 'I wanted to be the best . . .' Reg Park
'The man who engages . . .' and following, from
Cosmopolitan, August 1977. 'Muscle Madness:
The Incredible Boom in Male Body-Building'
by Leonard Todd
p. 58. 'Can you imagine, now, that a teenage
boy . . .' ibid.
'Can you imagine the effort . . .' *Time Out*,
7/10/77, by Scott Meek
Gustav wanting Arnold to be in army, from N.A.
interview Franz Hermann
'you have to be a little "off" . . .' *Time*, 24/12/90,
by Richard Corliss
p. 59. 'You have to think back . . .' N.A.
interview George Butler
'You can guess how they earned . . .' N.A.
iinterview Wayne DeMilia
'twelve different pamphlets . . .' and following,
from N.A. interview George Butler
p. 60. Arnold's earnings from *Los Angeles Times*,
10/9/89, by Jack Matthews
p. 61. Pumping ice cream and 'They were always
thirsty . . .' from *California Business*, June
1986, by Susan Peters
'We had to go to a shop . . .' *After Dark*, February
1977, N. M. Stoop
Pumping bulls' balls from ARNOLD
SCHWARZENEGGER: A PORTRAIT by
George Butler
Pumping mail order, from *Family Weekly*,
30/8/81, by Kathleen Beckett, Wendy
Leigh's ARNOLD and N.A. interview Ricky
Wayne
p. 62. 'We had sixteen people . . .' *Interview
Magazine*, October 1985, by Jonathan Robertsw
'We needed to eat . . .' *Sunday Times Magazine*,
26/4/92, by Russell Miller
'Franco did the bricklaying . . .' 'You' magazine
(*Mail on Sunday*), 22/11/87, by Douglas
Thompson
Tearing down Valentino's home, from *Esquire*,
March 1985, by Lynn Darling
Tarzan and 'We laid on our backs . . .' from
California Business, June 1986, S. Peters
'Charles Gaines invented . . .' ARNOLD
SCHWARZENEGGER: A PORTRAIT by
George Butler
'means nothing to me . . .' *Sunday Express*,
5/11/89, by Sue Russell
'He was gonna move . . .' N.A. interview Joe
Weider
p. 63. Arnold buying buildings, from 'You'
magazine (*Mail on Sunday*), 22/11/87, D.
Thompson, and *Sun*, 8/8/90, by Allan Hall
'Once he did about . . .' *California Business*, June
1986, S. Peters
Palmdale purchase, from GQ, July 1986, J. Vallely
Virginia coalmine, from *Observer Magazine*,
3/7/77, by Joan Juliet Buck
'Whenever a democratic . . .' *Playboy*, Jan. 1988, J.
Goodman
'I invest the money . . .' *Times*, 26/1/91, by
Kate Muir
Wisconsin degree, from *New York Times* 26/5/80

Arnold–Lorimer partnership and following, from
N.A. interview Jim Lorimer
$10,000 for seminars, from *Washington Post*, 9/1/8
M. Michaels
p. 64. Burt Reynolds partnership, from *Chicago
Tribune*, 31/1/77, by Marilyn Preston
'I mapped out . . .' *San Francisco Chronicle*,
13/10/85, by Stu Schreiberg

Chapter 8

p. 65. 'I knew that in the past . . .' *Time Out*,
7/10/77, S. Meek
Arnold and Barbara Outland, from Wendy
Leigh's ARNOLD and EDUCTION OF A
BODYBUILDER
p. 66. 'I think she realised . . .' and following,
from EDUCATION OF A BODYBUILDI
'She was very level-headed . . .' N.A. interview
George Butler
'I was not a well-balanced man . . .' and following
EDUCATION OF A BODYBUILDER
Arnold and agents, from *Options*, January 1989
'Look, Arnold . . .' from transcript of *Naked
Hollywood* TV series, Arnold interview
recorded 3/4/90
'I stopped bodybuilding . . .' *USA Today*, 30/6/8
by Tom Green
p. 67. 'I sat there . . .' *Los Angeles Times*, 16/10/8
by Deborah Caulfield
p. 68. 'I said, well, Bob . . .' and following, fro1
N.A. interview Eric Morris
'Waiting for Arnold . . .' L.A. *Herald-Examiner*,
5/4/88, by Bill Higgins
p. 69. Two months fiddle coaching, from Unite
Artists press notes on STAY HUNGRY
'I have a love interest . . .' *Playboy*, Jan. 1988, J.
Goodman
'I tapped a well . . .' *Sports Illustrated*, 7/12/87
'Acting was an enormous challenge . . .' 20th
Century Fox press biography, August 1982
p. 70. 'What happened was . . .' N.A. interview
Eric Morris

Chapter 9

p. 71. 'I'm coming day and night . . .' from the
film PUMPING IRON
p. 73. Hidden microphone reported in
Times–Picayune, 19/1/79, by Bob Thomas
'When you make a film . . .' N.A. interview
George Butler
'He had a Satanic ability . . .' N.A. interview
Vinve Gironda
'Arnold said at one point . . .' and following, fr(
N.A. interview George Butler
p. 74. 'No one in America will buy . . .'
and following, from ARNOLD
SCHWARZENEGGER: A PORTRAIT
Whitney Museum exhibition from *Vanity Fair*,
June 1990
PUMPING IRON funding details from *Premiere*
March 1993

Chapter 10

p. 76. 'Sure I get treated . . .' *Daily Express*,
23/5/77, by Victor Davis
Picking up women, from *Toronto Globe and Mai*
29/4/82, by Jay Scott (Chicago)
Felxing a tricep, from ARNOLD
SCHWARZENEGGER: A PORTRAIT by
George Butler

SOURCES

'an eye for the ladiies' N.A. interview James Karen
Woman at San Francisco party, from *Daily Express*, 23/5/77, V. Davis
Woman who 'ripped her clothes off' from *Daily Mirror*, 19/8/82, by William Marshall
French chambermaid and 'She became very excited . . .' from *Daily Express*, 23/5/77, V. Davis
'People were bugging him . . .' N.A. interview Joe Weider
p. 77. Women who offered $1000, from *Daily Express*, 23/5/77, V. Davis
'He stayed here the whole day . . .' N.A. interview Francesco Scavullo
'When you train . . .' *Time Out*, 7//10/77, S. Meek
'When it comes to sex . . .' *New York Times*, 15/10/76, by Cliff Jahr
'Why should I mind . . .' *Cosmopolitan*, August 1977, L. Todd
p. 78. 'I've spent so much time . . .' and following, from *Gay News*, no. 128, 1979, by Alison Hennegan
'I was up at Andy Warhol's . . .' N.A. interview Arthur A. Seidelman
p. 79. Arnold conversing with Sargent Shriver and Rose Kennedy, from *Sunday Express*, 27/10/85, by Roderick Mann
'My biggest challenge . . .' *San Francisco Chronicle*, 12/8/85
'Don't look at him as a Republican . . .' *Variety*, 25/5/95, by Army Archerd
p. 80. Jackie Kennedy and Greek sculpture, from *Daily Express*, 23/5/77, V. Davis
'I like hanging around . . .' *Evening Standard*, 11/1/85
'a typical evening's conversation . . .' *News of the World*, 16/2/86, by William Hall
Conversing with Rose, from *Sunday Times*, 27/4/86, by Will Ellsworth-Jones
'I can make her understand . . .' *Sunday Telegraph Magazine*, 22/8/82, by Pearson Phillips
'They think so much . . .' *Interview* magazine, October 1985, J. Roberts

p. 81. 'Dad said to pay attention . . .' and gift of 'Conan', from *People*, 7/6/82
'Girls giggle . . .' *Hollywood Reporter*, 18/11/81
Sue Moray and Arnold, from Wendy Leigh's ARNOLD
'Arnold said at the beginning . . .' N.A. interview Ben Weider
'I don't think he planned . . .' N.A. interview Joe Weider
p. 82. Maria's job, from *Company*, November 1986, by Julia Orange

Chapter 11

p. 83. 'I've been round the world . . .' CHECK
p. 83. 'If the first picture . . .' *Time Out*, 7/10/77, S. Meek
p. 84. 'All I had was one take . . .' *Hollywood Reporter* 48th anniversary issue
'He was beginning . . .' N.A. interview Karl Malden
STAY HUNGRY weight-shedding, from *Time Out*, 7/10/77, S. Meek
'The nicest weight . . .' *Me* magazine, 15/8/77
'He's terribly articulate . . .' *People*, 31/1/77
Natalie Wood duologue, *Hollywood Reporter*'s 48th annual
'I just do Arnold . . ' *San Francisco Chronicle*, 21/3//78, by David Scheiderer
p. 85. Selling books story, from GQ, July 1986, J. Vallely

'We're only here . . .' *Los Angeles Times*, 4/8/91, by Paul Ciotti
p. 86. 'When you saw me . . .' *Rolling Stone*, 17/1/85, N. Collins
'To sell something on TV . . .' *Time Out*, 10/8/88, Brian Case
'If you tell people . . .' *Rolling Stone*, 17/1/85, N. Collins
'America is so money-oriented . . .' *Time Out*, 7/10/77, S. Meek

p. 87. 'He had a real serious personal drive . . .' and following, from N.A. interview David and Barbara Stone
p. 88. 'The rush one gets . . .' *Chicago Tribune*, 17/6/87, by C. Lavin

'A lot of actors . . .' *Los Angeles Times*, 10/9/89, J. Matthews
'If you do those press junkets . . .' transcript *Naked Hollywood* TV series, Arnold interview 3/4/90
p. 89. 'I don't want to be another . . .' *Chicago Tribune*, 31/1/77, by Marilyn Preston

Chapter 12

p. 90. 'When you have a unique look . . .' *San Francisco Chronicle*, 15/6/86, by Dan Yakir
Turning down SEXTETTE, from Wendy Leigh's ARNOLD
'I'm much too pretty . . .' *San Francisco Chronicle*, 14/8/79, by Jennifer Seder
Close to playing Superman, from *Time Out*, 7/10/77, S. Meek
'A Road Runner done with live people', N.A. interview Hal Needham
p. 91. 'worked out perfect . . .' and following, from ibid.
p. 93. 'Studios can't do . . .' *Playboy*, January 1988, J. Goodman
'Universal, the distributor . . .' *Muscle and Fitness*, December 1994, 'My Mr Olympia Comeback' by Arnold Schwarzenegger (orig. printing 1981)
'One day, just a few weeks . . .' ibid.
Butler visiting Arnold, from ARNOLD SCHWARZENEGGER: A PORTRAIT by George Butler
p. 94. 'He said to me . . .' N.A. interview Reg Park
'I think Arnold . . .' N.A. interview Ben Weider
p. 95. 'Arnold was the only one . . .' and following, from N.A. interview Boyer Coe
'we didn't have enough footage . . .' N.A. interview Paul Graham
'I'm the kind of character . . .' Arnold interviewed in THE COMEBACK
Arnold's injury and 'On the plane to Australia . . .' from *Muscle and Fitness*, December 1994, A. Schwarzenegger
p. 96. Columbu on stage, from ARNOLD SCHWARZENEGGER: A PORTRAIT by George Butler
Uproar in Sydney opera house, from Wendy Leigh's ARNOLD and N.A. interview with Boyer Coe
'I met up with Mentzer . . .' N.A. interview John Citrone
'A fair placing for Arnold . . .' N.A. interview Boyer Coe
'What happened fourteen years ago . . .' N.A. interview Mike Mentzer
p. 97. 'I didn't think Mentzer . . .' N.A. interview Reg Park

278

'They couldn't take the fact . . .' N.A. interview Paul Graham

'I know a lot . . .' and following, from N.A. interview George Butler

Rows with journalists and 'I know I am getting a hard time . . .' Wendy Leigh's ARNOLD and N.A. interview Rick Wayne

Chapter 13

p. 99. 'It's a big picture . . .' *Time Out*, 7/10/77, S. Meek

De Laurentiis meeting, from *Atlanta Journal*, 14/6/87, by Eleanor Ringel and *Sports Illustrated*, 7/12/87

p. 100. Robert E. Howard information from *Washington Post*, 9/5/82, by Lois Romano

p. 101. 'It's one of the typical things . . .' ibid.

Pressman and Arnold, and CONAN directors' 'musical chairs', from N.A. interview Edward S. Pressman

'Probably the biggest mistake . . .' N.A. interview Hal Needham

p. 102. Training for CONAN, from Starburst, December 1982, by Phil Edwards

'I had to practice . . .' *Washington Post*, 9/5//82, L. Romano

'a time that had no religion . . .' *Hollywood Drama–Logue*, 17/6//82, by Pat H. Broeske

'You're not going to find . . .' *New West Magazine*, 27/8//79, 'The Barbarian In Babylon' by Kenneth Turan

'I said to him, Whenever you kill . . .' *Rolling Stone*, 22/8/91, by Bill Zehme

Not flinching at sword and 'If it was an honour . . .' from *Hollywood Drama-Logue*, 17/6/82, P. Broeske

p. 103. 'Hollywood is filled . . .' *New York Times*, 17/5/82, C. Chase

'On the first day . . .' *Sunday Express*, 15/8/82, Roderick Mann

'kicked by a camel . . .' ibid.

'Pain is temporary . . .' ibid.

'once when I had to climb . . .' *Hollywood Reporter*, 18/8/81

Special effects and constructions, from Prevue, April–May 1982, 'The Making Of An Adventure Epic' by Ken Bruzenak

p. 105. 'If somebody would've asked . . .' 20th Century Fox press biography, August 1982

Milius researcher, Michael B. Gladych

p. 106. 'He's not a natural . . .' *Prevue*, April–May 1982, K. Bruzenak

p. 107. Universal lopping Arnold's dialogue, from *Washington Post*, 9/1/83, M. Michacis

Arnold's voice-coaching, from N.A. interview Robert Eastom

p. 108. 'I have problems . . .' *Moviegoer*, May 1982, by Stephen Farber

'I hope it doesn't show . . .' *Los Angeles Times*, 16/10/84, by Deborah Caulfield

'serious type of science fiction . . .' and following, from *Time Out*, 7/10/77, S. Meek

p. 109. 'There is no way . . .' *Moviegoer*, May 1982, S. Farber

'With any luck . . .' *Washington Post*, 9/5/82, L. Romano

'Originally when Conan's mother . . .' *Moviegoer*, May 1982, S. Farber

'You deserve Mitterrand!' *Toronto Globe* and *Mail*, 29/4/82, J. Scott

'Fantasy is definitely . . .' ibid.

Sequel less bloody, from *Time Out*, 18/10/84, Mike Bygrave

p. 110. 'The first film took itself . . .' and following, from N.A. interview Richard Fleischer

'For two hours every day . . .' *USA Today*, 5/10/83, by Victoria Balfour

Dino's gymnasium, from *USA Today*, 29/11/84, Stu Schreiberg

p. 111. 'There was a lot of grease . . .' Wendy Leigh's ARNOLD

'Any time you deal . . .' *Winnipeg Free Press*, 2/10/85, Tom Sabulis

Arnold on set and 'He had to cope . . .' from N.A. interview Richard Fleischer

Chapter 14

p. 113. 'Americans are very positive . . .' *USA Today*, 5/10/83, V. Balfour

Arnold's naturalisation, from *Los Angleles Times*, 17/9/83

'When East Coast snobs . . .' *Hollywood Reporter*, 18/8/81

'I wouldn't be where I am . . .' *Times-Picayune*, 19/8/79, B. Thomas

'Any time you deal . . .' *Winnipeg Free Press*, 2/10/85, Tom Sabulis

Arnold on set and 'He had to cope . . .' from N.A. interview Richard Fleischer

p. 114. 'We Europeans . . .' *Time Out*, 7/10/77, S. Meek

'Look where Ronald Reagan . . .' *Girl About Town*, 31/8/82, by John Preston

'I wish I could . . .' *Sunday Times Magazine*, 26/4/92 R. Miller (quoting from book PUMPING IRON)

'I think Arnold . . .' N.A. interview Vince Gironda

p. 115. Arnold and Milton Friedman, from *Los Angeles Times*, 17/9/83, by Carol McGraw

'I am more comfortable . . .' *Rolling Stone*, 17/1/85, N. Collins

'A fine man . . .' *Daily Mail*, 10/3/88, by Sara Barrett

'He told me a hundred times . . .' and following, from N.A. interview Rick Wayne

p. 116. Portland, Oregon story from *San Francisco Chronicle*, 14/8/79, by Jennifer Seder (*L.A. Times*)

'To me my fame . . .' *Sunday Times Magazine*, 26/4/92, R. Miller

'I like running . . .' *San Francisco Chronicle*, 15/8/86, D. Yakir

'When pictures go out . . .' *Moviegoer*, May 1982, S. Farber

'I do tests . . .' *Washington Post*, 9/5/82, L. Romano

'Ego is a thing . . .' *Toronto Globe* and *Mail*, 29/4/82, J. Scott

p. 117. 'My goal is to stay . . .' *U.S. magazine*, 11/11/80

Milius for police chief, from *Sunday Times Magazine*, 26/4/92, R. Miller

'My political point of view . . .' *Playboy*, Jan 1988, J. Goodman

Chapter 15

p. 118. 'THE TERMINATOR . . .' N.A. interview Rick Wayne

Palm Springs jeep story; first version, *San Francisco Chronicle*, 30/12/83 (U.P. report), second version, *Los Angeles Herald-Examiner*, 5/10/84

'Everyone around me . . .' 'The Making Of T2' by Don Shay and Jody Duncan (*Titan Books*, London)

p. 119. Early development script and project THE

SOURCES

TERMINATOR, from THE FILMS OF
ARNOLD SCHWARZENEGGER by John L.
Flynn (Citadel)
p. 120. Making Hemdale sales presentation, from
Premiere, August 1994, by John H. Richardson
'As we sat there . . .' N.A. interview Rick Wayne
p. 121. 'Arnold said to me . . .' N.A. interview Joe
Weider
'The hardest part . . .' Rolling Stone, 17/1/85, N.
Collins
'In action films . . .' Playboy, Jan 1988, J. Goodman
'I think people root . . .' Time Out, 10/8/88,
B. Case
p. 122. 'There are a hundred rules . . .' GQ, June
1990, by Alan Richman
p. 123. Three months with weapons, from Naked
Hollywood TV series transcript, 3/4/90
Terminator walk Arnold's idea, from Premiere,
August 1994, J. Richardson
Arnold in make-up room, from 'The Making of
Terminators 1 and 2' promotion video
'He has great cheekbones . . .' and following, from
N.A. interview Adam Greenberg
p. 124. 'When he attacked . . .' and following,
from N.A. interview Lance Henriksen
p. 125. 'He's not the kind of guy . . .' and
following, from Premiere, August 1994, J.
Richardson
'He was very frightened . . .' and following, from
N.A. interview Linda Hamilton

Chapter 16

p. 127. 'Ten years ago . . .' People, 7/6/82
Procrastinating engagement, from Los Angeles
Times, 10/9/89, J. Matthews
Thalersee proposal and 'I can use that', from ibid.
p. 128. 'He and I were sitting . . .' N.A. interview
Jim Lorimer
Maria background from (mainly) USA Today,
18/4/86, 'A Problem Like Maria's' by Monica
Collins, and Wendy Leigh's ARNOLD
Tunisia story, from Washington Post, 31/5/89, by
Martha Sherrill
p. 129. The 'Event', from Wendy Leigh's
ARNOLD
Maria in her office and quotes, from USA Today,
18/4/86, M. Collins
p. 130. 'It makes me respect her . . .' Interview
magazine, October 1985, J. Roberts
'He asked me . . .' Naked Hollywood TV series
transcript, 3/4/90
'Dino could get him . . .' N.A. interview Richard
Fleischer
p. 131. 'We looked for places . . .' ibid.
p. 132. 'tempest in a teacup' and following, from
N.A. interview Jim Lorimer
'I'm very naive' N.A. interview Richard Fleischer
Further adventures Arnold and Brigitte, from
Wendy Leigh's ARNOLD

Chapter 17

p. 133. 'Le narcissisme . . .' Positif, February 1994,
'Stallone et Schwarzenegger, ou l'acharnement
du phenix' by Michel Cieutat
'The difference between . . .' Atlanta Journal,
14/6/87, E. Ringel
'I think Stallone . . . New Musical Express, 19/1/85,
by Derek Ridgers
p. 134. 'He didn't have that much . . .' USA
Today, 30/7/85, by Jack Curry
'If you're doing . . .' GQ, July 1986, J. Vallely

'I'd be angry . . .' News of the World, 27/10/85, by
Ian Harmer
p. 135. 'I make every effort . . .' and following,
from Playboy, Jan 1988, J. Goodman
'There's enough competition . . .' L.A. Herald-
Examiner, 16/12/87
Stallone-Arnold phone call, from Los Angeles
Times, 3/1/88
Stallone in nightclub, from New York Post,
17/9/88, cited in Wendy Leigh's ARNOLD
p. 137. NCTV statistics from Independent on
Sunday, 6/6/93, by Phil Reeves
Lieberman quote from Evening Standard, 16/3/93,
by Peter McDonald
'American fascist art . . .' Sunday Correspondent,
1/7/90, by Ian Penman
'repellent to the last . . .' Sunday Correspondent,
30/9/90, by Gilbert Adair
'Do you think before movies . . .' TV Guide,
11/4/92, by Susan Littwin

Chapter 18

p. 139. 'The guy was in shock . . .' Montreal
Gazette, 25/10/85, by Bill Brownstein
'I saw it as a James Bond . . .' and following, from
N.A. interview Mark L. Lester
Script genesis, from Lester and 'The Films of Arnold
Schwarzenegger' by John L. Flynn
p. 140. 'We sat across . . .' N.A. interview
Jeff Corey
p. 141. 'of course the film . . .' San Francisco
Chronicle, 13/10/85, by Stu Schreiberg
'You're always trying . . .' The Cable Guide, 5/9/85
'In one scene, I chop . . .' USA Today, 30/7/85,
J. Curry
'I went to the studio head . . .' Montreal Gazette,
25/10/85, B. Brownstein
'No, no, it's too campy . . .' N.A. interview
Mark L. Lester
p. 142. 'Let's be logical . . .' N.A. interview
Vernon Wells
p. 143. Arnold dislocating arm story, from
Starburst, April 1986, by Alan Fox
Arnold commando knife 'stunt', from N.A.
interview Mark L. Lester
'Two exploding jeeps . . .' San Francisco Chronicle,
27/10/85
'He'd sit for days . . .' N.A. interview Mark
L. Lester
'I am a publicity genius . . .' San Francisco
Chronicle, 13/10/85, S. Schreiberg
'What's a bunch . . .' Interview magazine, October
1985, J. Roberts
p. 144. 'shootouts' . . . and following, from USA
Today, 12/6/86, by Stu Schreiberg
'very self-aware . . .' N.A. interview John Irvin
'John is an actor's director . . .' San Francisco
Chronicle, 15/6/86, by Dan Yakir
'Things are changing . . .' Saturday Evening Post,
March 1989, by Ryan P. Murphy
p. 145. 'After COMMANDO . . .' N.A. interview
John Irvin
Bringing in Devore, from ibid.
'Casablanca-isation', from San Francisco Chronicle,
15/6/86, D. Yakir
p. 146. 'He's got a sensitive, classic head . . .'
People, 31/1/77
p. 147. 'He couldn't do it . . .' N.A. interview
John Irvin

Chapter 19

p. 148. 'My wife . . .' Daily Mirror (Mirror
Woman), 23/3/88, by Christine Appleyard

280

'embarrass the life . . .' *Daily Express*, 10/1/85,
V. Davis
'Violence is good fun . . .' N.A. interview
John Irvin
Cutting COMMANDO love scene, from
Washington Post, 15/10/85, by Rita Kempley
p. 149. Wedding details from (inter al.) *San
Francisco Chronicle*, 26/4/86 and 27/4/86
Today 27/4/86, *People* 12/5/86, *Time* 5/5/86,
Andy Warhol's DIARIES and Wendy Leigh's
ARNOLD
p. 151. George Butler story from Butler's
ARNOLD SCHWARZENEGGER: A
PORTRAIT
p. 152. Fischler dontating sculputre, from *GQ*, July
1986, J. Vallely

Chapter 20

p. 153. 'The first half I have clothes . . .' *Atlanta
Journal*, 14/6/87, by Eleanor Ringel
'in assence a battle . . .' 20th Century Fox press
handout for PREDATOR
'I am part of a team . . .' *Today*, 9/6/87, by Joan
Goodman
p. 154. 'The worst thing . . .' *Rolling Stone*,
17/1/85, N. Collins
'Even though many . . .' Fox press handout
'In Mexico . . .' ibid
p. 156. 'All these claims . . .' *Sunday Times
Magazine*, 26/4/92, R. Miller
Waldheim asking if Arnold minds meeting being
reported and Arnold quotes, from *Penthouse*,
January 189, by Sharon Churcher
p. 157. 'As to my father . . .' *Sunday Times
Magazine*, 26/4/92, R. Miller
'I don't suppose . . .' *News of the World*, 21/2/88,
by Wendy Leigh and Sharon Ring

Chapter 21

p. 158. 'I love the world . . .' *You* magazine
(Mailon Sunday), 22/11/87, D. Thompson
Moving house, from ibid.
Crashed pier, from *Evening Standard* 11/1/85
'Ninety percent . . .' and Oak Plaza details,
from *California Business*, June 1986, by
Susan Peters
p. 159. 'He presents them . . .' *Hollywood Reporter*,
24/11/86, by Leonora Langley
Arnold's vehicles, from *Interview* magazine,
October 1985, J. Roberts
p.160. L.A. Sports Arena story, from *Esquire*,
March 1985, by Lynn Darling
Coffee prank, from *News of the World*, 16/2/86, by
William Hall
Pontchartrain incident, from Wendy Leigh's
ARNOLD, confirmed by N.A. interview
Boyer Coe
p. 163. Wiesenthal Center contributions, from
N.A. interview Rabbit Marvin Hier
p. 164. 'He's the embodiment . . .' Hollywood
Reporter special Schwarzenegger issue, 9/3/93
Looking after Patrick, from Wendy Leigh's
ARNOLD
Prison seminars, from *Time Out*, 10/8/88,
B. Case, and *Mail On Sunday*, 27/5/90, by
Victor Davis
'That's much better than . . .' *Time Out*, 10/8/88,
B. Case
'Not at all . . .' *Mail on Sunday*, 27/5/90, V. Davis
p. 165. Hollenbeck Youth Centre, from *Hollywood
Reporter*, 9/3/93

'He has done so much . . .' N.A. interview Simon
Wiesenthal
'I don't need to get married . . .' *Sun*, 7/6/77, by
Jean Dobson
'have no heavy plans . . .' *L.A. Herald-Examiner*,
7/6/87, by Candace Burke-Block
p. 166. 'I believe kids . . .' *USA Today*, 18/4/86,
by Dan Yakir
'Let them? . . .' *Los Angeles Times*, 1/6/86
'I'll get in the car . . .' *You* magazine, 22/11/87, D.
Thompson
'I'm from a socialist country . . .' ibid.
'When we play . . .' *Today*, 9/6/87, J. Goodman
'so comfortably and sweat . . .' and 'This of
course . . .' *Playboy*, Jan 1988, J. Goodman
'I don't like to dictate . . .' *Today*, 9/6/87, J.
Goodman
'She also is not allowed . . .' ibid.
p. 167. Maria 'Regent' from *New York Times*
29/10/86
Maria contract non-renewal and pay cut, from *New
York Times* 1/7/86 and 10/10/86
'On the way home . . .' *GQ*, July 1986, J. Vallely
'I've got a relationship . . .' *USA Today*, 18/4/86,
by Monica Collins
'We fly back and forth . . .' *People*, 2/6/86
p. 168. 'The joy in public office . . .' *Entertainment
Weekly*, quoted in 'Nietzsche's Boy' by J.
Hoberman (*Sight and Sound*, September 1991)
'I don't think . . .' *GQ*, June 1986, J. Vallely

Chapter 22

p. 170. Location details and 'There are elements
. . .' from THE FILMS OF ARNOLD
SCHWARZENEGGER by John L. Flynn
p. 171. 'coming in today . . .' and 'much
more systematically . . .', plus shooting
schedule, from *Hollywood Reporter* 57th
anniversary issue
'There's a formula . . .' *Daily Mail*, 10/3/88, by
Sara Barrett
p. 172. NATO awards and Arnold quotes, from
Atlanta Journal, 14/6/87, E. Ringel
Tokyo phone call, from *USA Today*, 30/6/87, by
Tom Green
p. 173. 'The reality is . . .' *Hollywood Reporter* 57th
anniversary issue
'In my family . . .' *Chicago Tribune*, 17/6/87.
C. Lavin
'Why so early? . . .' *Playboy*, Jan 1988, J. Goodman
Maria's nephews' visit, from N.A. interview
Robert Easton
p. 174. 'How can a husband . . .' *Daily Mirror*,
26/9/84, by Noreen Taylor
Arnold at home, from N.A. interview Jim Lorimer
Arnold dancing with daughter, from *Playboy*, Jan
1988, J. Goodman
'She has very good instincts . . .' *Time*, 24/12/90,
by Richard Corliss
'She thinks I'm a workaholic . . .' *Playboy*, Jan
1988, J. Goodman
'I was trying to show Arnold . . .' N.A. interview
Walter Hill
p. 175. 'She plays the same kind . . .' *Los Angeles
Times*, 14/7/88, by Bob Thomas
'What we should have done . . .' N.A. interview
Walter Hill
p. 176. 'Amazing changes . . .' *Los Angeles Times*,
14/7/88, B. Thomas
'The Russians are fed up . . .' *Mail on Sunday*,
15/7/88, by Victor Davis
'I think one reason . . .' *Options*, January 1989
p. 177. 'He used to say . . .' and following,

SOURCES

from N.A. interview Walter
Hill

Chapter 23

p. 178. 'I'm not a stern character . . .' *New York Times*, 10/6/90, Richard Bernstein
'A week or so . . .' *Vanity Fair*, June 1990
'I have no patience . . .' ibid
'I want people to know . . .' *New York Times*, 10/6/90, Richard Bernstein
p. 179. 'The critics used to call me . . .' *Mail on Sunday*, 15/7/88, V. Davis
'I believe in systematically . . .' *Interview* magazine, October 1985, J. Roberts
'When we cut . . .' N.A. interview Walter Hill
Friars Club 'roast' from *L.A. Herald-Examiner*, 5/4/88, by Bill Higgins
p. 180. 'I do the washing up . . .' *Time*, 20/7/87
'You must be crazy . . .' *Sunday Express*, 5/11/89, S. Russell
Frontera visit, from *Time* 20/7/87
'Sorry, Arnie . . .' *Daily Mail*, 10/3/88, S. Barrett
'He appears to be . . .' *Time Out*, 10/8/88, B. Case
p. 181. 'My clients accept . . .' *Los Angeles Times*, 21/12/89
'When the press . . .' N.A. interview Rabbi Marvin Hier
p. 182. 'I never heard . . .' N.A. interview Simon Wiesenthal
'My reply to the press . . .' and following, from N.A. interview Rabbi Marvin Hier
p. 183. Fleming on Arnold and Wiesenthal Center, *San Francisco Chronicle*, 26/3/92, 'Arnold's Propaganda Machine'
'Sieg Heil' story and Hitler impersonations, from N.A. interview Rick Wayne
'but we did a lot . . .' N.A. interview Joe Weider
Posing 'classic', from N.A. interview Wag Bennett
P. 184, TWINS scriptwriters' story, from *You* magazine, 15/1/89, by Douglas Thompson
p. 185. 'In my last five . . .' Universal publicity notes on TWINS
'You can imagine . . .' TV Entertainment Tonight, 27/7/88
'He has this lovely . . .' TWINS publicity notes
'I changed the rhythm . . .' *You* magazine, 15/1/89, D. Thompson

Chapter 24

p. 187. 'I'd like to be a father. It's time.' *USA Today*, 30/7/85, J. Curry
Maria tells Arnold of baby, from *USA Today*, 1/6/90, by Ann Trebbe
Fertility experts, from *Daily Mirror*, 9/3/90, by Drew Mackenzie
Fights and night of love, from *Star*, 6/6/89
p. 188. 'It's great to be part . . .' *Daily Mirror*, 9/3/90, D. Mackenzie
SERGEANT ROCK details, from *Chicago Tribune*, 27/5/90, by Iain Blair
'I have my soft side . . .' ibid.
'I couldn't do . . .' *Mail on Sunday*, 27/5/90, V. Davis
p. 189. Baby shower story, from GQ, May 1990, by Alan Richman
'Although it's wonderful . . .' *Today*, 14/5/90
TOTAL RECALL project history, from *Los Angeles Times*, 10/9/89, by Jack Matthews
p. 190. 'You believe you've actually been . . .' *Chicago Tribune*, 27/5/90 Iain Blair
p. 191. 'It is strange . . .' ibid

Chapter 25

p. 193. 'I sometimes do feel . . .' After Dark, February 1977, N. M. Stoop
'Michael Dukakis . . .' *Sunday Telegraph*, 21/7/91
p. 194. 'That same day . . .' N.A. interview Jim Lorimer
'There are all kinds . . .' *Saturday Evening Post*, March 1989, by Ryan P. Murphy
'Some fifty-five percent . . .' and following quotes, from *New York Times*, 6/1/91, article by A.S. on fitness in schools
p. 195. 'If a kid grows up . . .' *Time Out*, 10/8/88, B. Case
Great American Workout, from *USA Today*, 25/5/90, by Ann Trebbe and Saturday Evening Post, July–August, 1990 by Maynard Good Stoddard and Cory SerVaas M.D.
'I have been very impressed . . .' *Saturday Evening Post*, July–August 1990, M. G. Stoddard and C. SerVaas
'I think it's great . . .' *USA Today*, 1/6/90, A. Trebbe
p. 196. Arnold Classic, from *Wall Street Journal*, 6/3/90, and N.A. interview Jim Lorimer
Naked Hollywood interview, details and transcript from Nicolas Kent
p. 197. Monaco gym, from *Mail on Sunday*, 27/5/90, V. Davis
TOTAL RECALL party, from *Los Angeles Times*, 4/6/90
Weights to Saudi Arabia, from *New York Times* 8/11/90
Grand Marshal at Hollywood parade, from *Hollywood Reporter*, 17/10/90
Lajos Goncz action, from *Today*, 18/7/90, by Mike Graham

Chapter 26

p. 199. 'Because I come . . .' GQ, June 1990, A. Richman
p. 200. Publishing history of ARNOLD, from *Chicago Tribune*, 31/5/90, by John Blades, and *San Francisco Chronicle*, 26/3/92, by Charles Fleming and *Sunday Times Magazine*, 26/4/92, R. Miller
'The subject has . . .' *L.A. Herald-Examiner*, 5/5/90
Articles and TV shows 'dropped', from *Montreal Gazette*, 15/7/90, by John Anderson and *Spy* magazine, March 1992, by Charles Fleming
Larry King show details, from *Montreal Gazette*, 15/7/90, J. Anderson
p. 201. Cannes press buffet, from ibid
'Why should I be mad? . . .' *Sunday Times Magazine*, 26/4/92, R. Miller
Deletions to ARNOLD in U.K. and British libel laws, from *The Times*, 11/8/93, by Roy Greenslade
'I think people should care . . .' *Chicago Tribune*, 31/5/90, by John Blades
p. 202. 'Mr Schwarzenegger has at no time . . .', from *Sunday Telegraph*, 6/7/93
'Schwarzenegger is in his metier . . .' N.A. interview Nicolas Kent
'I think she believed . . .' ibid.
p. 203. 'I am an organisation freak . . .' GQ, June 1990, A. Richman
Sliding doors story, from ibid.
p. 204. Miss America contest, from *Star*, 26/9/89

Chapter 27

p. 205. 'I'm looking forward . . .' *Naked Hollywood* TV series

'Having a baby . . .' *Sun*, 26/12/90, by Antonella Lazzeri
'Ivan Reitman is . . .' *Guardian*, 25/1/91, by Sarah Gristwood
p. 206. KINDERGARTEN COP project history and 'played on the concept . . .', from *New York Times*, 28/12/90
Ron Howard details, *Naked Hollywood* TV series
'Ivan Reitman took me . . .' *Guardian*, 25/1/91, S. Gristwood
'There'll be a writer . . .' *Naked Hollywood* TV series
p.208. 'The nation's health costs . . .' and following, from *New York Times*, 6/1/91
Face-stuffing discouragement and thumbs-up for veal and swordfish, from *USA Today* (Usa Weekend) 26/4/91
p. 209. 'Can you lift up? . . .' *USA Today*, 1591, by Wendy Benedett.
KINDERGARTEN COP junket, from *Times Saturday Review*, 26/1/91, K. Muir
Mrs Bush breaks leg, from *Guardian*, 25/1/91, S. Gristwood
Injuries list, from Health Watch, March 1993, by Mary Roach
p. 210. 'Since I just went through . . .' *Times Saturday Review*, 26/1/91 K. Muir
Wiesenthal Center Awards, from *Daily Mail*, 12/7/91, L.A. Magazine, August 1991 by Nikki Finke, and *San Francisco Chronicle*, 26/3/92 by Charles Fleming
'We honoured him . . .' N.A. interview Rabbi Marvin Hier
p.211. Special Olympics Torch, from *Variety*, 13/5/91
Hans and Franz, from *TV Guide*, 30/9/89
Milius and motorbikes story, from *Rolling Stone* 22/8/91, by Bill Zehme
New daughter, from *National Enquirer*, 13/8/91

Chapter 28

p. 213. 'Don't think my character . . .' *Los Angeles Times*, 19/5/91, by Pat H. Broeske
'It was actually Arnold . . .' *The Making of T2* by Don Shay and Jody Duncan (Titan Books)
'It would have meant . . .' ibid.
p. 214. 'The Terminators exist . . .' *Los Angeles Times*, 19/5/91, P.H. Broeske
'I would not consider . . .' *The Making Of T2* by D. Shay and J. Duncan
p. 215. 'I clowned around . . .' ibid.
'filthy sense of humour' and following, from N.A. interview Linda Hamilton
p. 216. 'I had to walk . . .' *Starlog*, August 1991, by Marc Shapiro
'Because I was . . .' ibid.
p. 218. 'Nietzsche's Boy' by J. Hoberman, *Sight and Sound*, September 1991
p. 219. 'Arnold is very Nietzschean . . .' *Forbes*, 25/5/92, by Matt Rees

Chapter 29

p. 222. 'We never stay on top . . .
'Schaltzi' details from *Los Angeles Times*, 16/2/92 and 15/3/92, and *The Great Life*, 27/2/92
p. 223. Planet Hollywood details from (inter al.) *Time Out*, 17/3/93, by Anita Chaudhuri and *Daily Telegraph*, 18/5/93, by Jasper Gerrard
'It's a matter of intelligence . . .' *Orange County Register, 18/6/93*
p. 224. 'Every time she comes . . .' and following, from *Time Out*, 17/3/93, A. Chudhuri

'He was very embarrassed . . .' and party details, from N.A. interview Michael Winner
p. 225. 'I think it's a big challenge . . .' *Time*, 28/5/90
'After I directed . . .' *Time*, 24/12/90, R. Corliss
p. 226. 'At first I thought . . .' N.A. interview Dyan Cannon
'He storyboarded . . .' N.A. interview Stanley Brooks
Dubbing session and 'You cannot just observe . . . from *TV Guide*, 11/4/92, by Susan Littwin
p. 227. Directors Guild junket, from *Los Angeles Times*, 8/4/92, by Bill Higgins
A.F.M., from *Hollywood Reporter*, 4/3/92
'Because I said so' ibid.
'We've stopped overpaying . . .' *New Yorker*, 28/2/94, by James B Stewart
p. 228. 'The country is going . . .' *Premiere*, June 1993, by Nancy Griffin
A.S. for 'Count of Monte Cristo', from ibid.
A.S. for 'Curious George', from *Variety*, 18/5/92
A.S. for 'Sweet Tooth', from *Screen International*, 19/6/92
Action doll and script evolution, from *Premiere*, June 1993, N. Griffin
p. 229. 'When I got to Culver City . . .' and following, from N.A. interview Charles Dance
p. 230. Arnold and Maria on screen, from *TV Guide*. 3/7/93
p. 231. 'I played two whole scenes . . .' N.A. interview Charles Dance
Post-production pressure and 'There was no panicked . . .', from *Los Angeles Times*, 30/6/93, by Terry Pristin
Test screening denial, from *Los Angeles Times*, 6/6/93, by Jeffrey Wells
LAST ACTION HERO opening, from *Hollywood Reporter* 18/6/93
p. 232. Arnold in Cannes, from *Variety*, 17/5/93
New Yorker article, 28/2/94, by James B. Stewart
'JURASSIC PARK had opened . . .' N.A. interview Stanley Brooks
p. 233. *Modern Review*, 'Pumping Irony' by Ed Porter, October – November 1994
p. 234. 'In one way. Arnold S . . .' *Independent*, 29/7/93, Adam Mars-Jones
Spy magazine article, March 1992, by Charles Fleming
p. 235. 'It was wonderful . . .' *Hollywood Reporter*, 26/2/92
'It was such a bad . . .' N.A. interview Francesco Scavullo

Chapter 30

p. 237. 'You get to be . . .' *New York Times*, 4/3/93, by Bernard Weinraub
'Bob Rafelson said . . .' ibid.
p. 238. Daughter Katharine on set, from *GQ*, June 1990, A. Richman
'I am looking straight . . .' ibid.
Resigning as national fitness chief, from *Variety*, 2/6/93
California fitness chief, *People*, 26/2/93
p. 239. Details of Arnold's office, from *In Style* magazine (*People*), December 1994, by Mark Morrison
'In the garage . . .' *Sunday Times Magazine*, 26/4/92, R. Miller
p. 240. Humvee details, from *Orange County Register, 18/6/93*, and *Los Angeles Times*, 13/6/91
'She hated it . . .' *GQ*, June 1990. A. Richman

SOURCES

Details of Gulfstream jet, from *People*, 30/12/91, and *Los Angeles Times*, 29/7/91

NASA rocket, from *Chicago Tribune*, 16/7/93, by Jessica Siegel

p. 241. Arnold's tank, from *Hollywood Reporter*, 28/7/94, and *Daily Telegraph*, 18/8/94

Bobby Shriver, James Cameron, motorbiking and LA TOTALE, from *Times-Picayune*, 23/7/94, by David Baron

p. 242. Maria's 1990 contract, from Down Jones, 9/4/90, and *Washington Post*, 9/4/90, by John Carmody

'The past ten to fifteen . . .' *Los Angeles Times*, 17/7/94, by David Kronke

'Bond's an aging Brit . . .' ibid.

p. 243. Cameron vetoes bathrooms, from *Premiere*, August 1994, by John H. Richardson

$15,000-an-hour fuel, from *Variety*, 14/7/94, by Army Archerd

'I am suspended . . .' *Showbiz Today*, 12/7/94

'Dis is where de money is!' N.A. interview John Bruno

'In a scene on the rooftop . . .' *Los Angeles Times*, 17/7/94, D. Kronke

'The trick to that . . .' ibid.

p. 244. 'There's probably a way . . .' ibid.

'The movie will increase . . .' *Variety*, 19/7/94

'This film is a work of fiction . . .' *Los Angeles Times*, 2/7/94

Washington demo and banners, from *A.P.* 15/7/94

'No, I let my wife . . .' Scotsman DATECHECK

'It's like RAIDERS . . .' *Times-Picayune*, 23/7/94

p. 245. 'There was this whole thing . . .' *The Valley Vantage*, 14/7/94, by Michael Cartel

New baby, Los Angeles Times, 22/9/93

Buying a new house, from *Los Angeles Times*, 12/9/93

Lobbying for land, from *Hollywood Reporter* 25/2/94

Hollywood star dug up, from *USA Today*, April 1994

Chapter 31

p. 248. 'I think that you could play . . .' *Washington Post*, 15/10/85, by Rita Kempley

Brillstein project, from *L.A. Life*, 13/12/93

p. 249. Maria's screenplay, from *Los Angeles Times*, 28/10/92, by John Lippman, and *Variety*, 27/10/92

CRUSADE details, from *Variety*, 22/9/94, and *Hollywood Reporter*, 17/11/94, by Kirk Honeycutt, and Screen International, 25/11/94

p. 250. 'The more I know . . .' *Variety Weekly*, 22/5/95, by Michael Fleming

Gorbachev meeting, from *Los Angeles Times*, 23/10/94

'When you're a stud . . .' *Times*, 11/8/94

p. 251. 'I remember her . . .' *Entertainment Today*, 25/11/94, by Reed McColm

'I've always been fascinated . . .' *Evening Standard*, 9/12/94, by Michael Owen

'It's not a sympathetic story . . .' N.A. interview Adam Greenberg

Arnold's children from *Daily Mail*, 10/8/94, by Bax Bamigboye

p. 252. 'picked the dress . . .' *The European*, 16/12/94, by Steven Goldman

'When I was dropped' *Premiere*, December 1994, by Rachel Abramovitz

'It was not the obstacle . . .' ibid.

JUNIOR's law office performance and Chris Conrad, from A.N.' 25/12/94, by John Horn

p. 253. 'I think the movie was done . .t.' N.A. interview Adam Greenberg

p. 254. 'Personally, I think that Arnold's Spy pic . . .' *Musclemag*, June 1992, by Robert Kennedy

'When I hear Lacey . . .' N.A. interview Mike Mentzer

p. 255. 'The Hollywood reporters . . .' N.A. interview Charles Fleming

'He's got tremendous pressure . . .' N.A. interview Jim Lorimer

'PUMPING IRON was an exercise . . .' N.A. interview Lacey H. Rich

p. 256. 'It was talked about . . .' N.A. interview Bernard Weinraub

'If you compare him . . .' N.A. interview Sam Popkin

'I don't know if this is good . . .' N.A. interview Simon Wiesenthal

p. 257. 'Why should I run? . . .' *New York Times*, 4/3/93, by Bernard Weintraub

'He hasn't warmed . . .' N.A. interview Jim Lorimer

'That's too facile . . .' N.A. interview Pauline Kael

Supporting Ted Kennedy, from *New York Times*, 8/10/94

Mid-East peace making, from *L.A. Times*, 7/7/95

Chapter 32

p. 259. 'There's something . . .' *Empire*, June 1993, by Tom Hibbert

Arnold's house purchase, from *L.A. Times* 18/6/95

Arnold in Miami, from *Miami Herald* 21/4/95

Atlanta wallbreaking, from *Atlanta Journal*, 2/2/95

Bruce Willis birthday, from *Globe*, 25/4/95

p. 260. Planet Hollywood, from *The Times* 14/11/94

Stallone award, *USA Today* 22/5/95

Love child scandal, *Globe*, 25/4/95

p. 261. Arnold and 'Heidi', from N.A. interview Stanley Brooks

p. 262. 'For the price of a cup of coffee . . .' and following N.A. interview Tony Purycar

p. 263. British fan's shooting, from *The Times*, 17/2/95, by Richrd Duce

p. 265. 'There's something essentially mysterious . . .' N.A. interview Walter Hill

p. 266. 'There was a natural . . .' N.A. interview George Butler

'I'll get you a million dollars . . .' and following, from ARNOLD SCHWARZ-ENEGGER: A PORTRAIT by George Butler

'Some time when I met . . .' N.A. interview Simon Wiesenthal

p. 267. 'I wake up . . .' N.A. interview Wag Bennett

'He feels that when he arrived . . ." N.A. interview George Butler

p. 268. Gore Vidal prophecy, from *Daily Telegraph*, 12/12/94, by Martyn Harris

'I'm more than happy . . .' *Empire*, June 1993, by Tom Hibbert

Index

INDEX